A Compassionate ROAR

RAISING AN URGENT VOICE IN OUR WINDOW OF MERCY

JOHN O ANDERSON

Bridge-Logos

Gainesville, Florida 32614 USA

ENDORSEMENTS

"I recommend A *Compassionate Roar* to every Christian and minister in America and throughout the West. John Anderson is a modern-day Jonah with a message from God for America. May we return to the Lord in repentance, faith and wholehearted obedience."

—PIERRE BYNUM,
THE ALLIANCE FOR REVIVAL AND REFORMATION

"A *Compassionate Roar* powerfully points to the Church's role as salt and light. The prophetic message of this book cries to the Church and says, 'It is time to seek the Lord.' This book has a message of urgency wrapped in humility. It is an extension of John Anderson's heart and life."

—JOE BIDDLE, PASTOR,
CALVARY TEMPLE, FALL RIVER, MA

"John Anderson speaks with the authority of a prophet and the heart of a pastor. Once again, he sounds a timely trumpet that the Church must heed. May we have ears to hear the message that this modern Amos has delivered!"

—REV. ROB SCHENCK, PRESIDENT,
THE NATIONAL CLERGY COUNCIL
WASHINGTON, DC.

"John Anderson's message blows like a crisp, cool wind through the fog of compromise and sloppy thinking that envelopes so much of the contemporary church. For Christians to keep silent at a time like this, is, in effect, to renege on their commitment to Christ. I feel that these judgments are closer at hand than most of us are willing to recognize, and that God may not prove to be so 'nice' as many contemporary preachers depict Him."

—THE LATE DEREK PRINCE

"This book is a much needed trumpet call to the Church and nation. Many of us are convinced that our nation could experience devastation as did Jerusalem, Babylon and Rome. John is right, we only have a 'window of mercy' in which to awaken and roar. "

—DR. JAY GRIMSTEAD, DIRECTOR, COALITION ON REVIVAL, MURPHYS, CALIFORNIA

"This book is a must-read for every Christian. To understand what is going on in today's society and how it relates to the Bible, John Anderson's latest book delivers a thought-provoking message."

—DR. AND MRS. PAUL BROWER (PH.D.)

DEDICATION

Dedicated to the memory of

PASTOR LARRY SQUIRES

A cherished friend who felt deeply about this book's message
and played a pivotal role in this edition.

CONTENTS

PREFACE

WILL WE AWAKEN?

"You can discern the face of the sky and the earth; but how
is it that you cannot discern this time?"
—JESUS, IN LUKE 12:56

Each of us remembers where we were on September 11, 2001, when we first learned of that day's terrible events, a day that sobered and shook us. The common mantra afterwards was: "On 9/11, things changed; we'll never be the same." Certainly 9/11 awakened a burst of patriotism as American flags and "God bless America" banners went up everywhere. For a while we had a religious upsurge as people prayed and attended places of worship. We rallied with national resolve both to repair the awful destruction and to begin a war on terror. Since then we've had a war in Iraq, and are now in a huge undertaking, often deadly, to rebuild that nation.

But the case is there that 9/11 and since awakened everyone except the Church. Many months after 9/11 the esteemed Henry Blackaby said: "I've been in many, many, many churches. I go and look at the bulletin, and I look at the topics of the sermons—you'd never know in most of the churches that 9-11 ever happened . . . I am convinced that a number one priority ought to have been a huge movement of prayer in the life of the churches." I also heard Mr. Blackaby say, "On 9/11 God was saying to the Church, 'You have sinned. And I am removing my hedge of protection from your country.'"[1] Mr. Blackaby's observations mirror those of others, such as the late Bill Bright and David Wilkerson.

But look around. What is our post-9/11 message? Isn't it still primarily the success-promising, user-friendly, prosperity and money-focused one we had before 9/11? And aren't we still just about as centered on our programs, church calendars, and contemporary music and worship as before, with our model for preaching the motivational speaker? Where is our call to repentance? Or our passion for a national day of humiliation, fasting and prayer such as Lincoln called several times in the Civil War? Or our asking whether 9/11 could be a remedial judgment? Shouldn't 9/11 at the least have been a wake-up call to these and similar issues?

Sadly, the seminal moment of 9/11 could go down as one of the most egregiously missed opportunities the Church has ever had. It birthed good questions such as, "If God was speaking to us, what was He saying?" Assuredly, one thing God was saying on Sept. 11 was the same thing He was saying on Sept. 10 and before, "Come back to Me!"

But we didn't hear "Come back to Me!" Grievously what we principally heard, from liberals to charismatics, were variations of, "A God of love would not have had anything to do with the events of 9/11," an objection that echoes that other one we've all heard, "A God of love wouldn't send anyone to hell." Both objections of course distort God's holy, gracious love, brush aside His justice, and ignore the gravity of sin. A proper question is not, "Would a God of love have had anything to do with 9/11?" But rather, "Given the weight of America's sins, such as our killing 40-plus million of our unborn, why were we not completely destroyed?" (The answer is rooted in the mercy of God.)

In this post-9/11 hour, perhaps we should ask ourselves if the classic conflict between the false prophet and the true prophet (such as Ezekiel, Jeremiah, Amos and others) is with us? A false prophet could, and can, be false in either of two ways: 1) by overtly teaching error, 2) by omitting part of the message. Usually it is easier to detect the false prophet who overtly teaches error; harder to discern the false prophet who simply leaves out part of the message. These latter false prophets might teach some true things, uplifting things, using Scripture. But their treachery–even unwitting treachery–lay in the vital things they usually omitted–God's justice, exposure of sin, warnings of judgment, compassionate calls to repentance, and, today, the Cross, things which God wanted the people to hear and which were included in the balanced messages of the true prophets. The true prophets, impelled by God's love, spoke *all* of God's message!

Essentially false prophets were the archetype preachers of the positive message–the "peace-peace" message which omitted "negative" things, a form of triumphalism which was very popular, and still is. They misused Scripture by teaching from selected areas of Scripture which seemed to support their sunny doctrines which people of course loved to hear. Today we might say they had crowds and their books and tapes sold well. But the Apostle Paul warned Timothy that, "the time will come when men will not put up with sound doctrine. Instead, to suit their own desires, they will gather around them a great number of teachers to say what their itching ears want to hear."[2] He exhorted Timothy, "Preach the Word."

Nevertheless the treachery of false prophets was, and is, deadly, particularly in times of flagrant national sin and looming judgment, when "Come back to Me!" was the urgent, pivotal message the nation needed to hear but didn't hear from these misguided preachers. God rebuked them, "The visions of your prophets were false and worthless; they did not expose your sin to ward off your captivity. The oracles they gave you were false and misleading."[3]

Over recent years we've had calls for "Forty days of fasting and prayer," "Forty days of purpose," and similar emphases–all worthy endeavors. However it's time for, "Forty days and we shall be over-thrown,"[4] echoing the prophet Jonah's urgent proclamation of judgment to Nineveh which resulted in massive repentance and God graciously withdrawing judgment. Jonah's strong word is the kind Peter proclaimed on the Day of Pentecost, "Save yourselves from this corrupt generation," which resulted in three thousand being baptized. Both Jonah's and Peter's messages were catalysts God used to send spiritual awakenings.

Can such spiritual awakenings happen again? We believe they can, and will, as today's Church raises a true prophetic voice, a voice motivated by God's heart which omits none of His message, which "cuts [us] to our hearts,"[5] stirs us to repentance, and calls, "Come back to Me!"–what might be termed "a compassionate roar."

. Let the roar be raised. Our society is sinning boldly. With abandon. And we face the consequences. Let the Church speak. America and the West will confront their sins at one of two times: either now in repentance while we have God's mercy–as Nineveh did and was saved; or later in judgment when there is not God's mercy–as Sodom did and was destroyed.

In Chapters 5 and 6 are particular issues and sins I passionately believe we will face either in repentance or judgment. One of them increasingly gripped me as I wrote. It was **the enormity of the evil in teaching our children to sin–and the peril in which this alone puts our nation**. I was sobered by Jesus' strong words in Matthew 18:6, "But if anyone causes one of these little ones who believe in me to sin, it would be better for him to have a large millstone hung around his neck and to be drowned in the depths of the sea." I trembled that our egregious teaching of our children to sin has put a collective millstone around our neck and we teeter on a cliff above the sea. I don't believe I said this strong enough in these pages.

A prime test in this post-9/11 time, underscored by the constant specter of more terror, will be whether we in the Church will be compassionate enough to roar. Will we intercede? Will we re-insert the gravity of sin and the terror of judgment back into our message?

True compassion, the First Corinthians 13 kind, coming from the heart of our gracious, holy Lord, will impel us to so roar. Spurious compassion, false love, will not.

But if we truly do roar the effect could be profound: It could be a catalyst for a spiritual awakening, starting with revival in the Church. Just the thought of this brings tears to my eyes.

There is an encouraging sign. There's a rising cry to see such an awakening. It's coming from many who are dissatisfied with the barrenness of their own spiritual lives and the superficiality of the message from parts of the Church; and are grieved at society's moral and spiritual direction. They are interceding. They are humbly repenting. They are searching the Scriptures.

As we journey together in these pages, may we join them. A few can be very pivotal. Let's pray for a spiritual awakening. Pray it starts with revival in the Church–the nation will not awaken unless first the Church awakens. And pray the awakening sweeps from the church house to my house to your house to the White House to every house.

PREFACE ENDNOTES

1 At "Heart-Cry for Revival Conference at The Cove at the Billy
  Graham Training Center in Asheville, North Carolina, April,
  2002.
2 II Timothy 4:2,3
3 Lamentations 2:14
4 Jonah 3:4 NKJV
5 Acts 2:37

Prologue

A COMPASSIONATE ROAR

"The Lion has roared—tremble in fear. The Lord God has sounded your doom—I dare not refuse to proclaim it.
—The Prophet Amos[1]

"It is my belief, Watson, founded upon my experience, that the lowest and vilest alleys of London do not present a more dreadful record of sin than does the smiling and beautiful countryside."
—Sir Arthur Conan Doyle
"The Copper Beeches,"
The Adventures of Sherlock Holmes, 1892[2]

America and Western nations need to hear a roar—a clear, compelling and compassionate roar, with tears, straight from the heart of God delivered by the Church!

It could be a most pivotal action that the Church can take in these post-9/11 times when war, the threat of terrorism, international turmoil, economic uncertainties, and other challenges are particular realities. Plus, there is no question that America and other Western nations rival Sodom in their aggressive, bold sinning.

As we in the Church face the realities of our present world, we might respond in various ways: wring our hands; go into a form of denial by hiding in our sanctuaries and busying ourselves in our programs and church calendars; distract ourselves by being caught up in the hype of the latest fad; focusing our message on success, prosperity, and similar things. Or we might take biblical action and, motivated by God's love, become a defining, prophetic voice; a voice urgently, passionately, and with tears, proclaiming the Word of the Lord for this day—this post 9/11 hour—aiming that Word toward the heart and conscience of both the Church and our society, calling us to return to the Lord. It's what we are calling *a compassionate roar*.

We believe deeply that such a roar could well be used by our Lord as a catalyst for revival.

Our roar must be compassionate for several reasons. One is that one of the most compassionate actions the Church can take in our present world is to speak of sin; warn of its consequence, judgment; call for repentance; and passionately preach the good news, the Gospel. It is doing what Scripture calls us to do. It is a spurious love, a compromised compassion, which avoids discussion of sin, or bypasses mention of eternal judgment and eternal life, or omits the need of repentance. True love expounds on all aspects of God's character—His love, grace, justice, wrath, mercy, judgment. True love tells all parts of God's message—sin, judgment, His love, repentance, salvation through Christ. True love warns. True love impels biblical integrity. True love compels a prophetic voice.

Another reason for compassion draws on that aphorism, *people do not care how much you know until they know how much you care*. This is a time for humility, tenderness and grief. It is not a time for finger-pointing; it's a time to take the world by the hand and lead it back to our gracious God. But it must be done honestly, biblically completely, accurately, and courageously holding nothing back of God's message. Under the Spirit's anointing, people respond to such compassionate integrity.

Still another reason for compassion—and the most important— is that our motivation absolutely must reflect the heart of our holy, just, and gracious God. This will be coupled with Scriptural accuracy. Certainly we can look out at our nation and see its sins, such as killing our unborn and betraying our God-given heritage, and exclaim, "Judge the nation, Lord; bring down your thunder on them. They deserve it." We'd be right; they do deserve it—of course "they" are "us"; and we're overdue for judgment; and the only reason we remain a nation is because of the mercy of God.

At the same moment we call for God to judge our nation, we might also look over our shoulder toward our Lord, fully expecting to see His fist, raised, poised to smash down in judgment on us. But we might be surprised—even shaken—by what we do see; because what we view is not His fist, but instead His open hand with arm outstretched toward our terribly evil and judgment-deserving nation. And then, looking beyond His open hand, we see His face, and the soft lines of concern. In His eyes, tears, tears of compassion, grieving that we may persist in our iniquity and fall in judgment. If we listen, we'll hear Him say, "Come back to Me!"

We could immediately recall this was the face of our Savior when He looked over Jerusalem and wept, "If you, even you, had only known on this day what would bring you peace—but now it is hidden from your eyes." And He described their coming brutal judgment, which, of course, happened—all "because [they] did not recognize the time of God's coming to [them]."[3] What a picture of God's heart expressed by our Savior!

Truly "God so loved the world . . ." And because God so loved, He roared. Certainly the most thunderous roar ever heard on this earth came from the Cross where God's Son died, where both God's wrath against sin and His love for us sounded forth. The Cross was the place where the Word of God and the Love of God were heard. So as God loved, let us love; and speak.

THE CAUTION OF OUR SAVIOR

In looking ahead to challenging days, our Savior cautioned us not to be taken up with "eating, drinking, buying, selling, planting, building, marrying, being given in marriage" like Noah's time and Sodom was.[4] Sadly, too many of us in the Church are ignoring this command of our Lord as we have joined the world in its frolic.

But no matter how well everything seems to be materially in our nation, we've learned from Sodom and Noah's time that our high standard of living will not determine our future, but our low standard of morals—our grievous sins will. As they do now, our sins will define our future: certain judgment. Contrary to the way things appear, we are racing toward judgment, the just consequences of our sins—and we are kicking aside God's warning signs as we go.

Enormously alarming is that we are doing what judgment-bound nations have done before: we're being mesmerized by trifles. America and the West are like firemen who late one night sped to a fire in a two-story house occupied by a young widow and her baby. The house was swallowed in flames, so a fireman swiftly climbed a ladder to a second-floor bedroom and peered in the window, looking for the woman and her child. He was astounded by what he saw: smoke was filling the room and to one side was a crib with the baby. However the woman was on her knees, crawling and *picking up bobby pins.* The fireman quickly smashed the glass, climbed through the window, grabbed the baby, pulled up the woman, and shouted: "*Woman, why are you picking up bobby pins when your house is on fire? Let's get out of here!*" Hard to believe. Hard to believe that a mother, or anyone, could be so foolish.

Yet others have been so foolish. In 410 A.D. Alaric the Visigoth led his barbarian army in the sack of Rome. Apparently the Roman Emperor Honorius, who had fled to Ravenna, received the grim news from one of the eunuchs who cared for the emperor's poultry. "Rome has perished," the eunuch declared. At that, Honorius cried out, "And yet it has just eaten from my hands!" Honorius had a large rooster named "Rome." The eunuch explained that it was the *city* of Rome which had perished at the hands of Aleric. The emperor with a sigh of relief, answered quickly: "But I, my good fellow, thought that my fowl Rome had perished."[5]

With our national iniquities, such as legally sanctioned blood-shed in the killing of our unborn and our pervasive immorality both heterosexual and homosexual, we have the signposts signaling that our ethical house is burning, and it could go to the ground. But we remain concerned with bobby pins and roosters—detached, self-absorbed, proud, focused on materialistic toys or pleasures or what-ever strikes our fancy. We certainly dismiss any suggestions of judgment. And our pulpits are largely not speaking of it. We should recall what Billy Graham said several years ago, "We cannot claim to be God's pets. We have no dispensation from judgment. If we continue in our present course, the moral law that says the `wages of sin is death' (Romans 6:23) will mean the ultimate death of our society."[6]

And take to heart what Dr. Henry Blackaby, special assistant to the presidents of several boards of the Southern Baptist Convention and co-author of *Experiencing God*, said in 1999 at a conference at the Billy Graham Training Center at The Cove in Asheville, North Carolina. When asked his view of the future of America, Dr. Blackaby said, "If you put the U.S. up against the Scriptures, we're in trouble. I think we're very close to the judgment of God." Dr. James Dobson of Focus on the Family agreed: "Sadly, I believe Dr. Blackaby's assessment of America is entirely accurate."

INDIFFERENCE TO JUDGEMENT-TALK

In spite of the warnings, we remain indifferent to judgment-talk and pre-occupied with a thousand economic, political, social, environmental bobby pins. We need to listen to the wake-up calls. What will it take to get us to do so? What will it take for the Church to do so? Another 9/11? Some other national tragedy? Another war? Economic disintegration? Natural disasters? A combination of these? Or something else unforeseen? Or, are we so set in our sin, so determined to go our own way, so self-deluded with our chosen lies and so indifferent and complacent that nothing will get our attention?

Ideally, God wants any wake-up call to come from the Church and its pulpits as it proclaims the Word of the Lord. But with the cacophony of voices today, a roar from the Church will have to be strong. *It will have to be a voice so motivated by the heart of God that it will be willing to roar!* It will come from men and women whose passion is to know God, are humble, whose only purpose is to please Him, and who we are undistracted by fads, hype and celebrity. They'll speak even at great cost, calling us to repentance and a return to the gracious God who gave us this grand country.

Is it possible that such a roar can rise the Church and from its pulpits in our day? We dare to believe it is. And we believe that such a voice could be a catalyst for the revival so many so desire to see and which many believe is our nation's and Western society's only real hope.

We should remind ourselves that God has spoken to us from both His Word and through events. But have we heard? At a conference in the fall of 2000, I heard Dr. Walter Kaiser, Jr. ask, "Is anybody listening? Is anybody at home?" Dr. Kaiser, a professor at Gordon-Conwell Seminary, declared that God has been speaking to America many years through event after event. "As I read the Scriptures," Dr. Kaiser added, "God is exceedingly angry with America. Therefore we stand under the judgment of God unless there comes a 180-degree turning to God—repentance!"[7]

One of the events to which Dr. Kaiser might have been referring to us as they voice of God in a wake-up call, could have been the 2000 presidential election (Other events could be September 11, 2001, and the War with Iraq, but for now we'll use the debacle of the 2000 presidential election.) Who can forget those 36 agitating days of wondering who our next president would be, arguing all the way to the Supreme Court, debating over our Constitution, quarreling over dimpled and hanging chads, watching the spectacle of ballot-counters holding up ballots to the light trying to discern whether they were to be tallied, and facing how divided we are?

That election challenge, which erupted in the middle of the writing of this book, had the earmarks of a "remedial judgment of God" (something that we will look at later). It appeared that we were poised at pivotal crossroads with two markedly different futures before us. We stood between "hastened judgment" and "delayed judgment"—a time of mercy. Our Lord was again asking, "Is anyone listening? Is anybody at home?" Some indeed did hear, because a focused segment of believers across our nation and across the world cried out to the Lord in intense intercession that was both amazing and wonderful.

A "WINDOW OF MERCY" NOW

Our Lord answered by graciously giving us a *"window of mercy,"* which we are in now. It's a time for the Church to come humbly before our gracious Lord in repentance and intercession, followed by calling for national repentance, and as said a bit earlier, taking our nation by the hand and leading it back to God. This is a time we must not squander because without action, *we could be headed for a time when we will have virtually abandoned all restraint in the bloodshed of killing our unborn, sexual licentiousness, pride and other public sins. Our cup of iniquity could be overflowing.* Richard Owens Roberts said, "Historically, unheeded remedial judgments have turned into final judgments. America, as a nation, is ripe for destruction."[8]

During this post-9/11 time, with a struggle in Iraq and the ongoing threat of terror, we need the same kind of commanding, unwavering voice which the Northern Kingdom of Israel needed— and got—in the Eighth Century B.C. during the reign of Jereboam II. Those times were similar to ours, much like Charles Dicken's statement in the opening lines of A *Tale of Two Cities*: "It was the best of times; it was the worst of times." There was great wealth, there was great sin. Israel had known God, but had rejected Him. The good times flourished; but so did injustice, pride, idolatry, immorality, and violence. Prosperity *and* sin defined the nation. It was the time of the Northern Kingdom's golden age; and it was its last age. The prosperous nation was headed for judgment and destruction.

Israel's situation was critical. Looming ahead—though they did not know it, and would not have admitted it if they did—was the ominous year of 722 B.C., when the unrepentant nation, after many warnings from God's prophets, would fall brutally to the Assyrians under God's judgment. This meant that Jereboam's Israel had about forty years left—from 762 B.C. to 722 B.C.—just forty years! In the rise and fall of nations, especially a nation like Israel that could trace its ancestry back over a thousand years to Abraham, forty years was a very short time.

Notwithstanding, like America now and Sodom before, prosperity was Israel's national sedative; she was indifferent to her peril. "Disaster will not overtake us," they said.[9] "Prosperity," Edward Gibbon wrote in *The Decline and Fall of the Roman Empire*, "ripened the principle of decay. As soon as time or accident had removed the artificial supports, the stupendous fabric yielded to the pressure of its own weight."

So Israel had to have a commanding, compelling voice to get their attention. And that is what God gave them. In His vast mercy God raised His voice through Amos with thundering words: "The Lord roars . . ."[10] using the image of God as a lion about to pounce on its prey. It was meant to jolt Israel and wake her up.

God's roar gripped Amos' soul: "The Lion has roared—tremble in fear. The Lord God has sounded your doom—I dare not refuse to proclaim it."[11]

The Lord's roar at His people in His chosen nation staggers us as we read it today. However, when God roared, He acted consistent with His character. With Israel in peril, roaring a warning of danger revealed the tender aspect of His love and mercy.

Certainly love roars when it sees a loved one in danger. Imagine you are deeply asleep at 2:30 a.m., and someone comes into your bedroom, gets about nine inches from your ear and thunders, *"Wake up!"* That would be a heart-stopping experience. And if they were just playing a little practical joke, you could be expected to be upset. However if your house were on fire, after the initial shock you would be grateful your "roarer" saved your life.

Or imagine a child, say about 2 1/2, sitting blissfully in the center of the street in front of your house, playing. Would you call others to view the "cute" scene? Not likely. What you'd probably do, at the risk of your own safety, is dash into the street. grab the child, and roar, "Don't play in the street!" (The child might interpret the aggressive action as judgment day, not comprehending the caring that motivated the action.)

When people are asleep in a burning house or a child is playing in the street, whispering or silence are the responses, not of love, but of indifference.

The catch-phrases of our day reveal our house is burning: Every woman has the right to control her own body. . . An unborn is not a person. . . Fathers can't protect their unborn. . . Partial-birth abortion is a woman's right. . . America doesn't have a Christian heritage. . . Give condoms at school without telling parents. . . Provide abortions to teens without telling their parents. . . Get rid of the Ten Commandments. . . Sexual license is a right. . . Homosexuality is an acceptable alternative lifestyle. . . Same-sex marriage should be permitted. . . Teaching our children about homosexuality in our schools must be allowed. . . Physician-assisted suicide is each person's decision. . . The anguish of aging and senility could be averted by voluntary death. . . Genetic engineering can yield a perfect humanity. . .

We are dying from a thousand wounds; yet we are oblivious that we stand at the abyss of judgment.

We dare not whisper—let the roar God gave through Amos be sounded again.

RIGHTEOUSNESS EXALTS, SIN IS A DISGRACE

"Righteousness exalts a nation, but sin is a disgrace to any people," God declares in Proverbs.[12] So sin is a disgrace to America—and every nation of the West. Killing our unborn is a disgrace. Teaching our children to sin is a disgrace. Pride is a disgrace. Self-absorption is a disgrace. Fornication is a disgrace. Adultery is a disgrace. Sodomy is a disgrace. Same-sex marriage is a disgrace. TV, movies, music and any media that honor these sins are a disgrace. Americans that practice these sins are a disgrace. Christians and preachers who watch these sins in silence are a disgrace.

America was born of the grace of God; it is beneath her calling to be so disgraced with vile sin. We are called the land of the free and the land of opportunity—a nation with the soul of a church. But we've defiled ourselves; we've settled for Sodom; we've consented to the values of barbarians. When Alistair Cooke, the British-born American journalist and broadcaster, was asked about Chesterton's famous remark that the United States was a nation with the soul of a church, he replied, *"That's true, but also the soul of a whorehouse."*

Several years ago *Slouching Toward Gomorrah*, Robert Bork's excellent and best-selling incisive analysis of the declining state of our culture, was published. Bork used "Gomorrah" as a metaphor for the debasement of American society. More commonly, of course, it is "Sodom"—the other degenerate city usually paired with Gomorrah—which is used as such a metaphor. As we know, Sodom, Gomorrah and the surrounding towns were destroyed by fire under God's judgment because they "gave themselves up to sexual immorality and perversion [homosexual practice]," and "serve as an example of those who suffer the punishment of eternal fire."[13]

The late James Montgomery Boice believed that America and the nations of the West are cultures of barbarians. He excellently defined a modern barbarian as *"a person who lives by power and for pleasure rather than by and for principle."* By that definition, some of us preachers who "live for power and pleasure rather than by and for principle" are barbarians. And who knows how many Christians and churches "live for power and pleasure rather than by and for principle"? Consider the mass appeal—the hype—continually being made in the Christian world promoting "power and pleasure." We find them in the promotions of the trendy success slogans, new "moves of God," power religion, prosperity, positive mental images, pop psychology, self-esteem, winds of doctrine, moralisms, and such which are so big in the Church today. We've proclaimed them from pulpit, magazine, radio, TV, book and bookstore. Because they've boosted our Sunday attendance and expanded our "ministries," we've competed with each other to shovel-feed them to our audiences.

Boice observed, "Is the Church not barbaric when it forgets its unique message and identifies with the aspirations and values of the world culture instead?" As examples Boice cites pragmatism, entertainment, competition, self-help programs, and "soporific pep-talks in order to keep people coming and giving with little thought for the ultimate well-being of their souls."[14]

We need to be very careful because our "barbarian" message today has the earmarks of being a 21st Century version of the sunny "peace, peace" message of the false prophets Jeremiah condemned in the 6th Century B.C. That message was like that of the success-focused window cleaner who was heavily into "the latest move of

God." He fell from the 22nd floor. As he plummeted, those who had open windows heard him cheerfully confessing, "So far, so good! So far, so good!" For Jerusalem, it wasn't so good. As the city scorned Jeremiah and listened to the utopian false prophets, it fell to the barbarous Babylonians in 586 B.C. under the judgment of God.

Dr. Steven Muller believes one reason America is barbarian is its "failure to rally around a set of values." This "means that we are turning out highly skilled barbarians," Muller said. "Society as a whole is turning out barbarians because of the discarding of the value system it was built on."[15]

Charles Colson says, "Today in the West, and particularly in America, the new barbarians are all around us. They are not hairy Goths and Vandals, swilling fermented brew and ravishing maidens; they are not Huns and Visigoths storming our borders or scaling our city wall. No, this time the invaders have come from within. We have bred them in our families and trained them in our classrooms. They inhabit our legislatures, our courts, our film studios, and our churches. Most of them are attractive and pleasant; their ideas are persuasive and subtle. *Yet these men and women threaten our most cherished institutions and our very character as a people.*"[16]

The idea that America and the West is a barbarian Sodom doesn't sit well with most of us. The likely reason is that we've succumbed to that delusion that has infected most all judgment-bound cultures. It's the hubris which assumes we are better, smarter, more sophisticated, and have made more progress than those who have lived before us. It is epitomized by that elitist statement of Sigmund Freud: "But these ancestors of ours were far more ignorant than we."

Irving Kristol said, "We are arrogant and condescending toward all ancestors because we are so convinced we understand them better than they understood themselves."[17]

Delivering a barbarian message in the Church comes not only from what we teach and preach; it comes from what we don't say. In the Old Testament Ezekiel and Jeremiah spoke of prophets who say "peace-peace when there is no peace." In the New Testament the Apostle Paul referred to a time when "men will not put up with sound doctrine," and there would be "teachers [who] say what their itching ears want to hear."[18]

What tends to happen is a strong focus on selected "positive" themes while omitting such principles as God's justice, sin, accountability, judgment, and eternal damnation.

An example might be teaching or preaching on the topic of success, prosperity or victory (various forms of triumphalism) and presenting these as "the blessings of grace." However, how is grace defined? A common definition is "unmerited favor"—acknowledgement that we have sinned and should face justice and eternal damnation; yet God loves us and sent Christ to be our Savior (*see Romans 5:8 and Romans 6:23*). So, scripturally, grace is defined "against justice." However, if God's justice is omitted, then grace becomes a distortion of God's character; it becomes unanchored grace, or as Dietrich Bonhoefer termed it, "cheap grace." It's the promise of blessing without repentance, and allows people to go to hell feeling good about themselves, successful and prosperous.

Unanchored grace results in all kinds of free-wheeling views, usually involving further distortions of God's character which effectively reduce the great and majestic God to a heavenly butler or Santa Claus and a formula for getting blessings, with the preacher the one who knows the formula.

Preaching about unanchored grace, of course, can be very popular, but it mistakenly reduces grace to sentimentalism. And such preaching is, as Fred Craddock said, like trying to "plant trees on clouds."

"I believe the greatest danger we face in America is the casual Christian," noted the late Roger Hull, former president of Mutual of New York. And the late Pastor Richard Halverson, once chaplain of the United States Senate and Washington, D.C., said, "The problem in America is the people who profess to believe in God and live as though God is nonexistent, the people who profess faith in God and live as though it doesn't make any difference. I'm concerned about the evangelicals who have embraced the secular way of life: materialism, the love of money. That's where the danger is in America."

VILE VALLEYS AND BEAUTIFUL COUNTRYSIDES

Sir Arthur Conan Doyle had Sherlock Holmes put things in splendid perspective: "It is my belief, Watson, founded upon my experience, that the lowest and vilest alleys of London do not present a more dreadful record of sin than does the smiling and beautiful countryside."[19]

So, except for our "smiling and beautiful countryside" made possible by the very highest standard of living in history, we are not so different from the "lowest and vilest alleys" of our barbarian fore-fathers, or of Rome, Noah's time, Israel, Judah, or Sodom.

"Pagan rebellion in ancient times actually escalated until God irrevocably 'gave them over' [see Romans 1:24-28]," says Carl Henry, speaking of judgment. "The Creator responded to mankind's insistent and unyielding rejection of Him by finally abandoning rebellious humanity to its own determinate intellectual depravity, degrading passions, and moral impurity."[20]

And speaking as Henry does of God "abandoning rebellious humanity," here is what Joseph Rowlandson said in 1678 in his sermon on a special day of prayer and fasting: "God's forsaking the people He has been near to is a thing of such weight and solemnity, and has such bitter effects that it is a very difficult subject, especially in a dark and mourning day, for ministers to speak of and for people to listen to. But servants of God must warn of the danger and the people of God must act so as to avoid such a judgment. As God's presence is the greatest good His people can experience on this side of heaven, so His absence is the greatest misery they can know on this side of hell."[21]

There is no time to waste. Our national urgently needs a clear, prophetic voice whose message is shorn of bobby pin frippery, a voice compelled to roar because it loves us enough to do so, a voice so filled with the singular Word of God it will get in the face of all of us in our barbarian Sodom and tell us the gravity of our sin and the terror of our certain judgment, and a voice which will "confront [us] with all [our] detestable practices,"[22] speak to us straightly about "righteousness, self-control and the judgment to come,"[23] "command [us] to repent,"[24] and summon us to "save ourselves from this corrupt generation."[25]

May such a roar arise from the Church. America needs revival. Such a roar has the genuine prospect of being the catalyst our Lord uses to ignite deep, biblical revival across our land. Jonah's roar in Nineveh ignited revival there. Peter and the Church's roar in Jerusalem on the Day of Pentecost ignited one there—one that still affects us.

Let us weep as we roar. It is how the prophet Jeremiah spoke. That great prophet saw his beloved, but willfully deluded Jerusalem in their idolatry, iniquity, and smugness. He saw their certain coming judgment. And he wept. His tears were the vehicle for the word which God gave Him to proclaim. With an intensity, that burned within him, Jeremiah declared—roared—resolutely and courageously all of God's message, giving no quarter to the false prophets of blessing, peace, and prosperity.

Let that voice today have the same clarity and passion of the prophet Elijah, who confronted Israel when Ahab and Jezebel ruled, when that nation waffled between God and Baal.

Elijah challenged the indecisive nation on Mount Carmel, "How long will you waver between two opinions? If God is God, follow Him; but if Baal is God, follow Him." The late Peter Marshall Sr., once chaplain of the United States Senate and pastor of New

York Avenue Presbyterian Church in Washington, D.C. preached about Elijah's confrontation with Israel on Mount Carmel. Marshall concluded his powerful sermon with the closing line from an article in Life Magazine: "We need a prophet who will have the ear of America and say to her now, 'How long halt ye between two opinions? If the Lord be God, follow Him; but if Baal be God, follow him—and GO TO HELL!'"

A contemporary chorus says, *These are the days of Elijah, declaring the Word of the Lord / And these are the days of Your servant, Moses, Righteousness being restored / And though these are days of great trials, of famine and darkness and sword / Still we are the voice in the desert crying, "Prepare ye the way of the Lord."*

While we have this window of mercy, our prayer is that the following pages will be part of a roar—for revival in the Church and awakening in America and Western nations.

As urged, we hope you will join in the prayers at the end of each chapter; and raise your voice in intercession and proclamation.

A compassionate roar will be enormously pivotal in our particular hour.

Let us pray together: *Our gracious Heavenly Father, thank You for Your blessing upon this nation. Everything we have comes from You. However, we have turned away from You and have embraced and excused terrible evils. We deserve judgment. And our judgment could have been hastened; but You, Lord, have given us a gracious window of mercy, which we must not squander. Your hand is extended to us; tears are on Your face. May we in Your Church seize this moment and seek Your face in humility and repentance. And speak up—roar—and call our nation back to You. Oh, Lord, may we weep as we roar. May this*

happen in America and every nation in the West from Australia and New Zealand to Great Britain and Switzerland. As we journey through the pages ahead, speak to each of us, starting with me. Let us understand the urgency of this. May our beloved America see a sweeping spiritual awakening from the White House to my house, to every house. In Jesus' name, Amen.

PROLOGUE ENDNOTES

[1] Amos 3:8, Living Bible.

[2] Sir Arthur Conan Doyle, "The Copper Beeches," *The Adventures of Sherlock Holmes*, 1892.

[3] From Luke 19:41-44.

[4] From Luke 17:26-30.

[5] David Willis McCullough, *Chronicles of the Barbarians*, (New York, NY: History Book Club, 1998), p.144.

[6] Billy Graham, *World Aflame*, Fleming H. Revell, 1965.

[7] Walter Kaiser, Jr., speaking at *The Power of Gospel Preaching* conference in Atlanta, GA, October, 2000.

[8] Richard Owen Roberts, in his article, *The Solemn Assembly*.

[9] Amos 9:10b.

[10] Amos 1:2.

[11] See #1 above.

[12] Proverbs 14:34.

[13] Jude 7.

[14] Ibid. p.30.

[15] Steven Muller, "University Professor Speaks Out," *NFD Informer* (September 1983), p.64.

[16] Charles Colson with Ellen Santilli Vaughn, *Against the Night: Living in the New Dark Ages* (Ann Arbor, MI: Servant, 1989), pp. 23-24.

[17] Irving Kristol, *Reflections of a Neoconservative* (New York, NY: Basic Books, 1983), p.79.

[18] II Timothy 4:3.

[19] See #1.

[20] Carl Henry, from his speech to the 40th National Religious Broadcasters Convention.

[21] Reverend Joseph Rowlandson, from his sermon, *The Possibility of God Forsaking a People,*" given Nov. 21, 1678 in Weathersfield, CT, on a special day of prayer, fasting and humiliation.

[22] Ezekiel 22:2; 23:36.

[23] Acts 24:25, Paul speaking before the Roman governor, Felix.

[24] Acts 17:30 Paul preaching in Athens.

[25] Acts 2:40.

PART ONE

OUR SIN, SILENCE
AND SELF-DELUSION

"There is a generation that is pure in its own eyes, yet it is not washed from its filthiness."[1]

"In his own eyes he flatters himself too much to detect or hate his sin."[2]

"Take heed, you senseless ones among the people; you fools, when will you become wise?"[3]

"The Lord knows the thoughts of man; He knows they are futile."[4]

Awhole generation is growing up with no awareness of regeneration by the Holy Spirit, a species without clear ideas about sin and sacrilege, a race for whom God and the supernatural are virtually eclipsed, individuals with no interest in the *imago Dei*, no eternal concerns.

"The forerunner of these half-men are being nourished wherever a pulpit no longer preaches the commandments of God and the sinfulness of man, the ideal humanity of Jesus Christ and the divine forgiveness of sin, and the fact of saving grace. Obscure the vitalities of revealed religion, detour churchgoers from piety and saintliness, and in the so-called enlightened nations not only will the multitudes soon relapse to a retrograde morality, but churchgoers will live in Corinthian immorality, churchmen will encourage situational ethics, and the line between the Christian and the worldling will scarce be found.

"**Even in the church, barbarians are breeding**: beware, the Scripture says, of the lawless one who will occupy the temple of God (2 Thess. 2:4). Savages are stirring the dust of a decadent civilization and already slink in the shadows of a disabled Church."[5]

—CARL F.H. HENRY, SPEAKING OF AMERICA

They had been taught that obedience to the laws of God was the only foundation for national greatness, liberty and security. As long as the nation recognized God as Supreme it could stand.

"But something had been happening in the national life. The faith and division of the founding fathers had faded. National decay had set in. There was confusion in the minds of the people. They were beginning to forget the principles that had made them a nation. They begin to love things more than principles. All around them paganism flourished. They took a little of Jehovah and a little of Baal. They became by degrees more and more broad-minded. Was it not a free country? Who wanted to be old-fashioned? So morality became a relative thing. The old absolutes were regarded as far too intolerant. The national moral standards were lowered. The worship of Baal and Jehovah got mixed. Somehow it was hard to draw a line of distinction. Materialism and idealism were often confused.

"Now Elijah saw the danger, he saw what would happen to the nation when its moral fiber was weakened. He knew the end of confusion and in decision. He knew with all of his heart that national ruin and disaster were inevitable if the nation forsook Jehovah and departed from its charter and constitution. Though a challenge, he summoned the leaders of the country together on this day of destiny, *'If the Lord be God follow Him, but if Baal then follow him.'*"[6]

—THE LATE PETER MARSHALL, SR,
COMPARING ISRAEL WITH AMERICA

PART ONE ENDNOTES

[1] Proverbs 30:12 NKJV

[2] Psalm 36:2.

[3] Psalm 94:8.

[4] Psalm 94:11.

[5] Carl Henry, *Twilight of a Great Civilization*, (Westchester, IL: Crossway Books, 1988), p.17.

[6] Peter Marshall, Sr, from his sermon, *Trial By Fire*, given in 1944.

1

DISCOVERY TRAIN

"There is no faithfulness, no love, no acknowledgment of God in the land. There is only cursing, lying and murder, stealing and adultery; they break all bounds, and bloodshed follows bloodshed. Because of this the land mourns."
—GOD, SPEAKING THROUGH HOSEA[1]

"Have we now lost?
Our country's dying now
Does it matter to you now?
We aren't free now
People dying in the streets now
Doesn't it matter to you now?"

—ANNE HERRING[2]

THE TRAIN RATTLED ALONG THE TRACKS, AND I JOSTLED slightly in my seat as it went. My stepfather had died, and I was returning home after the funeral in California.

My schedule as a pastor was continuously active, something I was very happy in; but the trip was a welcomed break. Taking the train gave me a few extra hours of solitude, for relaxation, for study.

I had brought along a book to read—a Bible commentary, not exactly your popular paperback variety of book, but something I was very much looking forward to. It was something relatively new by Francis L. Anderson and David Noel Freedman, one of Doubleday's Anchor Bible series of commentaries, on the prophetic book of Hosea. I was preparing for a series of messages I would give in my church on this Old Testament prophet, and his contemporary, Amos.

But that trip, and that book, changed my life.

By the time I got off the train I had reflected deeply inside. I had been shocked and scorched in my spirit; my intellect had been confronted and challenged as never before.

And that train ride was not the end of it, but rather a beginning. As the engine slowed and the brakes hissed, I was only beginning a journey that would take me through the Word of God again and again, and through scores of other books and commentaries, into secular history, and finally into my own church pulpit, and on to public platforms from my city to Rome and across the world, until I had been completely consumed by the gripping revelation that God began to give me on that train.

The journey began with Hosea, that extraordinary prophet who obeyed God and married a women who became a prostitute. That marriage and the children born were a living pageant of Israel's unfaithfulness to the Lord.

It was the eighth century before Christ, a pivotal time for both of the twin kingdoms of Israel and Judah. Both nations were at high moments in political influence and economic security. Jeroboam II and Uzziah, kings over the north and south, had defeated their enemies on a grand scale, expanding their borders and influencing civilization far beyond their national boundaries. The people realized they had entered upon an era of unsurpassed well-being. They believed their wealth and good fortune were God's reward for their supposed allegiance to Him.

But all was not as it seemed. The second half of that marvelous eighth century B.C. brought that bright age to a disastrous end— and the tragic decay of a nation began.

This is where Hosea's exceptional, profound ministry comes on the scene. His recorded work began during the latter years of the reign of Jeroboam II—a man responsible for a number of crimes against God and His people. As I read the commentary on Hosea, I read of Jeroboam's flagrant violations of his nation's sacred covenant with God. In fact, Jeroboam's regime saw gross sins practiced during that era of peace and prosperity. Not only Hosea, but also Amos, spoke to that self-satisfied, sinning culture. Amos looked at "the gap between the covenant requirements in the social and economic spheres and the realities in the kingdom of Israel," while Hosea spoke "even more vehemently about religious commitments and cult practices, charging the establishment with nothing less than idolatry, apostasy and cultic enormities, including sexual promiscuity and human sacrifice."[3]

The prophecies of Hosea and Amos pointed to the eventual downfall of Israel under the judgment of God. In 722 B.C. Israel was sacked by the cruel, invading Assyrians; in 586 B.C., Judah fell captive to the fierce Babylonians.

Essentially, Hosea and Amos were "end-times" prophets, speaking at a time the society was indulgent and self-absorbed— reveling in sinful practice. They spoke to a society that scorned their looming judgment.

Unlike our contemporary end-time expositors, Hosea was more concerned with the *message* of God for His people as they faced their "last days" than the schedule of events. He wasn't concerned with *when* the demise of Israel would occur. Hosea was concerned with *why* the people were subject to God's coming judgment, and *how* they could avoid spiritual disaster and find redemption. Hosea's concern was the salvation of God's people.

As the train rumbled along, I realized that there were even more similarities between Hosea's time and our own. And those similarities intrigued me. I wondered what exactly the elements were that led to Israel's downfall.

And then, a phrase from Hosea 4:2 jumped from the page, and began resounding through my mind: "they break all bounds. . .bloodshed follows bloodshed."

Carnage begets carnage. Murder spawns murder. Killing of innocent life begets more killing of innocent life.

As this recurring phrase played in my mind, bits and pieces of recent news articles and magazine stories and other sources flashed in counterpoints.

A quote by Albert Schweitzer surfaced: "If a man loses reverence for any part of life, he will lose his reverence for all of life."

As all of these thoughts began to congeal, an awful realization began to dawn: Israel's judgment and downfall came as they degenerated to proud, nonchalant, inhumane barbarians who, as God would say, became worse than the debauched barbarians they drove out centuries before. Evidence of their corrupted, arrogant character included an ultimate sin: the killing of innocent victims by official sanction. They "shed innocent blood," according to Psalm 106:38, "even blood of their sons and of their daughters, whom they sacrificed unto the idols of Canaan: and the land was polluted with blood."

And because of this "was the wrath of the Lord kindled against his people insomuch that he abhorred his own inheritance" Psalm 106:40.

But it was a single striking paragraph in the commentary on Hosea that deeply sobered me:

Idolatrous and apostate worship has two outstanding features, on both of which the prophet pours out his vehemence. Sexual promiscuity in the fertility cult undermines the moral structure of the covenant and is a gross violation of the basic requirements on community life under God. Furthermore, it is *sin against God and people*, that is, the *shedding of innocent blood*. This is not ordinary murder, but *officially sanctioned human sacrifice.*"4

When I read those words again, I stopped reading and put the book down. One word came flooding into my mind: *Abortion!*

But it was a question that gripped me, *Could abortion biblically be the shedding of innocent blood?*

That question haunted me. I thought of America, my country regarded as a great nation. And yes, my nation was a sinning nation; but could we have the same kind of barbarian character as Israel which rationalized and perpetrated the shedding of innocent blood, the same kind of ultimate sin that brought Israel's judgment?

Through an aggressive study of Scripture and history, I would come to believe that abortion is that kind of defining sin.

While it's true that brutal child sacrifice does not exist today as it did in Israel's day, abortion is its ghastly counterpart. Today, millions of innocent unborn babies are heedlessly destroyed by our cocksure culture who aggressively excuses its barbarian conduct with willful self-deceptions: "the right of a woman to her own body," "every child should be wanted," "the viability of the fetus," or "the right to choose."

In fact, we are slaughtering the most innocent of the innocents: unborn babies. And it is done through the decree of law, having been legalized by the Supreme Court in the famous *Roe vs. Wade* decision of 1973.

I looked out the window of the train.

Suddenly, as I sat in that rumbling train car, I realized that the issue—the sin—was more than a passing social concern. Abortion was carnage—but worse, carnage against the helpless, the defenseless, the weak, those the Lord speaks up for. It was the shedding of innocent blood; and, by the standard God had set for His people, most terrible of all—the shedding of innocent blood by official sanction.

Later I would read a searing statement by James Dobson that would stir me again: "I see abortion as the most significant moral issue of our times. In fact, I feel that the ministers of this country (of the world) are someday going to have to answer for their unwillingness to confront this issue head-on. It cannot be right to take an *innocent little child* whom God is forming in his mother's womb, and leave him to die on a porcelain table."[5]

My inquiry would expand and I would include other sins such as pride, self-absorption, and our pervasive immorality—both heterosexual and homosexual—as among the defining ways we as a nation, or any nation, reveal our barbarian arrogance deserving of judgment.

And I would struggle with why we in the church, and particularly we in the pulpit—starting with myself—were not addressing our national sins. Why were most of us mute?

For the next eight months I would find myself researching the message series on Amos and Hosea in a far more extensive way than I had ever done for any other series; and I would particularly focus on the message from Hosea 4:1-2, "My people ask counsel at their stock, and their staff declareth unto them: for the spirit of whoredoms hath caused them to err, and they have gone a whoring from under their God." That preparation and the message would remarkably launch a new ministry. Studying in those months, I would notice other parallels: Israel once knowing God and then forgetting Him; the same in America. Israel's arrogance and pride; ours. Israel practicing barbarism like the pagan nations; our doing the same. Israel's prosperity becoming a sedative dulling their conscience; the same here. Israel's indifference toward sin and judgment; ours.

Drawing those parallels would be ahead, but for the moment the implications of legalized abortion riveted my thoughts. Our easy, public-approved killing of our unborn suddenly seemed to line up precisely alongside Israel's ritualized child-sacrifices in several frightening ways. And even as their incredible violation of God's covenant sowed the seeds of their own destruction, so I saw, in my mind's eye, America reaching that same outer limit.

The only possible outcomes are catastrophe and judgment. Our urgent need is national repentance.

Let us pray together: *Our most gracious Heavenly Father, thank You for insight into Your Word. Teach to understand what we are doing both as a nation and as individuals. Father, we do face catastrophe and judgment for our grievous sins of bloodshed, licentiousness, all expressions of our deeper pride and self-absorption. May the following pages help us to understand where we are and what we must do which is repent and humbly seek Your face. May we in Your Church lead our nation back to You. In Jesus' name we pray. Amen.*

CHAPTER 1 ENDNOTES

[1] From Hosea 4:1-3.

[2] Anne Herring, from her song, *Killing Thousands,* 1981, Latter Rain Music.

[3] Francis L. Anderson and David Noel Freedman, *Hosea,* (New York: Doubleday, 1980), p. 38.

[4] Ibid., p. 49.

[5] James Dobson, *Theism and the Modern Mind,* Christianity Today, May 7, 1982.

2

MUTE LIONS

"Before I formed you in the womb I knew you, before you were born I set you apart; I appointed you as a prophet to the nations. 'Ah Sovereign Lord,' I said, 'I do not know how to speak. . .' But the Lord said to me. . . 'You must go to everyone I send you to and say whatever I command you."

—GOD SPEAKING TO JEREMIAH[1]

"Now when our land to ruin's brink is verging / In God's name let us speak while there is time / Now, when padlocks for our lips are forging / Silence is a crime."

—JOHN GREENLEAF WHITTIER

EIGHT MONTHS AFTER THAT TRAIN RIDE I SAT ON THE PLATFORM on Sunday morning in the church where I was pastor. The church was very full. We were singing. Later I would preach. No one could have anticipated the remarkable way the Lord would move that morning, nor that the message would launch a ministry.

I spotted two families seated on opposite sides of the sanctuary. Both were happily worshiping. But my heart stopped—I thought of the sermon I was to give later, and I reproached myself, "Why didn't I take them aside before today? They're going to think that I am just targeting them." I became very anxious. I thought, "I'll not give the message this week; I give it next week. And I'll talk to them."

But quietly pressed to my heart was, "Go ahead, preach the message; it will be all right."

"But they'll misunderstand," I argued. "I don't want to use the pulpit as a club to beat on people!"

Again pressed to my heart, "Go ahead, it will be all right."

At issue was that in each of the two families, a family member had been involved with a sin that I would discuss in my message from Hosea—and the two were there in the service. I knew I would be saying some very strong things. Plus my wife Esther and I had been deeply involved about two or three months before in working each family through the ordeals that resulted. At that same time I was preparing this mornings's sermon. If I didn't talk to them I reasoned, they would misunderstand; and I wanted those families to know I loved them. More important, that God loved them. They were not being singled out.

After several minutes of wrenching hesitation, I finally decided to go ahead and give the message that day.

Later, I reflected on the whole episode, and realized that behind all my grappling and my desire to assure those dear families of my love and God's, was a larger question: *Would I preach the truth?*

I also realized that muting scriptural truth can be accomplished in a variety of ways such as by avoiding certain parts of the Word of God, by softening the "hard" messages of Scripture; by getting caught up with some faddish wind of doctrine or new "move of

God;" by being distracted by hype, celebrity, entertainment, church growth, pop-psychology, by just plain fearing man; etc.

There is agony in the minister who aspires to be preach the truth—to be true both to the Word of God and the heart of God. He is tempted to be more faithful to one or the other. On the one hand he may focus on speaking the exact letter of the Word; on the other he may give place to speaking what he imagines is the love of God. One way he will tend to become strict, cold, without passion, pharisaical and subtly proud of his orthodoxy; the other way he will tend to become flaccid, sentimental, antinomian and subtly proud of his accommodating attitude. Both are false, producing false, mute prophets and spurious ministry.

But Truth and Love are not mutually exclusive; they are entwined in the very character of God. They are to be rooted in the soul of every true minister and in the fabric of every message he preaches.

Facing the dilemma of whether or not I would preach the truth was part of two questions which arose when I was doing the research for the Hosea and Amos series. At the time they seemed very difficult to answer. The first question was: *In sanctioning the killing of our unborn today, could we be doing the same kind of thing that brought judgment on Old Testament Israel and Judah when they shed innocent blood?*

I came to the conviction from Scripture that killing our unborn in abortion is shedding innocent blood and that we as a nation (or any nation) face judgment for it and for our other defining sins. Abortion is not a political issue; it is a national sin.

THE SECOND QUESTION

The second question came from trying to answer this first question: *Is it possible for a minister of the Gospel who accepts the Bible as the Word of God, and who believes Christ is our only Savior and Lord, who* believes the essentials of Christianity, to be someone who the Bible calls a false prophet?

You see, pondering the first question led me to think, *"If scripturally abortion is the shedding of innocent blood, we face judgment. But why are we not judged? And why haven't we preachers been saying something?"* In a way, I had a "King Josiah moment." When the Book of the Law was read to him, he had become greatly alarmed at the truth he was hearing and had exclaimed, "Great is the Lord's anger that burns against us. . ."[2]

I wrestled intellectually and spiritually with this question for quite awhile. Looking back, that now surprises me. Perhaps my struggle was caused in part by the fact that the Christian community in America and the West was dominated by a lavish style of Christianity. There were massive television ministries that were led by larger-than-life personalities who enjoyed luxuriant lifestyles and were accorded great celebrity. There was an extensive emphasis on Christian health and wealth. Many were teaching, or strongly implying, that as a Christian you had a Christ-given right to great material benefits—which could be yours if you had faith or believed correctly. Also, "entrepreneurial pastors," who developed megachurches and oversaw large staffs and massive budgets, had begun to appear on the Christian stage.

I wondered, "Have we in the Church effectively become a generation of false prophets?" I was freshly shaken by our Lord's clear warning "Watch out for false prophets, who come to you in sheep's clothing, but inwardly they are ravenous wolves."[3] *I had always put a "false prophet" outside the Church in a cult, or as some eccentric who claimed he was the Messiah. However, on closer reading of our Lord's warning, I saw that He doesn't warn of false prophets <u>outside</u> the Church, but <u>in</u> the Church—they "come to you in <u>sheep's</u> clothing."*[4]

In addition there is that disturbing passage from the Sermon on the Mount: "Many will say to me on that day, 'Lord, Lord, did we not prophesy in your name, and in your name drive out demons and perform many miracles?'" This puts this group clearly inside the Church as professed followers.

Jesus continued, "Then I will tell them plainly, `I never knew you. Away from me, you evildoers.'"[5] This is an uncompromising final judgment on a false ministry, which makes it a matter of great concern to all of us. The Lord also said, "Not everyone who says to me, 'Lord, Lord,' will enter the kingdom of heaven, but he who does the will of my Father who is in heaven."[6]

Just before the Apostle Paul left the elders at Ephesus to sail to Jerusalem, he exhorted them to "Keep watch over yourselves and all the flock . . ." He then cautioned them about a spiritual danger that would come not from outside the Church, but from inside: "I know that after I leave, savage wolves will come in among you and will not spare the flock. Even from your own number men will arise and distort the truth in order to draw away disciples after them. So be on your guard!"[7]

To find the answer to the question of whether a minister of the Gospel could become what the Bible defines as a false prophet, I also studied some of the writing prophets such as Amos, Hosea, Jeremiah and Ezekiel. Each of them had urgent, pivotal messages for their respective nations—Amos and Hosea for Israel; Jeremiah and Ezekiel for Judah and Jerusalem. Their messages, if heeded, would bring restoration and blessing. When the sin of these nations reached a crucial point and they headed toward their end in judg-ment, God in His loving care had sent them these and other prophets to warn them and call them back to Him. Their messages contained forceful and bold exposure of sin, and strong, repeated warnings of forthcoming judgment unless there was repentance.

But the nations did not listen; they displayed caustic scorn for both the message and the messenger.

Why didn't the nations listen?

We could say that it was because they were too settled in their prosperity and too materialistic, and the messages upset their lifestyles. That's partially true. We could also say that it was because they were violent and immoral, even amoral. That would also partially be true. We could add that it was because they had an active but distracted religion. Again, partially true. But even together, these answers don't add up to the real reason that they did not listen to God's prophets. We can only find that reason by looking at where the Lord Himself placed the responsibility for both the sin and the inattention of the people.

He placed that terrible blame at the feet of false prophets—those prophets who were charged with teaching the people the Word of God and or leading them spiritually, but who did not faithfully proclaim all of God's Word.

Take Judah's case. In language that should cause any of us Christians or preachers to tremble, God pointedly laid the blame for Jerusalem's fall to the false prophets : "The visions of your prophets were false and worthless; they did not expose your sin to ward off you captivity. The oracles they gave you were false and misleading."[8]

Now God judged Israel and Judah—and other nations—for their sins; they *were* guilty of committing them and they would be punished. But it is because of the false prophets that these nations were complacent in their sins, were unconvicted about them, easily continued to sin, and remained unconcerned about any resulting judgment. In fact, Israel and Judah stayed unconcerned about judgment in a large part because the false prophets put a continual emphasis on their national heritage and status, so the two nations simply would not believe that God would judge them.

Listen to F.C. Cook speak of the time of Jeremiah:

> *The false prophets assured the people of prosperity and deliverance. Their purpose was gain and popularity. The result for the people was being removed from the land—*

judgment . . . The false prophets in his days were so numerous and influential as to counteract and almost nullify the influence of the true prophet . . . But the secret of their power was MY PEOPLE LOVE TO HAVE IT SO. (Jeremiah 5:21)[9]

FALSE PROPHETS MESSAGE

The messages of the false prophets to the people were focused so continuously on positive and optimistic themes—"peace, peace"—and spoke so often of prosperity that Israel and Judah simply accepted by default the perilous delusion that the Lord would not deal with their sin, that He would not judge them. The people had itching ears, and the false prophets tickled them. Today their books and tapes would sell well. But God himself does not deal lightly with such matters. In the Scripture, His most trenchant and severe statements are those against false prophets.

Notwithstanding all this, I still had not been able to determine to my satisfaction if a minister of the Gospel today could be so defined. The question continued to trouble me, but I felt that I was on dangerous ground and wanted to move cautiously. I did not want to come to any quick conclusions, because throughout Church history, rash and unbalanced statements have often been made concerning who was or was not true, with accusations flagrantly thrown at servants of the Lord. But I couldn't leave the question alone just because of my concerns I had to have an answer.

I came to realize that the question had to be redirected if I was going to get anywhere. I was too concerned about those *outside* the Church who might or might not be false. I needed to start by being concerned about the ones *inside* the Church—especially me! Don't worry about seeing the mote in someone else's eye, I told myself; look into your own eye to see if there's a mote.

So the question became, *Could I—as one who believes he's a committed minister of the Gospel, and who accepts the Scriptures as the inspired Word of God and Christ as the only Savior and Lord—be defined as a false prophet?* Or, at the very least, could I have done what a false prophet does? Asking those questions about myself shook me.

I thought about my ministry, sermons, programs, and the things I had written. I tried to be as objective and fair as possible in my self-evaluation. My conclusion was that most of my ministry had been correct. But I also concluded that at times, perhaps unintentionally and even well-intentioned, I had done what a false prophet does!

If I had, pleading before God that I had been well-intentioned or meant well was no defense; nor was pleading that I had been uninformed, naive, green, mostly right, or that I came close, even though I might have been all of these. That was not enough! No, spiritual and moral issues are too crucial, the destiny and care of immortal souls too consequential, and the health and direction of society too pivotal for us to be inaccurate *for any reason* when delivering God's message. God places profound priority on His ministers getting His message RIGHT, and He accepts no alibis. CLOSE only counts in horseshoes, hand grenades, and haircuts. The lawyer's mistakes go to jail, the doctor's mistakes go to the cemetery, but the minister's mistakes go to hell!

This means, of course, that as ministers we'd better be certain of the scriptural truth of what we are teaching as we look closely at just what a false prophet is and does.

There are two kinds of false prophets mentioned in the Scriptures. The first are those who followed idols, such as the ones Elijah encountered on Mt. Carmel. The second are those who professed Jehovah. They were within the recognized religious community of either the Old Testament Hebrews or the New Testament Church, and knew the Scriptures well.

About false prophet in the Scriptures, Lynn Buzzard said, "Within the biblical tradition there were a host of prophets, even prophet bands, and most were unfaithful, false and political soothsayers. They were the culturally seduced, the fair-haired boys of the establishment, the assurers of victory.[10]

False prophets can get the spirit of Amaziah. You may recall that Amaziah was the priest at Bethel who told Amos to leave the country and go back to Judah.[11] Amaziah represented the established religion in Bethel. In his case, he was a priest for Jeroboam in the state church of Israel and enjoyed the considerable prestige and comfortable perks that the prosperous nation afforded a man in his position as head of the established religion.

An established religion can be any religious system or religious group, large or small.

Most of us think of the Amaziah spirit as the other minister's problem and are exceedingly blinded to it in ourselves. But conservative ministers—evangelicals, Pentecostals and charismatics—can be Amaziahs. In fact, they can be the most vulnerable precisely because they don't think they are vulnerable. As soon as any of us gets established in any ministry—from pastor to evangelist to missionary, from local church to para-church, from radio to television, we have a vested interest in perpetuating what we are doing or building. The Amaziah spirit becomes an enormous temptation. Churches have split because of the Amaziah spirit.

The Amaziah spirit lures the advocates of some new teaching, doctrinal fad, or "new revelation" program or scheme. The Amaziah spirit breeds celebrity and hype. Amaziahs can put out books and tapes, and have lavish ministries. And they can get so good at the activity of ministry and promote it so well that they think they are just fine and on track. Typically Amaziahs don't think they are Amaziahs.

However most tragically, Amaziahs lose the tender heart after God, humility, and the sheer, simple joy of pleasing and working for the sake of our Lord.

Under normal church conditions, the Amaziah spirit can stay well-hidden beneath a hypocritical facade of spirituality until true prophets like Amos show up. Amos made Amaziah uncomfortable. No doubt Amos was seen as one of those religious fanatics that Amaziahs have had to put up with throughout Church history.

AMOS, ROARING; AMAZIAH MUTE

If Amos as a prophet was a roaring lion, Amaziah was a mute one. All Amaziahs are. Amaziah had told King Jeroboam, untruthfully, that Amos was raising a conspiracy against the king. He said, "The land cannot bear all his words."[12] Amaziahs miss the real Word of God. What Amos was saying, Amaziah should have been saying: the nation is sinning and headed toward judgment. But Amaziahs have convinced themselves that such topics are out of place.

Yet here was this man of the cloth confronting the prophet of God and telling him, "Get out!" Perhaps Amaziah had been so compromised by prosperity that he figured that anyone showing up in Israel might just be there to pick up some of the country's plenty and cut into his share. "Go back to the land of Judah," he told Amos. "Earn your bread there and do your prophesying there." Then he defended Bethel's established religion, "Don't prophesy anymore at Bethel, because this is the king's sanctuary and the temple of the kingdom."[13]

What blindness! Here was the nation of Israel in peril, and before Amaziah stood Amos, a man with the one message that, if heeded, would save it. Yet, incredibly, Amaziah's first concern was to protect his religious turf. It was like telling someone with a medical cure for cancer to "Get out!" because you're making money by helping cancer victims.

No wonder the nation didn't listen to Amos, nor to Hosea. No wonder they didn't repent. Amaziah—and all of Israel's Amaziahs—kept them from it. Amaziah was so filled with the spirit of that thriving age, so comfortable in the perks of prosperity, and he so ignored the enormous iniquity of the country, that he let Israel continue its contented gaiety straight into judgment.

A mute Amaziah was Israel's real enemy. A roaring Amos was Israel's true friend.

Mute Amaziahs are America's and every nation's real enemies. Where are America's Amoses?

Today our cup of iniquity is filling. Do any of us want it on our conscience to live so comfortably in our churches or ministries, so at ease in our prosperity, so focused on our church program or special teaching or our ministry activity, that for whatever reasons we mute the truth about our nation's sins and its judgment? Will we not proclaim the hope that comes from national repentance, and thereby allow our nation to plunge blindly ahead into damnation? "I have made you a watchman," God said to Ezekiel. "When I say to the wicked, 'O wicked man, you will surely die,' and you do not speak out to dissuade him from his ways, that wicked man will die for his sin, and I will hold you accountable for his blood."[14]

This is a question I must, I repeat, I MUST ask about myself—whether I am a layman, pastor or television minister: "Am I now, or have I ever been, an Amaziah?" The work we do is too critical to the well-being of the eternal souls of countless millions, and our nation to ignore the very real possibility that somewhere in us may dwell tentacles of the Amaziah spirit.

It was in this context that I struggled that Sunday morning.

When I finally stood to preach I was deeply stirred; yet there was a flow, an ease to speak. Looking back, it was evident the Lord was there! I spoke for perhaps one-and-a-half hours. The message made comparisons between Old Testament Israel and modern America, including Israel's shedding of innocent blood in child sacrifice and ours in abortion. It spoke of Israel's judgment and the looming judgment for us in America. It spoke of repentance.

Then perhaps ten minutes before the end of the message I could stand it no longer—I wanted those two families to know I loved them, and our Lord did. In each family a young woman had had an abortion. Each family had struggled. My voice broke as I was gripped for them. In that same instant, something else happened as I continued to speak. In a flash I saw a panorama of the sin of America, our pride, arrogance, self-absorption, bloodshed in the womb, gross immorality, etc. It was like a vision. Then I was deeply aware of God's immense love for America, and for all of us there in that meeting. God's heart was breaking and calling, "Come back; I love you!" just as He did to Israel. My voice continued to break as the overwhelming awareness of both our terrible sin and our great God's compassion for us flooded my soul. In this way I concluded those final minutes and gave an invitation. Folks streamed to the front, many weeping, seeking the Lord. The Lord was graciously there.

It was a watershed moment. And it launched this ministry.

If I had put it off another Sunday, it would have not been the same.

> **Let us pray together:** *Our loving Father, thank You for Your Word, thank You for the Gospel of Redemption, and thank You for Your call to Your Church and its ministers to proclaim Your message. May we do so faithfully with courage, clarity and compassion. Forgive us for muting Your message for any reason. May the proclamation of Your Word become a roar into the heart and conscience of our nation that will be a catalyst to birth a deep spiritual awakening. Amen.*

CHAPTER 2 ENDNOTES

[1] From Jeremiah 1:5-7.

[2] II Kings 22:11-13.

[3] Matthew 7:15 (NKJV).

[4]. Matthew 7:15.

[5]. Matthew 7:22-23.

[6]. Matthew 7:21.

[7]. Acts 20:28-31.

[8] Lamentations 2:14.

[9] *The Bible Commentary, Volumes 5 and 6,* by F.C. Cook (Baker Book House, 1981).

[10] Lynn Buzzard, *Freedom and Faith,* (Westchester, IL, Crossway Books, 1982), p.21.

[11] Amos 7:10-13.

[12] Amos 7:10.

[13] Amos 7:12-13.

[14] Ezekiel 33:7-8.

3

BARBARIANS

"They shed innocent blood, the blood of their sons and daughters, whom they sacrificed to the idols of Canaan, and the land was desecrated by their blood."
— GOD, SPEAKING IN THE PSALMS[1]

"First Molech, horrid King besmear'd with blood / Of human sacrifice, and parents tears / Though for the noise of Drums and Timbrels loud / Their children's cries unheard, that passed through fire / To his grim Idol."
— JOHN MILTON, PARADISE LOST

I T WAS THE NIGHT OF SACRIFICE. THE AIR WAS HEAVY AND DAMP with sticky summer heat. Sweat covered one's body like an oily film.

Molech's image glowed against the dark, deeply clouded sky. The figure was ominous and awesome—a beautifully sculpted, dramatic bull's head atop a powerful, muscled body of a man. Tilka's heart pounded in anticipation of the night's sacrifice. It was anticipation bred of devotion, yet mixed with anguish and silent terror. It was her firstborn son who was to die in Molech's glowing, red-hot arms.

Tilka knew there was no alternative but to sacrifice her tiny son. It was the law and the way of her people. All her life, she had worshiped before Molech and Baal and the other gods and goddesses. When she had come of age, her family went to the temple together, each going in to the temple prostitutes. That was where she lost her virginity in the service to their gods. She knew it was the right thing to do.

And she had taken part in the sacrifices, watching other mothers place their innocent, newborn sons in the outstretched arms of the terrible, flames-filled Molech. It was a humbling experience. She always felt sympathy and pride for the mothers who gave up their children. It was necessary to ensure good harvests and even future fertility of the women.

Tilka knew that one day she would have the opportunity to serve the gods with the ultimate sacrifice. She knew she would have to give up her firstborn son, and knew she would. It had to be done. It was the law and the way of her people. She was always proud to be a servant of Baal and El and Molech.

She dressed in her most elegant and revealing gown. Tonight she would not only offer her son to Molech, but she would again offer her body to temple prostitutes at the height of the worship ceremony. As she prepared herself, she did her best to steel her thoughts against the pain of losing her child. She had to be perfectly numb and emotionless as her innocent infant son was rolled into the hungry flames—the ever ravenous flames. If she cried or gave any indication of sorrow, the sacrifice of her son would be meaningless, and she and her husband would be barred from the temple.

Tilka went over to where her son was sleeping. He had just nursed and was sleeping soundly. She wanted him to remain as quiet and peaceful as possible as he faced the ordeal. He was such a beautiful baby boy, with handsome features and a surprisingly full head of hair. He was flawless. As she wrapped him in his blanket, momentary regret and pain flashed through her breaking heart. Yet she didn't dare question the gods' motives, not even herself.

As Tilka and her husband approached the hill of sacrifice, the sounds of the ceremony drifted toward them. Loud drums were being beaten rhythmically, and other instruments added to the deep din. In the distance, to the west across the mountains, thunder rumbled in counter-point, and intermittent heat lightning flashed eerily. It was a perfect night for sacrifice, for the gods were joining the worship.

Tilka shivered in the chilly air, yet she was covered with a cold, slimy sweat. She and her husband walked into the circle of worshipers, and carried their son to the priest. As they moved nearer the blazing Molech, the music became louder and more frenzied. For a moment, Tilka wanted to scream and run, taking her child with her. Yet, from deeper inside, she knew the sacrifice was right and good. And she knew she would obey her gods as she had done all her life.

She placed her son in the priest's arms. The priest lifted the child toward the image and began chanting to the great god Molech. Attendants threw more wood into the furnace, making the fire roar with new intensity.

The music was raucous, a frantic din. It always got loudest during a sacrifice. Perhaps, Tilka guessed, it drowned out the cries of the dying infant as he screamed in agony and pain. The scantily clad temple prostitutes, both male and female, began to dance sensuously before the image of Molech, enticing the god to observe their ceremony and take heed of the sacrifice.

Tilka stood frozen, emotionless as she watched the priests handle her son. Each one took the child and intoned over him, praying to Molech, and blessing the sacrifice. Finally the child was handed to the high priest who stood before Molech's outstretched arms. Tilka had never noticed until tonight how frightening and evil Molech's image appeared.

The music reached a deafening peak. The dancers twirled in obscene frenzy, other worshipers joining them. It was as if a mass hysteria had begun to creep over the congregation of devout worshipers.

The priest slowly lifted the child skyward as he awakened and began crying innocently for his mother. But his mother stood still. Suddenly, the priest, not able to get too near the glowing, intensely hot image of Molech, threw the crying child into the god's outstretched arms. The innocent child screamed in terror and pain. The odor of charred flesh immediately filled the air with its awful stench. For several moments, the child's frantic death cries could be dimly heard beneath the noise of the instruments. The priest took a rod and pushed the blackened, charred body deeper into the flames, and the crying stopped.

The baby was finally dead. Molech was served.

The ceremony had now reached a fevered pitch. Tilka, feeling as if she had turned to stone inside, approached one of the male prostitutes. And they disappeared into the temple. The rest of the night, she buried the last traces of emotion beneath a torrent of sexual activity and drunkenness. She and her husband were well respected by the community, and devout followers of the gods. They would be honored for several days because of the sacrifice of their son. By the standards and laws of their land, they had done the right thing.

Twenty-eight centuries later, Mary moved about the bedroom slowly, gathering her belongings into a small suitcase. Today was the day she would go to the clinic. The summer sun glared brightly through the window. Mary was hot and sweating in spite of the air conditioning.

Mary was seven months pregnant. But she and her husband had both finally decided that, even at this late time in the pregnancy, they didn't want the child. They both had successful careers, and they had only been married three years. Her husband, John, felt it was too early for a child. A child, he had said, would be an intrusion on their time together. She had agreed, even though they spent very little time alone with each other. They were both very involved in their careers. And in addition, the doctor was not sure the baby "was quite right," and had implied that there might be something wrong.

Also, Mary wanted the abortion for another reason. She wasn't really sure if the child was her husband's or her lover's. She had been seeing Allen for slightly more than seven months.

Allen wasn't Mary's first lover, either. There had been one other since she married John, and several before her marriage. In fact, even John had been one of her premarital affairs. Mary was a modern, liberated, free-spirited woman.

She lost her virginity in high school. Her mother knew about it, and had even given her the pill. Mary was also aware of her parents' sexual activity outside of their marriage.

It was socially acceptable to be promiscuous. It had not even been much of a shock to learn that her husband, John, had had an affair with one of their old college pals, Elizabeth. Elizabeth was Mary's former roommate, and one of her best friends.

Mary had often discussed abortion with her friends. It was a common topic. Several in her social circle were actively involved in lobbying for pro-abortion laws, and many had had abortions. Although Mary conceded that their decisions to have abortions were selfishly motivated, she felt they were justified.

This was to be Mary's second abortion. After all, no birth control method is one hundred percent effective. That first one a few years back had been in her 10th week. A powerful vacuum tube is inserted into the uterus and suction tears the body of the baby into pieces before it sucks the pieces with the placenta into a jar. More than two thirds of abortions are done by suction.

For that abortion, Mary had taken great care to adopt a very rational, non-feeling air concerning what was happening to her. By careful practice she had begun to think of the baby growing inside as an "it." The doctors had even referred to what remained after an abortion as the "product" of an abortion. She decided that it was not much different than having a tumor removed. It wasn't a tiny human being inside her; it was merely an unwanted piece of tissue. The nurse had called it a "product of conception" or a "POC." Mary tried to adopt that same attitude toward this abortion, although something inside nagged her about this one being in the seventh month.

She reproached herself for waiting so long. After all, she could have had a saline abortion a couple months ago. But she shuddered as she recalled what she had read about that kind. A long needle is inserted through the mother's abdomen and directly into the sac containing the amniotic fluid surrounding the baby. A solution of concentrated salt is then injected into the sac. The saline solution is absorbed by the baby into its lungs and gastrointestinal track, producing a change in the osmotic pressure in his tiny body. The outer layer of skin is also burned off due to the high concentration of salt. Normally, the mother then goes into labor and hours later delivers a dead baby.

Mary just couldn't bring herself to have a saline. And anyway, she knew someone who had had one; and the baby lived for awhile. That young woman had told of having the baby thrash about in her womb, choking and burning in the poison saline solution. Then she expelled the badly shriveled and crumpled form. It had been a little boy. A nurse took him and laid him on a towel on another table. Then she heard a soft gurgling sound coming from his throat. *Oh my!* she thought. *He's still alive!* A nurse hurriedly wrapped the towel firmly around the baby, especially tight around the head, and quickly left.

Mary knew she couldn't handle anything like that, which was another reason she had waited so long.

Mary finished packing a few things and carried her bag through the living room and out to the car. John drove her to the clinic. They both were silent, not knowing what to say to one another.

Besides, they had already talked it out between them, and with their friends. They knew they were doing the right thing. They really weren't ready for children, and it would be senseless to have an unwanted child around.

Mary shivered in spite of the day's warmth. She and John walked into the reception room. Very nicely appointed. Other women and a couple of men were seated. She glanced out a window. Across a side street, children were playing in a park. A couple of mothers pushed strollers. Seeing the children touched something inside Mary. For a moment she felt panic, and she wanted to run away somewhere . . . where she could have her child and see him grow. But the panic subsided as she rationalized these silly urges away.

They filled out some papers, and John left. She was taken to a room where she changed, and got into a bed. Later the doctor came in. Since Mary was so far along in her pregnancy, she would have "D and X" abortion. The procedure would take three days; the first two to dilate, the third to perform the abortion. She would receive any medical treatment needed for severe cramping, sleep disturbances and blood loss. He assured her everything would be fine. He left.

Mary tried to relax. But she wrestled with her thoughts. She had to talk. Her throat was dry, but she began to make conversation with the others in the room. She found out that one of the others was getting a D and X, commonly called a "partial-birth abortion." The others were having suctions. Soon, among themselves—with a couple veterans of abortion taking the lead—they calmed each other's fears, and reassured themselves that they were doing the only right thing. There was no option. Besides, why feel guilty about something that society, even the law, sanctioned? Everyone was getting an abortion nowadays. Children were unnecessary nuisances where an individual's career or economics was concerned.

For Mary the two days for dilation seemed to drag by; then, finally, the day for the abortion. She was positioned by the abortionist. He used forceps to move the baby to a feet-first position, then he pulled until all but the baby's head was out of the womb—it was a girl. The baby moved her legs and arms, and for a brief moment grabbed the abortionist's finger. But the abortionist swiftly took surgical scissors and stabbed a hole at the base of the little girl's skull, reaming it slightly. She went limp. In quick succession, the abortionist inserted a vacuum tube and began suctioning the little girl's brains out. That finished, he collapsed her skull, and pulled the dead girl on out.

An attendant cared for Mary while the abortionist put the dead body aside—he noticed that it was an excellent specimen from which to dissect body parts to "sell." He then disinfected the scissors and placed them on the table for his next patient.

Later the abortionist began chatting with Mary, telling her how well the procedure had gone and asking how she felt. She felt OK, she said. Inside she was numb.

After a time of recovery, Mary walked down the hallway to the pay phone, and called John. Then she called Allen.

The abortion was over, and it was time to move on . . .

Mary's child was hardly different from Tilka's. Both were offered up to contemporary idols. Tilka's idol was Molech, a product of her society's depraved imagination. Mary's idol was convenience, a product of her society's twisted view of human life.

Both of the sacrificed lives were innocent.

Both societies were proud, prosperous and self-absorbed.

Both societies were blindly self-deluded.

Both societies had decayed to a place where sexual immorality had become the norm.

In both worlds, murder had become commonplace, barbarian murder of innocents had become typical, and officially sanctioned murder of innocents had become custom or law.

In both the killing was rationalized. But there was a difference. For Tilka, she rationalized the killing because her baby was so valued, it would make the gods happy. For Mary, she rationalized the killing because her baby was not valued and without her, she could get on with her life.

Tilka's barbaric society went down in judgment. So will Mary's!

Let us pray together: *Our gracious Heavenly Father, our Creator, the Giver of Life to each of us. Forgive us for so wantonly destroying life in the womb—our unborn children made in Your image. Our land is desecrated with their blood. Father, we have become barbarians. We face judgment—we deserve judgment! Do whatever is necessary in our nation to have us confront the enormity of this sin— pierce our indifferent hearts, and grant us repentance. And may there be a deep and holy revival in our beloved nation, starting in Your Church. In Jesus' name we pray. Amen.*

CHAPTER 3 ENDNOTES

[1] Psalm 106:38.

4

BLIND
SELF-DELUSION

"For they are simpletons who turn away from Me—to death. They are fools, and their own complacency will destroy them. But all who listen to Me will live in peace and safety, unafraid of harm."

—GOD, SPEAKING IN PROVERBS[1]

"Those are the greatest fools, that are wise in their own conceit; and those the worst of sinners, that feign themselves just men."

—MATTHEW HENRY

OUR GREATEST LIES ARE TO OURSELVES. OUR CAPACITY TO rationalize the greatest evils seems to know no bounds whether we self-delude as a nation, church, preacher or individual.

In his compelling play *The Visit* (which was later made into a classic film), Friedrich Duerrenmatt paints a vivid picture of the process whereby otherwise honest human beings rationalize themselves into deep hypocrisy. In the story, a small European town goes bankrupt. The only person who can save the community is a very wealthy woman who once lived there. Shortly after the bankruptcy, she returns for a visit, and when she does, she agrees to restore the town's economic base. But there is a price: she wants the life of the town's foremost citizen. It seems that when she was a girl, he got her pregnant and deserted her.

At first the entire town is disgusted by the rich woman's proposal, but as the story continues, the various segments of the community—the justice system, the educational system, the business community, the town council, the church, and eventually the man's own family—each segment caves in. Each group somehow finds a way to rationalize away the value of one man's life in exchange for the common good.

There is no happy ending to Duerrenmatt's story. The man is murdered; the town is restored; outrage is replaced by indifference; and hypocrisy prevails.

What a picture Duerrenmatt's story is of the rationalizations societies make to excuse increased levels of degeneracy. It doesn't happen overnight. Our national conscience once was appalled at killing its unborn, at sexual license, or at males marrying males or females marrying females. These were heinous evils. But then destructive philosophies slithered in, and our moral values were attacked. And attacked. Unrelentingly. Slowly we began to change our thinking. Eventually our national conscience began to find room for increasing evil. We didn't call it evil, of course; we called it social progress or something for the national good. It was all very pragmatic. But gradually the unthinkable became thinkable, the unacceptable became acceptable; evil became good; good became evil. And we arrived at a day like today.

This is how Nazi Germany came into being. Before World War II, the Germans couldn't have conceived that their nation would become so arrogant and deluded that they would slaughter six million innocent and helpless Jews, and millions of others. Yet it happened. Nazi Germany is now defined by one sin: GENOCIDE.

The alarming part is that today we in America are so cocksure in our self-delusions. "In his arrogance the wicked man hunts down the weak [our most weak are our unborn] . . . He blesses the greedy and reviles the Lord . . . In all his thoughts there is no room for God . . . He says to himself, 'Nothing will shake me; I'll always be happy and never have trouble.'"[2]

"They slay the widow and the alien; they murder the fatherless. They say, 'The Lord does not see; the God of Jacob pays no heed.'"[3]

"This is the way of an adulteress: She eat and wipes her mouth and says, 'I've done nothing wrong.'"[4]

Charles Simeon, an early 19th Century preacher, said, "By nothing are the delusions of men more strengthened than by a confidence in their own wisdom and judgment."

Men and nations and churches and ministries perish in their self-delusions when it is too late to rectify them. America will perish because we are willfully blind and purposefully deaf. It is not because the warning signs are not there, nor that God has not spoken to us and the West. Certainly God has spoken, and is speaking to us (which we'll examine later). It is because we are determined to believe our chosen lies about cherished sins such as abortion and gross sexual perversion—*we have decided we will not listen to the truth*. Such willful self-delusion is the most alarming part of our national character.

Pride, self-absorption, and indifference breed self-delusion. Nations get self-deluded. Individuals get self-deluded. Churches get self-deluded. Ministries get self-deluded. And Jesus warned of it several times.

JESUS USES A WEDDING STORY TO WARN

In one of His most penetrating stories, Jesus used the happy setting of a wedding to give us one His most forceful warnings of self-delusion. Weddings of course are usually festive times for families and friends to gather. No less in Jesus' day. Usually a wedding then was in the evening when the bridegroom, attended by friends, would go to the house of his betrothed, his bride. There the two wedding parties would join and form a joyful procession to walk through the city or village to his house for the wedding feast. As they walked others would join them, carrying lamps.

Jesus told of ten young virgins awaiting a wedding party[5]—and the coming of the bridegroom. Outwardly, neither they, nor anyone else could tell them apart. All ten were called virgins, carried lamps, and were together specifically to meet the bridegroom. They were a select group.

But Jesus divided them: five wise, five foolish. Five wise virgins brought oil for their lamps. The five foolish did not. Five were careful; five were careless. What is pivotal is the incredible depth of self-delusion in the five foolish, careless virgins who _thought_ they were completely okay—as they blissfully gathered to meet the bridegroom.

Jesus uses those foolish virgins to personify that vain confidence, that blind conceit which a person can assume about the alleged goodness of their condition. That self-absorbed focus can and does blind foolish people and nations to their unfit condition. Matthew Henry said, "Those are the greatest fools, that are wise in their own conceit; and those the worst of sinners, that feign themselves just men."

The ten waited and waited. They took a nap. Then suddenly the announcement at midnight, "Here's the bridegroom. Come out to meet him." The ten scurried to light their lamps. And perhaps for a moment, all lamps lit up. They waited. Then, one, two, three, four, five lamps went out. The foolish were identified. But they still didn't have a clue. They didn't understand the foolishness of their actions; they simply hurried up and asked the five wise women for oil. Those five wisely told them they had to get their own. While the five foolish were away getting oil, the wedding party arrived and the five ready virgins joined the gala procession with lamps held high, and walked on to the wedding banquet. The door was shut.

A bit later the five foolish virgins arrived at the door and called out, "Sir! Sir! Open the door for us!" They fully expected the door to open. But the voice inside answered, "I tell you the truth, I don't know you!"

"I don't know you" is an utterance no human soul will ever wanted to hear, especially a human soul who has blissfully lived as if everything is fine. There are not human words to describe the indescribable horror, the unspeakable shock that hits the person when the incalculable enormity of "I don't know you" dawns on them for the first time. Jesus let us know a little about that terror in another story about self-deceived people who were standing before a shut door.[6] He said they were knocking and pleading, "We ate and drank with you, and you taught in our streets." But He will replied, "I don't know you or where you come from. Away from me, you evildoers. There will be weeping there, and gnashing of teeth."

The somber, terrifying lesson of Jesus' story is that self-delusion can become so embedded in people that they behave like those who are genuine, They even associate with them and perhaps sincerely, but wrongly believe themselves to be genuine. Then they stand before the unopenable door. And like the virgins, the grim tragedy is that it is only there before that door through which they will never pass, that those self-deluded have the first inkling that they are unfit. Then it was too late. It is over. "Weeping and gnashing of teeth" is the stomach-wrenching anguish of the self-deluded when both the truth of their folly and the finality of their judgment hits them.

Jesus said, "Therefore keep watch." Be careful and vigilant; evaluate yourself. And the fool of fools is that person who, when they read or hear this story of Jesus, does not stop and take a deep, strong look at himself or herself.

Of course this story is primarily a warning to individuals. But societies, nations, churches and ministries, which are after all populations of individuals, get self-deluded.

America cannot continue as it is going. The vanity of the self-deluded virgins reflects our national character. Our pride rationalizes our aggressive sinning. Listen to us brazenly argue for them. We have the taste for the bloodshed of Cain, the Canaanites, Nineveh, and Babylon. Hear feminists, politicians, and the media assertively contend for shedding the innocent blood of the unborn children and defend partial-birth abortion. We have the spirit of the whoremonger. Listen to sexual Philistines attack moral values and promote licentiousness and homosexual perversion. We are so convinced that these national sins are worthy endeavors that we are teaching them to our children—a reality that immensely marks our foolishness and particularly places us near judgment.

WILL IT TAKE JUDGMENT ITSELF?

Our retribution is fast approaching. But we remain indifferent. We weep to consider the likely scenario for America that it will take judgment itself upon us for the truth of our self-deception and the finality of our punishment to hit us.

One reason God sent prophets (and sends modern preachers) was that He cared enough to have His prophets face self-deluded cultures and speak His delivering Word. He wanted people to come back to Him. The prophets became God-sent spiritual surgeons with an intense mandate to go after the nation's cancer—the self-delusion and the insidious false security, and to cut that foul tumor out, and to call the nation back to God. Roy Clements said, "God did not send prophets to Israel to amuse their bored minds or to soothe their anxious hearts. He sent them to turn people to repentance.

'The day of the Lord is coming. Be different, change, get ready.' That was their message."[7]

God's answer to the nation's chosen lies was Truth, His Word spoken by His prophets into the heart and conscience of the nation. Anderson and Freedman said, "In the mounting crisis . . . only the Word of God, drastic and devastating at it might be, could avail against the forces both internal and external which threatened the life of the nations and their inhabitants severally."[8]

Jesus certainly was such a surgeon. He used unmistakable language to describe how we are to confront sin: "*Woe* to the world because of the things that cause people to sin! . . . If your hand or your foot causes you to sin, *cut it off* and throw it away. It is better for you to enter life maimed or crippled than to have two hands or two feet and be thrown into eternal fire. And if your eye causes you to sin, *gouge it out* and throw it away. It is better for you to enter life with one eye than to have two eyes and be thrown in the fire of hell."[9] There is no room for self-delusion in a statement like this. And of course the New Testament has regular references to *sin, judgment, death, wrath,* etc.

SELF-DELUSION AND MINISTERS

Self-delusion hits even preachers. Here we visit again Jesus' warning, "Many will say to Me on that day, 'Lord, Lord, did we not prophesy in Your name, and in Your name drive out demons, and perform many miracles?' Then I will tell them plainly, 'I never knew you. [There are those sobering words again.] Away from me, you evildoers.'"[10] Certainly ministers who prophesy, cast out demons, or work miracles could believe they were okay, that the Lord knew them. Who could believe the Lord would ever call them "evildoers"? Or say, "I never knew you."? The seventy-two prophets Jesus sent out returned with joy and said, "Lord, even the demons submit to us in Your name." Jesus replied, "I saw Satan fall like lightning from heaven. I have given you authority to trample on snakes and scorpions, and to overcome all the power of the enemy; nothing will harm you. *However, do not rejoice that the spirits submit to you, but rejoice that your names are written in heaven.*"[11]

But the prophet Amos was not deluded. He understood his priorities and his relationship to the Lord, and he spoke God's message right. Bible scholars describe Amos as one of the fiercest, if not *the* fiercest, prophet in the Scriptures. *But fierce as compared to what?* Yes, Amos was fierce if his urgent voice is compared to the easeful sounds Israel's ears were used to. But assuredly his voice was not fierce when compared to the nation's peril and its advancing judgment. Irving Jensen says of that day, "The rich were getting richer, and the poor were getting poorer. Idolatry, hypocrisy, moral corruption, and social injustices were everywhere. The nation was truly on the brink of disaster."[12] It was this condition in the nation that raised the voice of God to a lion's roar through Amos; it was intended to wake the complacent Israel to the consequences they faced if they did not turn from their sins to Him. "With Amos [and Hosea] we stand among the conditions of our day," George Adam Smith said.

Amos is not the only prophet who used jolting language to arrest the attention of self-satisfied people. Hosea spoke of "whoredom." Other prophets employed "harlot," and "prostitute." The Holy Spirit's language through Jeremiah is graphic: "I will pull us your skirts over your face that your shame may be seen. . ."[13] John the Baptist confronted the crowds coming to be baptized, "You brood of vipers! Who warned you to flee from the coming wrath?"[14]

John White said, "The Holy Spirit's inspiration of a term like *'harlot, whore, or prostitute'* is designed to sting people into shocked awareness that their sins (whatever those sins might be) enrage God."[15] White calls this "the prophet's whip of cords,"[16] comparing their words to Jesus' words when He drove the moneychangers out of the Temple. Jesus said He spoke what His Father gave Him to speak.

Israel had lost the knowledge of God and mixed the values and life-styles of the surrounding pagan, barbaric nations with the "worship" of God. With their consciences seared and anchored in their self-delusion, they did "not know how to do right."[17] That produced an amoral society, which easily excused things once considered abominations.

Speaking as a prophet, Jesus warned of the massive self-delusion in the time when "the Son of Man is revealed."[18] He compared that day to "the days of Noah," and "the days of Lot" (referring to Sodom), cultures that both ended in cataclysmic judgments by flood and fire. The contrast between the view Noah's day and Sodom had of themselves and the view God had of them is striking. They saw themselves as fine, but God defined them by their sins, with their cups of iniquity full. Their future: judgment. God saw Noah's generation and "how great man's wickedness on the earth had become, and that every inclination of the thoughts of his heart was only evil all the time;" that "the earth was corrupt . . . and full of violence."[19] God saw Sodom as "arrogant, overfed, unconcerned, not caring for the poor and needy, haughty, who did detestable things before me."[20] One detestable thing practiced in Sodom was homosexual perversion which spawned an attempted sexual attack upon two of God's angels. The city gave the sin its name and recorded it forever in the pages of infamy: sodomy!

However, against God's view was Noah's day and Sodom's. They were indifferent to their sin and their coming judgment. They were eating, drinking, marrying, buying, selling, planting, and building. It was business as usual. Times were prosperous. The apathetic cancer was at work, and both cultures remained nonchalant to their true sinful condition. They remained optimistic about their future right up until the day when judgment's flood began in Noah's time,[21] and sulphur fire rained on Sodom.[22]

Today it is exceedingly probable that our violence exceeds that of Noah's day, since we kill millions of our unborn children and are striding toward "physician-assisted suicide." Our perversion goes beyond Sodom with our public debate about solemnizing sodomy right into Christian marriage, Holy Matrimony, through same-sex marriage.

JESUS WARNS HIS CHURCH OF SELF-DELUSION

Jesus most trenchant warning of self-delusion was to His Church. "I'll spit you out of my mouth," He said to complacent Laodicea. That warning was one of five He gave among His seven letters to churches in Asia in Revelation 2 & 3.

Jesus commended those He could; He condemned those He had to. He was not fooled with appearances. With His penetrating, unerring eye He looked beyond the veneer of each church's perception of itself to the true state of each church's heart. He "knew their deeds." Jesus commended two without reservation, Smyrna and Philadelphia. Jesus gave four, Ephesus, Pergamus, Thyratira, and Sardis, mixed reviews: praise mixed with things he hated. One, Laodicea, received only condemnation. Things the Lord detested included losing first love, holding to Balaam's teachings, tolerating Jezebel, and having a reputation for being alive, but dead, neither hot nor cold, but lukewarm.

Jesus shows us that churches can and do build collective life-styles based on self-delusion. They don't see themselves as they really are, the way He, Jesus, the Lord of the Church, sees them, which is the only evaluation that matters. Jesus wants us to understand there is to be more in His churches than a life-style of good works (Ephesus); there is to be first love. More than remaining true to His name and keeping the faith (Pergamus). There is not to be the teaching of Balaam or the Nicolaitans. More than love, faith, service and perseverance (Thyratira), they are not to tolerate the self-anointed prophetess, Jezebel, and her damning teachings; more than having a reputation for being alive and a having a few unsoiled members (Sardis), they are to wake up and strengthen what remains.

Jesus excoriated one Church, Laodicea, for building their collective life-style around the self-deception that they were rich, wealthy, and without a need. "But you do not realize that you are wretched, pitiful, poor, blind and naked," He said.[23]

Until Jesus x-rayed them, five of the seven church were blind to their true condition. We can assume that if He had not corrected them, they would have glibly continued to tolerate legalism, false doctrine, false prophets, paganism, immorality, dirty believers, illusions of prosperity, and such.

Jesus' judgment on the five was a prophetic roar. He would remove their candlestick. He would fight against them. He would make them suffer intensely. He would strike their children dead. He would repay them according to their deeds. He would come like a thief. He would spit them out of His mouth.

Were these five churches rocked by what Jesus said and did?

Every church wants to be stripped of self-delusion. Let each church—particularly its pastors, elders and deacons—regularly place themselves humbly before our Lord with the letters to the seven churches of Asia open. Let them pray concerning the things in those letters, and ask the Lord to show them what kind of a church they are and show them the things He commends and condemns in them. Then, with contrition, they should repent of those things He doesn't want; and with earnest heart ask Him for strength and wisdom to have those things He wants.

SELF-DELUSION IN MINISTRY AND WORSHIP

Jesus' incisive evaluation of the five churches provides us a graphic display of how embedded self-delusion can become in church life. These five churches may variously have had good preaching, good ministry, excellent programs, the latest contemporary worship, high standards, and alive reputations on which they congratulated themselves. But they still received rigorous censure from Jesus.

Ministry and worship may in fact be highly displeasing to our Lord—they can become despised by Him. "I hate, I despise your religious feasts," God says. "I cannot stand your assemblies. Even though you bring me burnt offerings and grain offerings, I will not accept them. Though you bring choice fellowship offerings, I will have no regard for them. Away with the noise of your songs! I will not listen to the music of your harps."[24] And God says again, "When you spread out your hands in prayer, I will hide My eyes from you; even if you offer many prayers, I will not listen. Your hands are full of blood."[25] God means to shake the very souls of all who were involved in any *routine of ministry or worship.*

What about our hymns, choirs, spiritual songs, dancing, our clapping, shouting, orchestras, and drama teams. . . those things we so much enjoy listening to or doing when we "worship"? Could God be saying, "Away with the noise. I will not listen."? Could that be possible? Could God not enjoy what we enjoy? Could we be the very opposite of what we have think we are? Could we be that deluded?

Modern church life is packed with Sunday and midweek services, seminars, spiritual celebrations, retreats, special days, city-wide campaigns, and camps. Read the brochures; read the magazines. Are these meaningless to God, nothing but religious activities we busily and blithely practice while evil multiplies around us and judgment looms? Could we our Lord actually look at us as "worshipers" who exult in abounding worship which we totally enjoy while we are surrounded in society by abounding sin that we totally ignore?

Could we be that deceived? Israel was. Five churches were. Others have been.

Could it be that while we delightedly skip from one happy spiritual event to the other, enjoying with abandon all the uplift, renewal, and blessing they appear to bring, God is saying, "I hate, I despise, I cannot stand them."?

It is a question we dare not ignore.

God was so fed up with Israel's well-established but sin-ignoring religion that He mocked it, "Go to Bethel and sin; go to Gilgal and sin yet more. Bring your sacrifices every morning, your tithes every three years. Burn leavened bread as a thank offering and brag about you freewill offerings—boast about them, you Israelites, for this is what you love to do."[26] For a lot of Christians today, those Words of God strike close to home.

Why does our Lord abhor so much of what we consider to be good, even Spirit-led and anointed, religious activities?

Well, what did the Lord want from Israel, from His chosen people? What could they have done that would have pleased Him? "But let justice roll on like a river, righteousness like a never-failing stream," God says through Amos.[27] "Wash and make yourselves clean. Take your evil deeds out of My sight! Stop doing wrong, learn to do right. Seek justice, encourage the oppressed. Defend the cause of the fatherless, plead the case of the widow," God says through Isaiah.[28]

There's our answer. *Justice. Righteousness. Cleansing. Right living. Defending the fatherless and widow.* These are what our Lord is looking for in His people. God wants them pouring abundantly from them at all times. Such things blessed and saved the nation of Israel, and such things will bless and save our nation or any nation of the West.

The Lord wants worship—liturgical or non-liturgical, evangelical, fundamental, Pentecostal, or charismatic—*that focuses on knowing Him more.*[29] "*Seek Me and live!*"[30] The people who *know* God care deeply about things that God cares about.

When we have neither heart nor desire to truly *know* God, and no concern about injustice and unrighteousness, God despises our multitude of religious events, our rituals, our kneeling at altars, and our lifting our hands in praise. They are empty words and sounds before Him, rattling noises that have no meaning to Him. He turns His ear away and does not hear. Unless we are spiritually dead and do not know it, surely we can feel the heat of His displeasure at our self-deceived worship.

Perhaps our greatest tragedy in such an atmosphere is that the false prophets of our day have cunningly diverted our attention from our sins and the clear warnings of the Scriptures to those more pleasing topics that tickle our ears and fill their meetings and pocketbooks. As in Noah's day, and in Sodom and the churches in Asia, we can dance to the tune of the flesh, and ignore the troublesome words of the Bible that warn us that all things today are as they were in those ancient societies upon which God poured out the wrath of His righteous judgment.

Let's be reminded that true worship and true ministry come out of a heart that wants to please God, not to please self. And true worship and true ministry motivate us to do those things that please God. Such as having compassion, acting justly, and living righteously. These are both a result and a sign of true worship and ministry. Otherwise they are nothing more than religious play, something that the person enjoys doing and has convinced himself or herself that God enjoys it. True worshipers, however, care first and foremost about what the heart of God cares about. They will use their hands, feet and voices to bring about what He cares about. The prophet Micah said, "And what does the Lord require of you? To act justly and to love mercy and to walk humbly with your God."[31] And James said, "Religion that God our Father accepts as pure and faultless is this: to look after orphans and widows in their distress and to keep oneself from being polluted by the world."[32]

Carl Henry said, "We must choose to cast our lot either with a society that admits only private faiths, and simply add another idol to modernity's expanding God-shelf, or we must hoist a banner to a higher Sovereign, the Lord of lord and King of kings."[33] The genuine Church has always hoisted such a banner. Churches such as Laodicea do not.

What demolishes willful self-delusion? *Repentance!* "Repent" is what Jesus commanded of Ephesus, Pergamus, Thyratira, Sardis and Laodicea. If Jesus used the word, "repent," we must.

Repentance in a church is to be part of its lifestyle. Repentance will be integral in the fabric of genuine revival.

The kind of church our Lord wants is humbled, has a heart after God, loves one another, is committed to holiness, seeks justice and righteousness, and speaks for the oppressed.

Self-delusion ravages America. It excuses our enormous sins. It revels in the prosperity of the moment. It ignores accountability. Like it did with Noah's day, Sodom, Israel, and other nations, self-delusion will take us to hell.

Only a repentant church who has severely dealt with its own self-delusion will have the moral coin and clear insight to speak compellingly to our deluded nation and call it to repentance and back to God.

That could bring a blessed spiritual awakening across our land!

Let us pray together: Our gracious heavenly Father of Truth and Wisdom, how we need—and desire—Your holy evaluation; how we need—and desire—the piercing insight of Your Word to search us. As Your Son looked deep into His church, look into our churches. Do not let us off easy; but show us how You see us, how we really are, what we really have become. Deliver us from self-delusion. Forgive us for blindly thinking we are wonderful when You see us as woeful; for haughtily confessing we are rich when in Your eyes we are poor; for raising our hands when You see them stained with blood. We only want to please You! Then enable us to speak to our self-deluded world Your anointed, penetrating Word. And may that Word convict and bring to repentance our nation. And with that, a gracious, fresh spiritual awakening. In Jesus' name we pray. Amen.

CHAPTER 4 ENDNOTES

[1] Proverbs 1:32-33 (NLT).

[2] Psalm 10:2-6.

[3] Psalm 94:6-7.

[4] Proverbs 30:20.

[5] The story comes from Matthew 25:1-13; it might be good to read it.

[6] Luke 13:23-28.

[7] 6. Roy Clements, *When God's Patience Runs Out*, Inter-Varsity, 1988, p. 92.

[8] Anderson and Freedman, Hosea (Doubleday, 1980), p.41

[9] Matthew 18:7-9.

[10] Matthew 7:22-23.

[11] Luke 10:17-20.

[12] Irving Jensen, *Minor prophets of Israel*, Moody Press, 175, p. 45.

[13] Jeremiah 13:26-27.

[14] Luke 3: 7.

[15] Ibid, p. 19.

[16] John White, *The Golden Cow*, p.7.

[17] Amos 3:10

[18] Luke 17:26-30.

[19] Genesis 6:5-13.

[20] Ezekiel 16:49-50.

[21] Matthew 24:39.

[22] Genesis 19:23.

[23] Revelation 3:16-17.

[24] Amos 5:21-23.

[25] Isaiah 1:15.

[26] Amos 4:4-5.

[27] Amos 5:24.

[28] Isaiah 1:16-17.

[29] Philippians 3:10.

[30] Amos 5:4.

[31] Micah 6:8.

[32] James 1:27.

[33] Carl Henry, *Twilight of a Great Civilization*, (Westchester, Il, Crossway Books, 1988), p. 181.

PART TWO

THE WEIGHT OF
OUR DESERVED
JUDGEMENT

"Can unjust leaders claim that God is on their side—leaders who permit injustice by their laws? They attack the righteous and condemn the innocent to death."[1]

"For only when you come to judge the earth will people turn from wickedness and do what is right. Your kindness to the wicked does not make them do good. They keep doing wrong. . . Look! The Lord is coming from heaven to punish the people of the earth for their sins."[2]

In the latter days of the Roman Empire we can see a similar disregard for human life. When burdensome regulations and taxes made manufacturing, trade, and even common labor unprofitable, individuals were locked into hereditary trades and vocations for life, and their sons and daughters could have no vocational mobility at all.

"Eventually children came to be seen as a needless burden; so infanticide which was forbidden by penalty of death in the glory days of Rome, suddenly became a convenient expedient. Abortion, strangulation of infants, and exposure to the elements were widespread practices in the closing centuries of the empire. In some cases, children were sold into slavery or prostitution. But almost no one could afford the luxury of bearing and raising children any longer. No one wanted the additional responsibility of caring for the young when life was so tenuous and pointless."[3]

—JIM NELSON BLACK, COMMENTING
ON AMERICA'S PRESENT SITUATION

And whereas, it is the duty of nations, as well as of men, to own their dependence upon the overruling power of God, to confess their sin and transgressions in humble sorrow, yet with assured hope that genuine repentance will lead to mercy and pardon, and to recognize the sublime truth, announced in the Holy Scripture and proven by all history, that those nations only are blessed whose God is the Lord;

"And, insomuch as we know that, by His divine law, nations, like individuals, are subjected to punishments and chastisements in this world, **may we not justly fear that the awful calamity of civil war, which now desolates the land, may be but a punishment inflicted upon us for our presumptuous sins, to the needful end of our national reformation as a whole people?**

"We have been the recipients of the choicest bounties of Heaven. We have been preserved, these many years, in peace and prosperity. We have grown in numbers, wealth, and power as no other nation has ever grown. **But we have forgotten God.** We have forgotten the gracious hand which preserved us in peace, and multiplied and enriched and strengthened us; and we have vainly imagined, in the deceitfulness of our hearts, that all these blessings were produced by some superior wisdom and virtue of our own.

"Intoxicated with unbroken success, we have become too self-sufficient to feel the necessity of redeeming and preserving grace, too proud to pray to the God that made us! It behooves us then, to humble ourselves before the offended Power, to confess our national sins, and to pray for clemency and forgiveness.

"All this being done, in sincerity and truth, let us then rest humbly in the hope authorized by the Divine teachings, **that the united cry of the Nation will be** heard on high, and answered with blessings, no less than the pardon of our national sins, and restoration of our now divided and suffering country to its former happy condition of unity and peace." 4

—ABRAHAM LINCOLN, CALLING FOR A
DAY OF NATIONAL HUMILIATION
FASTING AND PRAYER

PART TWO ENDNOTES

[1] Psalm 94:20-21.

[2] Isaiah 26:9-10, 21.

[3] Jim Nelson Black, *When Nations Die: Ten Warning Signs of a Culture in Crisis*, (Wheaton: Tyndale House, 1994) p.3.

[4] Abraham Lincoln, in his *Proclamation for a Day of National Humiliation Fasting and Prayer*, called for April 30, 1863.

5

OUR CHOSEN LIES

"There is a way that seems right to a man, but in the end it leads to death."
—GOD, SPEAKING IN PROVERBS[1]

"Deep down in his mind, every man knows that he is the creature of God and responsible to God. Every man, at bottom, knows that he is a covenant-breaker. But every man acts and talks as though this were not so."
—CORNELIUS VAN TIL[2]

I REMEMBER AS A YOUNGSTER HEARING SOME OLDER PEOPLE MAKE idle comment about a tall building in the city. I think it was a hotel. One said, "It doesn't have a 13th floor," and alluded to the superstition about the number 13 that causes builders to skip from the 12th floor directly to the 14th to avoid bad luck.

I don't know if tall buildings still are constructed without a 13th floor, but years later I realize that no matter what that floor above the 12th is numbered, it is still the 13th. It might make superstitious edgy people feel better to have that floor labeled the 14th; but that cosmetic change doesn't alter the truth that in the numerical sequence of the floors, it is still the 13th one.

I suppose that skipping the numerical designation of an "unlucky" floor is innocuous enough, but it's indicative of our cultures vulnerability to self-deception. We've learned to change the labels to alter the perception of truth. We call an unborn child a "mass of tissue," a "collection of cells," or even "fetus." We change the words to deny an unborn child's humanity. An abortion is the "evacuation of a uterus," a "termination of pregnancy," or a "repro- ductive right." Whoremongering is "promiscuity." Fornication is "pre-marital sex." Adultery is an "affair." Sodomy is "being gay." And on and on.

Several new tags have arisen in recent years, especially in polit- ical jargon where our politicians have made an art form of lying to us to escape scandal. A president told us, "is" and "alone" do not mean what they mean, and some kinds of sex are not sex. Perhaps the most notable newer political word is "spin," another name for political lying. We even have "spin doctors," professionals in public relations whose skill is to take a lie and spin it into the illusion of truth or take truth and spin it into deception. As Columnist Craig McMillan says, spin doctors work as if, "their lies had the power to heal a nation." Then there is "war room" a place where political operatives dig up things scandalous about opponents—even to twisting truth so it appears bad. Even our preachers can lie to us about the extent of their ministries, how their money is being spent, and how big their congregations are.

We are becoming a nation where "lying-chic" is accepted. Lying is a national contagion. McMillan said, "It is clear that our age has embraced the spirit of deceit. School principals endorse minor chil- dren lying to their parents about an abortion—while they prohibit school nurses from dispensing an aspirin tablet without parental approval. Husbands and wives lie to one another about their sexual liaisons. Factory bosses lie to their workers about plant closings, so they can obtain the advantage of an orderly shutdown with the workers must pass up good jobs in more honest, viable firms.

Employees lie to their prospective bosses about job qualifications on their resumes, so they can gain the edge over those who honestly report their experience and education."

"Yes," McMillan added, "we are drowning in a sea of deceit, tangled in a life jacket of lies, and going down for the third time—both as individuals and as a nation."[3]

The alarming part is that we seem indifferent toward standing truth on it head and nonchalant toward how this affects us as a people with regard to law or our heritage as a nation. "We have placed upon the throne lying and dishonesty and lack of integrity," presidential candidate Alan Keyes said. "And right now it looks as there are too many American tempted to go down on their knees and worship that vice."[4]

On January 19, 2001, the last full day that outgoing President Bill Clinton would be in office, one of his staunchest defenders was on a television debate program. The president's defender kept waxing eloquently about how the president was leaving office with such "high approval ratings," implying—"spinning"—that since the people approved so heartily of him, he had done a great job. Of course the administration of that president was the most scandalous in our history. In the words of George Will, Bill Clinton was "the worst person ever to have been president."[5] Values were ignored so that a president could commit adultery Sunday morning, and then pick up his Bible and go to church while many excused his sin and kept his approval ratings high. What that presidential defender failed to articulate were the tragic consequences of the president's various depravities—from immorality to lying under oath. Although his behaviors were (perhaps understandably) vigorously defended and excused by lawyers, politicians and leftists, many of **us** also excused them.. The real tragedy is that during that president's administration public outrage toward evil waned and cynicism toward politicians rose. When a high percentage of the people in the electorate affirm a president—or anyone—in his depravity while also excusing that depravity, that does not so much validate the president as it reveals, lamentably, the depravity of the society.

"They perish because they refused to love the truth and so be saved," II Thessalonians says. Verse 12b speaks of those "who have not believed the truth but have delighted in wickedness." Between these two statements is this sobering one: "For this reason God sends them a powerful delusion so that they will believe the lie and so that all will be condemned who have not believed the truth."

When a nation listens to "the lie," as The Rebirth of America says, "It dethrones God and deifies man's achievements; it exalts human reason as supreme; it trusts education and science to solve its problems; it believes that man is evolving into perfection; it replaces God's moral standards with situational ethics; it promotes sensual pleasure and instant gratification; it strives for a world utopia of prosperity and peace; it makes the State the sovereign dictator over everyone."[6]

What we see is God giving sinners what they stubbornly want. If they are defiant and don't want God and truth, then God gives them over to untruth. If they won't love truth, they will get powerful lies.

Consider the implications of rejecting truth for us as a society. We show little evidence for wanting truth; we prefer to believe lies—clever self-deceptions—because we want to sin. We want the legal right to kill our unborn children, so we turn our backs on the truth of the sanctity of human life and allow mothers to claim that legal right to abortion. We want sexual license, so we don't to love the truth of God's happy principles for sex only within the intimacy of marriage and believe the lie of whoremongering: "If it feels good, do it."

Now we are in the same process with such sins as same-sex marriage, physician-assisted suicide, adoption of children by homo-sexuals, and abortion. We seem to come up with new justifications to excuse whatever we want to do. We even turn these justifications into laws that legislate the sins and support the sinners.

These are all based on chosen lies.

And chosen lies are dangerous. They are the basis of self-delusion.

Our chosen lies now have our acceptance. They are now rooted in our national character. We are moving toward abandoning truth and restraint with growing ease. And worse, we are indifferent toward the consequences of our choices. The evidence is clear. America deserves judgment!

"I am against you," God said to Israel and to other nations.[7] Israel particularly couldn't believe God would say such a thing, caught up as they were in the hubris of their wonderful heritage. Like Israel, America probably doesn't believe that God could say "I am against you" to us either, and for the same reasons. But why should God be for us? What does America have to recommend itself to the great Almighty God of holiness and justice? Why should God bless liars? Can God be for us with our collective hands dripping with the blood of our unborn children and with no end to this butchery in sight? Why should God bless murderers who increasingly insist that such killing should be completely unhindered?

No, America is building its own case that it deserves judgment. Here are some of our chosen lies that make that case.

One chosen lie: **"We can disown our Christian Heritage with Impunity."**

"We hold these truths to be self-evident that all people are created equal, that they are endowed by their Creator with certain unalienable rights among which are life, liberty, and the pursuit of happiness," is the first sentence of the Declaration of Independence.

"We, the people of the United States, in order to form a more perfect union, establish justice, ensure domestic tranquility, provide for the common defense, promote the general welfare, and secure the blessings of liberty to ourselves and our posterity, do ordain and establish this constitution of the United States of America," is the preamble to the Constitution.

These remarkable sentences are from our foundational documents. They speak of "self-evident truths" and "unalienable rights." How out of place do "truth" and "unalienable" seem today when unchanging or absolute principles are so attacked? A "Creator"? The "created"? We're moving at warp speed away from those godly ideals. "We, the people of the United States." Consider how revolutionary, how radical the idea of "We, the people" establishing and ordaining a government in a day when monarchy was the political system, kings were sovereign, and people were subjects! Our forefathers took an amazing step.

But America's foundation is based upon is a sovereign *people*, not a sovereign government. How many of us understand this, when big government is standing the principle on its head?

The American system of government consists of a sovereign people, a government receiving its power from the people Its purpose is to secure human rights, which are ordained by God.

Our Pledge of Allegiance declares us to be "one nation under God." Our money has our national vow, "In God We Trust," which is also engraved on a bronze plaque in the Dirksen Office Building of the U.S. Congress.

Our Christian heritage is reflected throughout Washington, D.C. The Library of Congress has a multitude of scriptural verses on display. Each session of the U.S. Supreme Court opens with the cry, "God save the United States and this Honorable Court." On the stairwell walls within the Washington Monument are inscribed "Holiness to the Lord," and "Search the Scriptures." Engraved at the top of the stairwell is, "Praise the Lord." Abraham Lincoln's "Gettysburg Address" is enshrined on the wall of the Lincoln Memorial, and found in it are these words: "This nation under God." And among Lincoln's speeches engraved on the walls of the Memorial are references to "God," "the Almighty," and "the Bible."

Furthermore, when a president-elect is inaugurated, he places his hand on a Bible as he takes the Oath of Office and concludes the oath with the words, "So help me God."

Clearly, the government of the United States has vowed to honor God.

We need to re-connect with our heritage, recapture the value system on which we were founded, and once more celebrate being "under God." And we need to teach all this to our children. Again, Steven Muller warns, "Failure to rally around a set of values means that we are turning out highly skilled barbarians. Society as a whole is turning out barbarians because of the discarding of the value system in was built on."

Muller added, "To restore its lost value system, America would have to return to its faith in God. There can be no value system where there is no supreme value that transcends man's natural self-centeredness, where one man's values are esteemed as good as another's."[8]

In Scripture, over and over God wanted His people to remember their heritage. "Remember the wonders He [God] has done, His miracles, and the judgments He pronounced," David said.[9] Remembering would anchor them in the future, "Remember how the Lord God led you . . . Be careful that you do not forget the Lord your God, failing to observe His commands, His laws . . . Otherwise, when you eat and are satisfied . . . your heart will become proud and you will forget the Lord your God . . . You may say to yourself, 'My power and the strength of my hands have produced this wealth for me.'"[10]

Sadly, by the time of the Early Church, Israel had moved so far from their heritage that when Stephen attempted to return them to it in Acts 7, they were infuriated and killed him.

Today America is foolishly moving away from our unique heritage, and rejecting the God who made it all possible. We are pushing God away and removing Him from virtually every area of our national life. We almost seem on a rampage to become atheistic. Billy Graham said, "We talk of God, but we often act as though we are atheists. We have developed a sort of dual personality, a schizophrenia. We have 'In God We Trust' on our coins, but 'Me First' engraved on our hearts."[11]

The result is that our national recognition of God is more and more hollow lip-service, a book-cover facade hiding the pages in which are recorded the hideousness of our national hypocrisy. Sadly our national oath is a lie in the mouth of our country, a perjury, and a blasphemy of which we are increasingly guilty.

What if God takes us at our word, when we say, "God, we do not want You," and leaves us? What if He "gives us up," to use the phrase from Romans 1? Why should He not do so? If He did, our "In God We Trust" would be replaced with "Ichabod"—"the glory has departed." This judgment may already be happening.

I have given my wife Esther flowers. I have given her cut flowers she can put in a vase with water. Also I have given her flowers growing in a flower pot. There is a difference. In the flower pot, the flowers are connected to their roots; in the vase, they are not. And no matter how those cut flowers are watered and cared for, they will eventually die.

What do flowers have to do with a godly nation? They illustrate the vital importance of staying connected to good roots. Thomas Jefferson, third president of the United States and famous horticulturist, obviously understood the link between viability and healthy roots when he wrote, *"Can the liberties of a nation be secure when we have removed the conviction that these liberties are the gift of God?"*

We'd better answer that question! Because there are many in this nation who are working to sever the conviction that our liberties are the gift of God.

If they are successful, then, like cut flowers, such a severed nation will die.

A dead nation?

America?

Judgment?

Yes. Yes. Yes.

Another chosen lie: **"Changing the definitions of good and evil does not matter."**

"Woe to those who call evil good and good evil."[12] We're pursuing the delusion that standing good on its head is no issue. Moral absolutes are under attack. We're plunger deeper and deeper in the dark abyss of self-determination of our moral values.

Evils are being lifted to the status of "morally neutral." In worst cases they're being elevated even higher to "virtues." The slaughter of unborn children is no longer the evil our forefathers called it. It is now morally neutral—a "choice," as in "pro-choice." It is also now a virtue—a "right," as in "a woman's right," or a "reproductive right." Such a "right" has taken on an inviolable aura, as a constitutional right to freedom of speech, religion, or the press. Abortion is also now the virtue of "a compassionate action." The woman is unmarried, has too many children, has a career; he baby might be unwanted, or be in jeopardy of being born into terrible poverty or with a handicap—all giving him a "bad life." So the compassionate thing to do would be to kill that child. Compassion being turned into a rationale for killing is the ultimate expression of hypocrisy. Evil is called "good."

Of course, on the other hand, to deny a woman access to the alleged virtue of her "right" to abortion is opposed venomously. That's terribly wrong. To stand against a woman's choice to "compassionately" kill her unborn child is hard-hearted and callous. Good is called evil.

In killing our unborn children, we've simply declared it a "right"; but we don't want to discuss whether or not it is right!

Once marriage between heterosexual partners was the only one acceptable. In fact, no one even considered any other way. But now the immoral coupling of unmarried men and women, or homosexuals living together is equated with traditional marriage. In many states these arrangements are legally equivalent to traditional marriage. Evil is called good.

Even further, our immoral society has elevated homosexuality to the status of a third gender, as if there is male and female, and then there is homosexual. We've embraced this "three-sex" concept so deeply that we're teaching it to our children in our tax-funded schools and elsewhere. *Teaching our children to accept sin in this way or any other way could in itself bring down God's righteous judgment on us!*

We're seeing the created natural order of male and female overturned. Evil is called good.

And of course any opposition to such licentious reasoning meets strenuous objection to, since doing what is right in your own eyes is canonized. Moral judgments are out; right or wrong no longer exist; and whoever calls sin "sin" is quickly and automatically castigated. Good is called evil.

Again, Isaiah 5:20, from another translation, "Destruction is certain for those who say that evil is good and good is evil; that dark is light and light is dark; that bitter is sweet and sweet is bitter."[13]

"Destruction is certain . . ." can only mean one thing: America faces judgment.

Another chosen lie: **"Choices do not have consequences."**

"You will not surely die," the serpent hissed to Eve in the Garden of Eden. In other words, "Go ahead and sin [only it is not called sin], nothing bad will happen." Eve was convinced, and ate the forbidden fruit—only to discover the lie. *She did die.*

Satan's lie to Eve was the first version of that clever deception which claims that choices do not have consequences. To this day the deception convinces plenty of willing dupes, America included.

Duped like Eve, we're living as if we can choose to sin without reaping the consequences. We do this against the clear Word of God—what we sow is what we reap, and the wages of sin is death. Yet we live in denial like those the prophet Zephaniah wrote about, "The Lord will do nothing, either good or bad."[14] We live like Israel and Judah which the prophet Jeremiah referred to when he wrote, "They have lied about the Lord; they said, 'He will do nothing! No harm will come to us; we will never see sword or famine."[15] Of course we know that the sword did come—brutally—to Israel and Judah. They paid a tragic price for their chosen lies.

To say that a choice does not have a consequence is a contradiction. It's an absurdity, like saying water is not wet, fire does not burn, a dog is not an animal. *In fact, a choice is the selection of a consequence.* A choice equals a consequence; a consequence is a choice. If I choose to wear a blue shirt, the consequence is that I wear a blue shirt. If I choose to eat an apple, the consequence is that I eat an apple. If I choose to turn left at the light, the consequence is that I turn left at the light. When I chose to marry Esther (after asking her), the happy consequence (after she said yes) was that I married her. (Actually our marriage involved two choices, hers and mine; but the principle is the same.)

Our nation is living in a self-made fantasy with "We shall not surely die" as a national mantra. We've embraced the absurdity of neutered choices, which is an oxymoron.

We're living in a house of clouds, where circles have four sides, squares have seven sides, triangles are a straight line and parallels intersect. It's where you can plant weeds and grow roses, and breed rattlesnakes and get a house dog. It's where absolutes are maybes, and maybes are absolutes. It's where belief is feeling, and feeling is belief. It's where options are principles, and principles are preferences. It's where America is now.

In our fantasy we give "choice" to a mother who wants to kill her unborn baby; we give "choice" to fornicators who want to commit that sin, we give "choice" two men or two women who want to marry—all without consequences, all sans judgment.

Our fantasy produces delusional logic: The unborn child has no humanity. Killing the unborn child is legal. Therefore the unborn child is a legal non-human. And therefore we kill nothing. There can be no judgment for that!

Our fantasy is now our societal creed. "Choice" is reflected in Supreme Court decisions, in our laws, in the platforms of the political parties, in the speeches of political candidates, and, most notably, its what we teach our children (because it won't hurt them because there are no consequences). It's in our movies, on our televisions, and in our music. All without consequences.

The answer to fantasy is truth. And the Church must step into America's dream world and proclaim Truth. We must insist that our society stop basing so much on "choice" and start considering what choices are: consequences. America must be told from Scripture that there is no such thing as neutered choice, "Do not be deceived: God cannot be mocked. A man reaps what he sows." And we must tell America that there is a connection between moral anarchy and a debased society; and between moral probity and a virtuous society. That it's a contradiction to sow death in the womb and reap life in society. That it's impossible to cultivate immorality—heterosexual or homosexual—and garner strong families. That it's stupidity to publish pornography and expect to build people of character. "Human actions," Herbert Schlossberg said, "have moral consequences. There is a principle of moral accountability in the universe."[16]

However, at this point in our history, we are not heeding the "principle of moral accountability;" we are sadly choosing the smooth arguments of fools. We are as Isaiah said of Judah, "He feeds on ashes, a deluded heart misleads him; he cannot save himself, or say, 'Is not this thing in my right hand a lie?'"[17]

We may live in denial of the consequences of our chosen lies such as disowning our Christian heritage. We can invert the definitions of good and evil, or by fiat, declare that choices do not have consequences. But denial changes nothing more than it did for Eve.

Eve's deluded heart chose sin. As Eve learned, her choice had consequence: judgment.

We are headed for the same consequence. Because we are indifferent in nation and church, we grieve intensely.

What will it take for us to see the lies in our chosen lies? To reconnect ourselves with our heritage? To put Truth on the throne? To quit living in a fantasy? To turn our nation around before God's judgment?

There is an answer, a powerful one: the Church roaring.

Let us pray with one of our nation's founders, Thomas Jefferson: *Almighty God, Who has given us this good land for our heritage, we humbly beseech Thee that we may always prove ourselves a people mindful of Thy favor and glad to do Thy will. Bless our land with honorable industry, sound learning, and pure manners. Save us from violence, discord, and confusion; and from pride and* arrogance; and fashion into one united people the multitude brought hither out of many kindreds and tongues. Endow with the spirit of wisdom those to whom in Thy Name we entrust the authority of government, that there may be justice and peace at home; and that through obedience to Thy law, we may show forth Thy praise among the nations of the earth. In time of prosperity, fill our hearts with thankfulness; and, in the day of trouble, suffer not our trust in Thee to fail. All of which we ask through Jesus Christ our Lord, Amen.

CHAPTER 5 ENDNOTES

[1] Proverbs 14:12 and 16:25.

[2] Cornelius Van Til, *Apologetics* (1966), p. 57.

[3] Craig Macmillan, World Net Daily column, Dec. 14, 2000.

[4] Alan Keyes, in a campaign speech in California during the 2000 Republican presidential primary.

[5] George Will, in his Jan. 11, 2001 column, *"Clinton's Mark."*

[6] *The Rebirth of America*, Arthur S. DeMoss Foundation, 1986, p.143.

[7] For instance in Ezekiel 21:3; 25:7; 26:3; 29:3; 35:3.

[8] Steven Muller, "University Professor Speaks Out," *NFD Informer* (September 1983), p.64.

[9] I Chronicles 16:12.

[10] From Deuteronomy 8:2-17.

[11] Billy Graham, *World Aflame*, (Westwood, NJ: Fleming Revell Company, 1965), p.35.

[12] Isaiah 5:20.

[13] Isaiah 5:20, New Living Translation.

[14] Zephaniah 1:12.

[15] Jeremiah 5:12.

[16] Herbert Schlossberg, *Idols for Destruction*, (Nashville, TN: Thomas Nelson, 1983) p.293.

[17] Isaiah 44:20.

6

SINNING BOLDLY

"I am sending you to . . . a rebellious nation that has rebelled against Me; they and their fathers have been in revolt against Me to this very day. The people to whom I am sending you are obstinate and stubborn."
—GOD, SPEAKING TO EZEKIEL[1]

"It is our insensitivity to sin that prevents our realizing how hell-deserving sin is; our devilish dispositions make sin not appear 'horrid.'"
—JONATHAN EDWARDS[2]

TO UNDERSTAND WHAT WE HAVE DONE IN AMERICA, WE NEED perspective.

Let's visit a memorable place and time. Let's go to a bitterly cold December afternoon in Eastern Pennsylvania. It's snowing hard with about a foot on the ground and a biting wind blowing laterally. To the left is a forest of oak and elm; ahead are several miles of gently rolling hills and meadows. About 15 feet away a large, gray horse stamps his feet nervously. Astride the horse a tall man sits, with a dark cloak around his shoulders which are hunched against the cold, and a tri-cornered hat pulled low over his forehead.[3]

Out of the woods there emerge rank upon rank of ill-clad men. They shuffle silently past the man on the horse. Most of them are clad in what six or eight months ago must have been uniforms, but now are only rags and tatters. Some have cloaks, and some have pieces of burlap around their shoulders; but many are just in shirt-sleeves. Muskets are on most shoulders, but some have just fouling pieces, old shot guns or pistols stuck in their sashes. Some have boots, but others have just pieces of shoes or burlap tied about their feet. Incredibly many are bare-footed. It has been said that you can trace the path of these men across the frozen landscape by the bloody foot-prints they leave behind them in the snow.

A few of the men glance at the man on the horse, but most stare straight ahead. But they all know he is there. And for them that is enough. We are drawn to look closely at the man on the horse as he watches these men—11,000 of them—pass before him. He is weeping.

It is December 19, 1777, and General George Washington is reviewing what is left of the Continental Army of the United States of America as they enter their winter quarters at Valley Forge. It is the beginning of a long, dark chapter of American suffering, as there is nothing to eat at Valley Forge except a few barrels of flour which they will mix with creek water and bake on fire-stone, and call it "fire-cake." And disease will soon set in with typhus, diarrhea, tuberculosis, pneumonia, smallpox, and starvation so decimating their ranks that by February, nearly eighteen men a day were dying every day. Washington and Lafayette make the rounds everyday encouraging the men and praying with them. A young Lieutenant, John Marshall, is there; he would later become Chief Justice of the United States Supreme Court.

Almost a third of the 11,000—some 3,000—died; they lie buried at Valley Forge. The wonder is that they stayed. It would have been easy to melt away into the woods, go AWOL, and go back home. But they endured the suffering and were faithful to their call.

In that crucible of suffering at Valley Forge—so aptly named—God welded together a group of men through pain who remained committed to their vision of freedom, and their commitment to one another. Prior to Valley Forge, those men had been routed in battle again and again by the British army, then the most powerful army on earth. But after Valley Forge, they never lost another battle. In three years the war was over.

America was born.

Were we worth it?

Were we? Were we worth their sacrifice?

We could fast-forward to our bloody Civil War, or on to World War I, or to World War II, or to other wars before or since, where Americans have fought and died . And we could ask the same question: *Were we worth it?*

WHAT IF WE COULD INTERVIEW MEN AT VALLEY FORGE?

What if we could actually return to that bitterly cold December day in 1777 as those ill-dressed men marched past George Washington at Valley Forge? Suppose we could talk to them, and tell them a bit of what it is like now, some two-and-a-quarter centuries later, about our lifestyles, our homes, automobiles, computers, prosperity, airplanes, entertainment, TVs, movies, music, politics, etc.? No doubt it would amaze them.

However, what if they asked us about our values? What if they asked us about what we now believe? What would we say if they asked if the idea of freedom is still in our hearts? What would we say? What if somewhere in our conversation with them we said the following: "You know, your sacrifice, suffering, and even deaths, there in Valley Forge and throughout that Revolutionary War provided us with a most wonderful freedom. It gave us the special freedom to kill our unborn children!"

How do you think they would react?

They might say, "What do you mean, 'kill our unborn children'? Do you mean a baby in the womb, before it is born? To kill it then?"

"Yes! It's called abortion. This freedom has become very important to women."

"You mean a mother in your day would do that, kill her unborn baby? And that it is important to her to be able to so if she wishes?"

We might try to explain, "You see, two-and-a-quarter centuries from now, women will believe that the freedom for which you sacrificed gives them the right to decide to kill their unborn babies."

"What about the fathers? What do they think?"

"As far as the fathers are concerned, the freedom for the mothers means that the fathers can't say anything."

"But, then the fathers don't have any freedom."

"Yes, but the baby, I mean fetus, is in a mother's body. It's her body, so the freedom is only for her."

Before they could respond, perhaps we went on, "But another freedom you gave us through your sacrifice is to make it possible for children to be adopted by two men or two women who are living together, who are a couple."

"You mean, 'living together' and 'are a couple,' like husband and wife?"

"Precisely."

"Do people do that in your day, openly that is"?

"Yes! They're called 'homosexuals.' People believe they should have that right."

"And you put children with them?"

"Of course. It's part of the wonderful freedom you've given us; which by the way, has also made it possible for us to teach our children in school about the freedoms I've mentioned, like a mother being able to decide to kill her unborn baby, and people of the same sex living together and adopting children!"

"You mean that you teach children about those kinds of things?"

"Yes, in school and other places."

"Doesn't anyone in your day think these things are wrong?"

"Oh, some people object, religious people and some others. But most people either think these things are all right or don't care."

AFTER OUR INTERVIEW

After our interview, how inspired might those men at Valley Forge have been to stay there and bear the sacrifices of that war which birthed America, particularly when their generation produced the values in the Declaration of Independence.

The journey from the values of Valley Forge and the Declaration of Independence to abortion clinics; sexual license in movies, TV, and music; fatherlessness; same-sex couples adopting children; drug addictions and other evils of our day is sobering. Part of the problem is that our Christian heritage is getting edited out, most of us don't even know the story of Valley Forge. We've forgotten the values of the Declaration of Independence or other parts of our great heritage.

America (as well as Canada, Australia and New Zealand) was birthed in a virgin land filled with abundant natural resources. Our founders gave us a robust republican form of government and a robust political system. We worked to build our society and to create an impressive civilization, but in the words of Abraham Lincoln, "We have forgotten God . . . And we have vainly imagined, in the deceitfulness of our hearts, that all these blessings were produced by some superior wisdom and virtue of our own."[4]

The time since Valley Forge has taken us through the grief of the Civil War, a war of judgment. As Lincoln put it, "the awful calamity of civil war, which now desolates the land, may be but a punishment inflicted upon us for our presumptuous sins."[5]

We have enjoyed high materialistic ride; we've lived well. But we are being summoned by God to give an account of our steward-ship—to answer a question: How is it possible that in the two-plus centuries since Valley Forge and the Declaration of Independence, America has become a sewer of sin, violence and immorality?

And, why is it that our America is ignoring the warnings of judg-ment?

Look at Lincoln's answer in 1863, "Intoxicated with unbroken success, we have become too self-sufficient to feel the necessity of redeeming and preserving grace, too proud to pray to the God that made us!"

Intoxicated with success? Too self-sufficient? Too proud? This was Lincoln's prophetic evaluation of his day. When those attitudes get rooted deeply in a nation, they foster aggressive, argumentative sinning. When a society not only sins, but argues for its sins, vehe-mently contends for its sins, and quarrels if it doesn't get its way, it's called sinning boldly.

A boldly sinning nation lives for now. It forgets its heritage. It wants rights, personal pleasure, its needs cared for. And it bases its arguments on chosen lies—selected deceptions that provide the brazen excuses for their bold sinning—they are a culture of barbarians who live "by power and for pleasure rather than by and for principle," as James Boice said.

America is sinning boldly, and egregiously. It is showing that it deserves judgment. Here are several of the reasons.

BARBARIAN BRUTALITY

> "A murderous and cruel disposition, which, rather than have its plans frustrated, will imbue the hands with innocent blood—the blood of those who have done it no injury."
>
> —MUFFET

There he is on the cover of *Time Magazine* looking out a second story window to an approving crowd just below, happily holding his hands above his head, palms out, a look of glee on his face.

It's his hands that rivet your attention. They're bloody, very bloody. It's the blood of an Israeli soldier that the young Palestinian has just helped massacre and toss out the window. It's stomach turning, barbaric.

God hates "hands that shed innocent blood."[6] He hates such hands on any of us. "Your iniquities have separated you from your God . . . for your hands are stained with blood,"[7] the prophet Isaiah said to his nation. They were "swift to shed innocent blood."[8]

It pains to say that America holds up bloody hands to the God of heaven, reddened with the blood of the millions of its unborn children which it has slaughtered. We can hope that many Americans are not proud of what we have done, and continue to do, but are grieved. But we know that there are those in our country who vehemently believe in killing of our unborn children. Oh, they do not outwardly smile in glee at the blood that is spilled when unborn children are murdered; they do not stand in the windows of abortion clinics with hands up, proudly showing the blood of unborn just killed.

No, that would be too raw, too indelicate, too unbefitting. Modern barbarians are too sophisticated to do that. No, they stand on public platforms, in halls of Congress, at the White House, at the Supreme Court, in the media, on university campuses, in the offices of feminist organizations, and in our schools. They stand on those public platforms and bellow rhetoric about "rights" and "pro-choice" and "reproductive freedom" and "termination of pregnancy" and, well . . . you've heard it.

The ruse of rhetoric works. The clever words cover up the deadly, bloody reality of a human life destroyed. No hands are held up, but the hands are bloody just the same.

With abortion, our own American holocaust is raging. It is "feticide." The womb—once the haven of new life—is now the chamber of destruction. The womb has become a tomb. The bloodshed of abortion has become our leading cause of death.

With our abortion technology, we "have invented another way of doing evil."[9] Our abortion technology enables us to kill unborn children assembly-line quickly. In fact, we're more efficient than the Nazis were in destroying the Jews and the multitude of others who died in concentration camps. The spirit of Molech[10] lives in America; and our land is polluted by the shedding of innocent blood. "Bloodshed follows bloodshed"[11] as it did in Israel during the time of Hosea and Amos. And its "breaking all bounds"[12]—like a river overflowing its banks, flooding out of control, rampant, and without restraint. It's the language of wanton excess.

Part of our "breaking all bounds" in our bloodshed is that now we use our destroyed unborn or dead infants as a source of body parts. A foul "industry" now traffics in body parts, one of the largely unmentioned parts of the whole sordid business of bloodshed. Do you remember the body-parts scandal in England where some 100,000 organs were found being held by hospitals and medical schools? And of the weeping mother whose infant son died in a hospital, who later found his body parts pickled in 36 glass jars? She stuffed the jars into a bag and fled sobbing into the street.

Against our rampant bloodshed, the mantras of "rights" and "pro-choice" and other such public heresies sound empty and vacuous. These slogans do not absolve us of accountability for what we are doing. "They shed innocent blood, the blood of their sons and daughters, and the land was desecrated by their blood," Psalm 106 says.[13] "They have filled this place with the blood of the innocent,"[14] Jeremiah said. King Manasseh "filled Jerusalem with innocent blood, and the Lord was not willing to forgive."[15]

But again, we are determined in this sin; we intend to continue the bloodshed; and we will oppose venomously anyone who would deny our "right" to continue it. An example is the ferocious attack that John Ashcroft received when he was nominated by President George Bush to be Attorney General. Mr. Ashcroft, a godly man, who was strongly pro-life, received a vicious assault. Forget the inflamed rhetoric of that moment. What drove the attack was the sin of bloodshed with the consummate intention of Mr. Ashcroft's opponents to do whatever necessary to ensure that this sin remains a "right" in America.

It ought to frighten us—but it doesn't—to realize that every killing of human life, however secret, will be brought into God's light. Every killer, however unsuspected and unfound, will be exposed before God and punished. And every innocent victim will be avenged by the almighty Creator of heaven and earth. Said Isaiah, "The Lord is coming out of His dwelling to punish the people of the earth for their sins. The earth will disclose the blood shed upon her; she will conceal her slain no longer."[16]

Bloodshed? Forbidden by God? The Scriptures shout this out over and over again until we cannot miss it or deny it or ignore it.

But we do ignore it. We shut our ears and our hearts to it; so much so that as a nation, we have reason to be alarmed. The killing of our unborn children is neither a political nor social issue. It is a grave moral question that defines us as a nation and shows the extent to which we deserve and will face judgment. We dare not minimize this, for God will not and does not. As W.J. Deane said, "The shedding of innocent blood cries for vengeance, and pulls down God's heavy judgments on the murderer."[17]

Our great peril is that we have so seared our collective conscience that we are indifferent to our peril. We minimize our deserved judgment and continue the bloodshed, sinning boldly and insensibly to the enormity of what we are doing. We continue the killing, willingly believing our chosen lies and not understanding that the blood of each of those we destroy cries to God of heaven for justice. And each individual cry will be heard.

Our heavenly Father sees each of the millions of unborn that are cruelly and mercilessly destroyed each year, snuffed out as if they were only animals. (Animals would probably be treated more humanely.) Each one bears the heavenly Father's image, each one is an unrepeatable miracle. Each time one is destroyed, God is pained. His pain never subsides. He never "gets used to it" as we have. We turn our heads and hearts from the carnage, but God never does. The human destruction is always before Him.

As we get more and more determined to permit and practice our sin of bloodshed, and have less and less respect for human life, God moves His wrathful hand closer to us. For the blood of millions of aborted children cries to God, the heavenly Father, from clinics and hospital rooms for vengeance. His ear hears their silent screams; and they are loud.

Society's chosen lies tell women that killing the helpless innocent lives developing in their wombs is a right; it's normal; and it's moral. So they do it. And the number of cries keeps growing by thousands each day. Those cries are reaching a thunderous crescendo.

Unless we also hear their cries, and humble ourselves in repentance, God will answer their cries with judgment.

Returning to those men at Valley Forge: If they had known how we would become so barbarian and brutal, and practice such bloodshed using the freedom they won, it is reasonable to believe that those men at Valley Forge would have been horrified. And they might have considered their sacrifice of hardship and death not worth such "freedom!"

It is also reasonable that their generation would now rise—as Jesus said the Queen of the South would of His generation[18]—and will condemn us, affirming our judgment is deserved.

BARBARIAN ABANDONMENT

"Children crying in the night,
Children crying for the light,
And with no language but a cry."

—UNKNOWN

There is a silent yearning in our generation. It is the cry for a father. That it is a cry for someone to want them, to nurture and protect them, and only a good father can, particularly a biological one. And certainly now, with mother also gone out of the home, the cry for a father has added significance.

The cry for a father echoes in the heart of the heavenly Father who cares for the fatherless: "For the Lord your God is . . . the great God . . . He defends the cause of the fatherless and the widow";[19] "But You, O God . . . You are the Helper of the fatherless . . . You hear, O Lord, the desire of the afflicted . . . You listen to their cry, defending the fatherless and the oppressed . . ."[20]

Fatherlessness defines our society. Our fatherless generation is part of an unwanted generation. We're self-absorbed, so from killing babies in the womb to abusing them as children, from careers to lifestyle, our message to our children is, "We don't want you—unless it is convenient for us!" We'll allow you to be born at our convenience; but if you're conceived when it's not convenient, we'll destroy you. And if we allow you to be born, we'll spend time with you when it's convenient.

Our children are learning this message; and we're naive if we think they are not.

Fatherlessness is part of a larger challenge for manhood. Men only need to take a hard look at the evils of our culture—child molestation, violence in our streets, violence in our schools, rape, wife-beating, pornography, mugging, robbery, murder, homosexual perversion—and one reality jumps out: overwhelmingly these evils are committed by men—both young and old. They are principally male sins.

However, fatherlessness so defines us that it could be called a defining delinquency that stands us on the abyss of judgment. Today we've created a fatherless generation which if not corrected, will only bring our societal downfall.

We have a fatherless generation in two pivotal ways: in society and in the womb. And unless we get the "Daddy problem" handled both ways, we won't survive as a culture. As much as any situation does, this determines our future.

In our society, one of the fastest growing groups is single-parent families. Most of these are headed by women without husbands. And their children are without fathers. Tragically, well intentioned but misguided welfare dollars often support such fatherlessness, and help perpetuate the problem.

The devastating effect on our future from an enlarging segment of our society growing up without fathers, is immeasurable, particularly in our inner cities.

Adding to this somber situation is that increasingly there are homes where the woman and the man in the home are not married, just living together. Plus, as couples divorce and remarry in a seemingly endless shuffle, more and more the children in those homes are not the biological offspring of one or the other of the partners, usually the man. As a result, there are a growing number of homes in which men are raising other men's children while other men raise theirs. We are very thankful for men who do their best in these unfortunate circumstances, and in no way would we hurt them. But the reality remains that the children who are not living with their biological fathers are in some measure fatherless. In addition, in those homes where children are living with their biological parents, the fathers many times are struggling with fatherhood.

Strong homes anchored by fathers of character are essential to the stability of any society. Without that foundation, a society will drift. Fatherlessness threatens America. Our nation cannot sustain unendingly the level of fatherlessness we have and survive.

However, it is the fatherless generation we have created *in the womb* that is particularly damning to us. Consider how we are doing this. We've stubbornly embraced the "pro-choice right" of a woman to kill her unborn child if she chooses. We insist it is her decision alone to kill or not to kill the life in her womb. Consistent with this, we have also decreed that the father of the unborn child, whether married to the mother or not, has no legal part in her abortion decision. In 1992 the United State Supreme Court struck down the requirement that a wife has to notify her husband before she has an abortion. So today a father cannot keep his unborn child from being killed.

This means that every unborn child in America is legally fatherless!

Fatherless! Every unborn baby is fatherless. Can we grasp the enormity of the injustice this is? It is without equal. And the peril of judgment it portends for us is terrifying. We, as a nation, have not only determined that the fate of the unborn child will be in the hands of his or her mother, but we have removed the father from being able to protect his baby. This comes close to "assassin's insurance," the extra care a killer takes to make sure his murderous deed is successful (such as the bullet to the head after the victim is down).

We not only have the weighty sin of killing our unborn children on our heads, but also the grave offense of rendering them fatherless and removing all possible protection. This immeasurably increases our blame and our deserved judgment.

When we comprehend the gravity of such fatherlessness, it should put us all, but men particularly, on their faces in repentance before God, their heavenly Father. We should beseech Him for mercy on our country, on our unborn children, and on they themselves.

Perhaps we can go further in saying that when we in our obstinate emphasis, contend that it is the exclusive right of a woman to decide whether or not she kills her unborn child, we legally set the woman alone. We legally isolate her from the father of her child and effectively make her a widow.

Also, the exclusive "right" of a woman to an abortion has become so much a part of our public doctrine that in many states we let an underage girl decide for herself to have an abortion without her parents' knowledge or consent. This makes the girl fatherless. The baby in her womb is fatherless. And so is she! Our society only compounds the weight of its judgment.

Modern men have lost their fear of God and having to account to Him for their lives and the lives of the fatherless. Regardless of arrogance, every earthly father will face the heavenly Father to answer for the blood of the millions of babies who have been aborted. "Father" means the "giver and protector of life." Although the mother's role is important, the buck stops with the father. Every man will give a personal accounting for every act of sexual intercourse he has ever had and the consequences of that intercourse.

And he will give account to almighty God for every aborted baby that he fathered.

Give us "mighty in spirit" who know God and love and respect Him.

A final perspective: Again and again in the Scripture, God commanded His people to care for the aliens, the widows, and the fatherless—the three weakest groups in society. The barbarian, pagan nations around them were brutal toward human life. God tells His people to be different, and to take care of the very weakest and give them protection. Our heavenly Father demands justice for the fatherless, and if earthly fathers and nations will not speak up for them, He will. *And His voice will be heard!*

God gave the state "the sword." This puts the state in the strongest position in the society. That "sword," wielded as the strongest was to protect the very weakest from oppression and destruction. This is a fundamental reason God instituted government. It *is* government's reason to be.

By extension, within a family the strongest member is the father. He is to protect all of his family, particularly the very weakest among them. This *is* one of a father's reasons to be. He will be answerable to God for his wife and his offspring.

A nation and its fathers will be held accountable before God for the ways they did or did not fulfill their primary role. The question for a nation and it fathers is, "*How well did you protect your very weakest?*" This is the preeminent question for America and our fathers now. *How are we protecting our children in our society and in the womb?*

When a nation and its fathers abdicate their fundamental and vital role, they also abdicate their reason to exist. Such abdication carries fierce penalties: disintegration and judgment.

We are witnessing the wholesale abdication of America's and its fathers of one essential reasons to exist. Instead of protecting our unborn children, the "sword" is used to reach into the womb and kill those very weakest our nation is charged to care for. And most notorious, America is forbidding fathers from protecting their unborn offspring. This double damnation exposes how deserving of judgment we are.

Will we examine this? Or will we remain so determined in our bold sinning, that we continue on toward our certain disintegration?

May God give us a mighty spiritual awakening in our nation and in our manhood.

Again, let us return to those men at Valley Forge. What would they think of what America is doing today? Would they consider their sacrifice worth creating such a nation?

BARBARIAN INDOCTRINATION

> "And whoever welcomes a little child this in my name welcomes me. But if anyone causes one of these little ones who believe in me to sin, it would be better for him to have a large millstone hung around his neck and to be drowned in the depths of the sea."[21]
>
> —JESUS

It should give us pause that our greatest sins today are against our children: in killing them in the womb, fatherlessness, and especially "causing them to sin." And we don't seem to care.

Jesus emphasizes that when we *"welcome a little child in His name,"* we welcome Him. Scripture declares that children are *"the heritage of the Lord,"* and *"blessed is the man whose quiver is full of them."*[22]

However, "causing them to sin" is rampant, pervasive, and breaking all bounds. The following dialogue took place in a recent comic strip. Two young women are traveling together in a car to a family get-together. The first young woman says, "Do you think we should have told your sister we were living together?" The second young woman (the driver) replies, "People will find out anyway." FYW: "You almost told her we were married." SYW: "Liz is cool. She can keep a secret. Besides, my family doesn't pry into personal affairs. They're not gonna ask her a lot of questions." The last frame shows the two girls at the get-together being stared at by family members in a way to evoke a laugh.[23] Using humor to teach is powerful; and here we are to laugh at two young women facing family in a lesbian relationship. What we should be doing is weeping. What about young women or girls, say ages nine or ten to young teens, who read that comic? The comic strip seems to imply that lesbian relationships are normal and fine. It subtly seems to needle the family members.

Put that comic strip's message against Jesus' warning, "*If anyone causes one of these little one who believe in me to sin, it would be better for him to have a large millstone hung around his neck and to be drowned in the depths of the sea.*"[24]

Drowning by a millstone was used by Romans, Greeks and others to punish the worst class of criminals, especially those who commit "parricide" (murdering his father, mother, or near relative), and those guilty of sacrilege.[25] Jesus is saying it would be better to be executed the way the worst of criminals are executed than to cause one child—just one—to sin. This is stunning. And staggering. And trenchant. It leaves no doubt as to the gravity and wickedness such an action against a child is before God. In God's eyes, the utter treachery of such an evil comes, as we have seen previously, from His deep care for and defense of the weakest and most defenseless in society.

The damning reality is that our children have few morally safe places to be. This is compounded because we shrug off the weight of this sin.

Our homes are not safe. Sexual sins are paraded everywhere: on TV, in movies, in music, and in the gutter-values of rock stars invade the places our children live. TV sitcoms are filled with immorality, licentious humor, violence, and many times a homosexual character. Movies the same. And much of the music is so filthy, vile and degrading to women that it is unprintable here or in a family newspaper. But our children see and hear all of this in homes. They are growing up with it. They are being cultured in it. By the time they are age twelve, a huge percentage are deeply indoctrinated. (Churches need to MAJOR in children's ministry.)

Children's organizations are not safe. Even the Boy Scouts are now heatedly censured and their funds are cut off because they will not allow homosexual Scout leaders!

Our schools are not safe. Sexual libertines, feminists, gay rights activists and New Agers are too often given the ear of our children in school. Lesbian and homosexual lovers tell about their lifestyle and answer questions, using language that is unprintable. Homosexuality is presented as normal, as that "third sex." Children are told abortion is a right (and by implication, morally right). With a school's cooperation, a young woman can hurry off, get an abortion without her parent's knowledge and consent, and go home with her parents being none the wiser.

Sex education in the name of AIDS awareness and pregnancy prevention is vile. It can include instruction on birth control and disease control, including the use of condoms. Picture a sex education instructor before say twelve-year-olds, girls and boys together. Perhaps your child in the group. Imagine as the instructor shows how to put on a condom using a pickle as a prop, as those wide-eyed youngsters look on. Child pornography starts right there. Sex education may be promoted as progress and help for our children, but it marks our debauchery. Put Jesus' penetrating warning against that moment.

Our anti-child attitude has been building over the years. There was the sexual revolution of the '60s when long-held values about marriage and family were attacked; and the Pill made promiscuity "safe." Of course, a few years earlier World War II, had a role as women left home for the work place. Alfred Kinsey's abominable "research" in the late '40s on sexual attitudes and standards certainly got us going down our slippery slope. "Because of this fraudulent research," said Judith A. Reisman and Edward W. Eichel in their book *Kinsey, Sex and Fraud*,[26] "Kinsey's brand of social 'science' has led to one of the greatest hypocrisies of our time: the pretense of safe-sex instruction to children while in reality advancing his agenda, including indulgence in high-risk lifestyles and behaviors."

We now know that Kinsey used children and babies in his studies, even stimulating them to orgasm as part of his research, a despicable and criminal treatment of children which should have caused us to trash his entire research and imprison him. However, Kinsey's debauched studies affirmed—and affirm—our lust. We ignored the abominations on the children. We embraced Kinsey's "con-job on society," as Reisman and Eichel put it.[27]

Whenever a parent allows his or her child to view immoral entertainment on television, video or theater, or listen to debauched music, they cause the child to sin. Whenever anyone teaches a child or suggests to a child that sinful activity, whether heterosexual or homosexual, is natural, they cause the child to sin. *Whenever anyone teaches or exposes children to evil—whether that child is age five or eight or fourteen—they cause that child to sin; and they put a millstone around their own neck and deserve the judgment of God.* God will not permit us to offend our children ad infinitum.

It's time for the Church, with pastors and ministers leading the way, to come to our Lord as He told us, *as a little child* in humility and in repentance for our sins against our children. Churches must become vigorous "children protectors," "*speaking up for those who cannot speak for themselves,*" and "*defending the rights of the poor and needy.*"[28] We must become ardent "children welcomers," taking children into our arms as Jesus did and blessing them. Each one is *an unrepeatable miracles for whom Christ died.* "Join me and others in crying out for mercy and compassion on behalf of all children everywhere," P.E. Quinn said in *Cry Out*, the story of his terrifying life as an abused child. "Speak up, learn, get involved. Our children need us desperately. Even more, we need our children—healthy and alive."[29]

Do we want the Presence of the Lord? Jesus said, "Whoever welcomes a little child like this in My Name, welcomes Me."

It is not saying it too strongly that our egregious nonchalance toward causing our children to sin could be the mark where our cup of iniquity overflows. The only reason we remain as a society is the mercy of God. "The reason, then, why this awful day of wrath has not yet arrived," Eryl Davies of Wales said, "is owing to God's kindness and longsuffering towards us."[30]

We must return to those men at Valley Forge. Can we in any way ever believe that they would approve of the way we are indoctrinating our children?

Did those men at Valley Forge who sacrificed so deeply for us (and millions of other men and women in other wars and in other ways who sacrificed) go through all they did only to enable us to build a nation of barbarians and bring down the just judgment of God on us?

Those Valley Forge men might wonder what kind of moral and spiritual leadership we have in our time which would let such conditions exist challenged. Those men were used to churches that were clear on matters of righteousness, preachers who expounded Scripture powerfully, helped mold the public conscience, denounced as savage the killing of unborn children, and condemned as the foulest practices the abandoning of children and the teaching of perversion to them.

Arguments over rights and choices would have been branded as public heresies. Those men would have found incredible that churches and preachers now stay on the sidelines on matters of public sin because "these were political concerns which mixed church and state."

As it is, America stands teetering on a cliff above the sea with a deserved millstone around our collective neck. We deserve to be drowned. Our national judgment is justified.

At what point will our sin push us off?

Let us pray together with Josiah Gilbert Holland: God, give us Men! A time like this demands strong minds, great hearts, true faith and ready hands / Men whom the lust of office does not kill / Men whom the spoils of office cannot buy / Men who possess opinions and a will / Men who have honor; men who will not lie / Men who can stand before a demagogue and damn his treacherous flatteries without winking! / Tall men, sun-crowned, who live above the fog in public duty and in private thinking! / For while the rabble, with their thumb-worn creeds / Their large professions and their little deeds / Mingle in selfish strife, lo! Freedom weeps / Wrong rules the land, and waiting Justice sleeps / All of which we ask Through Jesus Christ our Lord, Amen.

CHAPTER 6 ENDNOTES

[1] Ezekiel 2:3-4.

[2] John Gerstner, *Jonathan Edwards on Heaven and Hell*, (Baker, 1980) p.81.

[3] This story, found in this paragraph and the next five paragraphs, is adapted from an address by Peter Marshall, Jr., *Restoration, Revival, and Repentance in America*.

[4] From Abraham Lincoln's *Proclamation for a Day of National Humiliation Fasting and Prayer* for April 30, 1863.

[5] Ibid.

[6] Proverbs 6:17.

[7] From Isaiah 59:2-3.

[8] Isaiah 59:7.

[9] Romans 1:30.

[10] Leviticus 18:21. A detestable Semitic deity honored by the sacrifice of children. See Chapter 3 also.

[11] Hosea 4:2.

[12] Ibid.

[13] From Psalm 106:37-41.

[14] Jeremiah 19:4.

[15] From II Kings 24:3-4.

[16] Isaiah 26:21.

[17] W.J. Deane, biblical expositor, *The Pulpit Commentary*, *Proverbs* (London: Funk and Wagnalls) p.131.

[18] Matthew 12:42.

[19] From Deuteronomy 10:17-18.

[20] From Psalm 10:14, 17, 18.

[21] Matthew 18:5-6.

[22] Psalm 127:3-5.

[23] Syndicated comic strip, *Better or Worse*, Saturday, Jan. 6, 2001.

[24] Matthew 18:6.

[25] James M. Freeman, *The New Manners & Customs of the Bible*, (North Brunswick, NJ: Bridge-Logos Publishers), p.444.

[26] Judith A. Reisman and Edward W. Eichel, *Kinsey, Sex and Fraud*, (Lafayette, LA: Huntington House, 1990), from an ad for the book.

[27] Ibid.

[28] Proverbs 31:8-9.

[29] P.E. Quinn, *Cry Out—Inside the Terrifying World of Child Abuse*, (Nashville, TN: Abingdon Press, 1984), p.200.

[30] Eryl Davies, *The Wrath of God*, Evangelical Press of Wales, 1984, p.21.

7

TREACHEROUS PROPHETS

"Preach the Word! Be ready in season or out of season. Convince, rebuke, exhort, with all long-suffering and teaching."

—PAUL, TO TIMOTHY[1]

"Hearers are led to deny the truth which the preacher leaves out. Omitting any truth intentionally leads to a denial of it."

—JOHN ELIAS[2]

T HEY NEVER ASKED ME IF MY LANTERN WAS LIT," THE RAILROAD worker said. I remember reading his comment sometime after he was called to testify in a hearing on a terrible rail accident, an accident that happened sometime in the 19th Century.

I cannot remember the details of the accident, but during the hearing the railroad worker was grilled about his whereabouts and activity at the time of the accident. Was he at the proper place? Yes, he said he was. Did he have his lantern? Yes. Was he waving it? Yes. They excused him.

What they didn't ask was whether or not his lantern was burning. A burning lantern waving at the proper place and time possibly could have averted the accident.

Do we need to make the analogy? Our nation—and nations of the West—does face judgment. There is an "accident" coming. What we need to avert it are people with lanterns positioned at the right time and place, waving their lit lanterns—lit with **all** of God's message, nothing omitted.

Lantern-waving is easy for us in the church or us in the pulpit. We're get very good at waving them, lit or not, in our programs, meetings, worship, some new teaching, church growth method, entertainment, loud music, whatever. But are our lanterns lit? I admit I've waved a few lanterns, and not all of them have been.

But a church or a minister without a lit lantern is like a surgeon without a scalpel, a fireman without a hose, a writer without a pen, a teacher without a book, a nurse without bandages, a grocer without food, a mechanic without tools, or a lion without his roar. In each case something they are known for, something they exist for, something they use is missing. A church or minister without a lit lantern is, well, treachery.

It has been said that "when God begins to judge a nation, the first thing He does is to give His people cowardly clergy." Perhaps, more accurately, another way to say this is, *"If God wants to judge a nation, all He would have to do is send them distracted churches and preachers who omit parts of God's message!"*

This may beg the reality a bit because over the centuries God has not had to send such distracted churches or preachers; churches and preachers have done the job themselves. To be honest, one of God's biggest problems over eons has been keeping His spokesmen on message. Usually when they drop some part of the message, it's generally the "negative" or "bad" aspects such as judgment, holiness, justice, wrath, accountability, repentance or such; and focus on the "positive" or "good" aspects such as blessings, love, prosperity, and success. To suit their ideas, they also tend to re-fashion "God," which of course leaves them without the God of Scripture—only a god, an idol. And they wind up with an unlit lantern.

Whether a church or minister has a lit lantern or an unlit one is an essential difference between true ministry and false ministry. The unhappy part is that we get so focused on waving our lantern that we don't notice or don't care if it is lit. That is treacherous.

America needs to be a country filled with churches and preachers armed with lit lanterns waving them clearly and furiously in our barbarian Sodom. It would be a form of roaring. We weep for our beloved America, willfully self-deluding, aggressively embracing lies it desires to believe, proudly pursuing bold sinning in shedding the innocent blood of its unborn children, arguing for sexual debauchery, abandoning its children in society and the womb, and nonchalantly teaching its children to sin. We are poised under judgment.

At a time like this, our nation deeply needs its whole land filled with lit-lantern wavers. However, as is the case much of the time, it is not a majority of those who are to speak for God who so wave, it's a dedicated minority who do so, sometimes a remnant.

God of course will have His true spokesmen. There were 7,000 in Israel, God told Elijah, who had not bowed to Baal during the time of Ahab and Jezebel. One of those was the true prophet Micaiah, son of Imlah, who had a tumultuous encounter with Ahab and about 400 of his prophets in a classic encounter between true and false prophets.[3] At issue was whether Ahab and King Jehoshaphat of Judah, who was visiting Ahab, should go to war against the king of Syria, Ben-hadad. Ahab had defeated Ben-hadad before, and in fact had spared his life. But now Ben-hadad held the Jewish fortress at Ramoth-Gilead and thus offered a standing menace to Israel.

"Shall I go to war against Ramoth Gilead, or shall I refrain?" Ahab asked his 400 prophets. "Go," they answered, "for the Lord will give it into the king's hand."

Pretty impressive, some 400 prophets prophesying and all with the same word from the Lord. "Attack Ramoth Gilead and be victorious, for the Lord will give it into the king's hand," they said with one voice. One of their number, Zedekiah, probably one of their leaders and certainly the most outspoken, dramatically held up iron horns he had made and said, "This is what the Lord says: 'With these horns you will gore the Syrians until they are destroyed.'"

It was not until Micaiah, the true prophet, was brought before Ahab that another message was given—the right one. At first Micaiah, seemingly disgusted, just muttered what the 400 had said; but Ahab remonstrated with him to tell what the Lord was saying. Micaiah told Ahab he would be killed. And he told of a vision he had of a lying spirit coming "in the mouths of all these other prophets of yours," emphasizing, "The Lord has decreed disaster for you."[4]

Micaiah was slapped by Zedekiah who wanted to know "which way did the spirit from the Lord go when he went from to speak to you?"

Micaiah held firm; and Ahab ordered him sent to prison. Ahab and Jehoshaphat and their army went to war, with Ahab disguising himself in an apparent attempt to escape his predicted death. But Ahab was killed and his body brought back to Samaria. His chariot was washed where the prostitutes bathed; and dogs licked up his blood.

From the perspective that history affords us, it is fairly easy to see who was right and who was wrong in this episode. However, it might not have been so easy up close and at the time. The story offers insight into what false and true ministry might look like.

A FALSE MINISTRY CAN SAY "THUS SAYS THE LORD"

The 400 prophets in Ahab's court all were speaking in the Lord's Name. The 400 said one thing "in the Name of the Lord." Micaiah was the lone dissenter. Four-hundred to one. Overwhelming odds. Who is to be believed? Does the majority rule?

In Jeremiah 28, Hananiah certainly used the Name of the Lord in his declaration before Jeremiah and the priests and the people. Jeremiah spoke several times of such prophets doing this. In Jeremiah 24:30-40, he has a strong condemnation. And in Lamentation 2:14, "The visions of your prophets were false and worthless; they did not expose your sin to ward off your captivity. The oracles they gave your were false and misleading."

The prophet Ezekiel says in 22:28, "Her prophets whitewash these deeds for them by false visions and lying divinations. They say, 'This is what the Sovereign Lord says'—when the Lord has not spoken." What is our Lord's attitude? "Indeed, I am against those who prophesy false dreams,' declares the Lord. . . 'They tell them and lead my people astray with their reckless lies.'"[5] Ezekiel also, in Chapter 13, has a penetrating denunciation of prophets like this. . . . which would be riveting to read, right?

Of course someone speaking false prophesy is *speaking thoughts of his own mind, not the Lord's.* They may claim that these selfish thoughts are scriptural, even given to them by the Holy Spirit; and they may teach their delusions to the people and give them false hope. "They speak visions from their own minds, not from the mouth of the Lord."[6] "These lying prophets ... prophesy the delusions of their own minds."[7] Where does the Lord place the responsibility for a nation's iniquity? At the feet of the false prophets. "Because from the prophets of Jerusalem ungodliness has spread throughout the land."[8]

Just because anyone uses the Name of the Lord—which, by the way, is close to blasphemy if used carelessly, and violates the Third Commandment—does not mean they are speaking from the Lord. In I Corinthians 14, someone may give an utterance, but others are to judge, or evaluate. This underscores that no one speaks "ex cathredra" or is infallible, no one beyond loving appraisal. Micaiah was quite ready to be evaluated, saying, "If you ever return safely, the Lord has not spoke through me."

A FALSE MINISTRY OFTEN OPERATES IN A SYCOPHANT SPIRIT

The sycophant spirit is a man-pleasing spirit; and those 400 prophets of Ahab were classic sycophants. They knew Ahab wanted to go to war at Ramoth Gilead, so they told him what he wanted to hear. They probably reasoned, "The king wishes it. Jehoshaphat assents to it. The people are set upon it. We would be going against common sense and our own interests to resist it."

There was a terrible end to their deception: Ahab was killed. He was not blessed and successful as the prophecy over him confidently declared. Of course there was a justice in it all: Ahab sowed lies, so he reaped delusions. "He who hates truth shall be the dupe of lies" it has been said. He wished for lies, and he had them. His own passions and pride were reflected and echoed in the voices of his 400 prophets. Ahab was lured to his death by the man-pleasing prophets he cherished and patronized. He was left to the prophets of his choice. No hand was raised to stop him. He went straight into the jaws of death as the victim of his own foolishness, cruelty and sin.

It is thus that God deals with deceivers. He leaves them to be deceived, to be the prey of their own disordered fancies. It is notorious how men find in the Bible what they *wish* to find there; how often and unsuspectingly they read their own meanings into the words of Scripture; how they interpret its injunctions by the rule of their own inclinations. We must beware.

Micaiah followed the Lord. He wanted truth. He said, "As surely as the Lord lives, I can tell him [Ahab] only what the Lord tells me." A true ministry loves truth, and wants truth and only truth. Truth is one of the absolute passions of true ministry—in a church or preacher. Love of truth is one of the earmarks of the true man or woman of God—truth is their integrity. To not love truth is to be given over to believe the lie.[9]

A sycophant spirit can be very subtle. A pastor ascertains what some in the congregation like to hear, and accommodates. He can learn what his congregation's "hot buttons" are and push them. Ministries can do this, developing new teachings that attract attention, saying things so that support will come in, not saying things that will cause support to sag. Many teachings can be, and are, developed around money and possessions.

A FALSE MINISTRY CAN PLAY TO FADS, HYPE AND CELEBRITY

This is actually a corollary of the previous one: the sycophant spirit, the man-pleasing spirit. I suppose we could say that the 400 prophets of Ahab were into a conquering fad which assured them of "victory over the Syrians." They certainly were confessing it. They were energetic in it. They had the trappings of a conquering fad—unanimous affirmation, vigorous pronouncements, even a set of iron horns. Perhaps Zedekiah was their celebrity, the chief promoter of that moment's fashionable emphasis.

Sadly today in parts of the Body of Christ, the focus is on whatever the latest teaching is, the newest revelation or such, and the hype and promotion that goes with it. Sometimes there is truth in some new emphasis, with the error coming in the lack of balance with other aspects of the Word of God. Sometimes, of course, the new teaching is a mixture of the true and the suspicious.

And of course celebrity is nothing other than man-focused idolatry. God has no celebrities in His Kingdom. There are men and women who humbly serve among us in ministry whom we are to respect, love, and hold in the highest esteem. But celebrities, no; celebrities are not needed in true ministry. Celebrities are needed in false ministry. Celebrities are needed to keep the new teaching going and the money flowing. Celebrities are many times those on whom hype is focused on. Certainly Micaiah was not a celebrity. Paul was not a celebrity. Jesus was not a celebrity. In fact, He told us we are to be servants. And when we move from servant to celebrity, we move from true ministry to false.

One enormous tragedy in all this is that false ministries squander the Word of God on the latest doctrinal fads, teaching, hype an celebrity, and do not use the Word with bold authority so that it penetrates the hearts and the souls of the hearers to bring them to God. Such squandering of the Word can produce "revivals" where the focus is on emotional responses and not on Christ and His cross.

However, the focus in revival should never be just on emotional responses. A revival is about "reviving," that is, "bringing to fresh life that which was stagnant or dead." It involves changes in char-acter, the renewed and blessed awareness of the Presence of our wonderful and holy God. It involves dealing with sin, particularly pride, so it involves repentance, renewal, and recommitment to knowing God, prayer, and holy living. Emotional responses are easy to generate and can deceive us, but genuine humility, holy living, a passion for the Lord, repentance and all only come from the Lord. If an alleged revival is primarily centered on emotional responses, two things are true: 1) the revival never happened; it was a hyped revival; or 2) it happened, but it is over.

By squandering the Word of God on fads, new teachings, hype and celebrity, we also move away from reliance on the power of the Gospel. This is the reliance that Paul spoke of when he said,, "When I came to you, brothers, I did not come with eloquence or superior wisdom as I proclaimed to you the testimony about God. For I resolved to know nothing while I was with you except Jesus Christ and Him crucified. I came to you in weakness and fear, and with much trembling [not much hype in these]. My message and my preaching were not with wise and persuasive words [hype?], but with the demonstration of the Spirit's power, *so that your faith might not rest on men's wisdom, but on God's power.*"[10]

A FALSE MINISTRY CAN REPLACE THE GOSPEL WITH THE THERAPEUTIC

James Davison Hunter wrote in *The Public Interest* about the curriculum of moral education at churches and synagogues around the nation. He finds the old categories of sin, repentance and redemption are out, and the therapeutic language of self-esteem and self-love are in. According to Hunter, it appears that at this moment in history, the secular world view is influencing the churches far more than the churches are influencing the surrounding society.

Apparently we are in an age that overvalues the therapeutic, which was immensely influenced the message of the Church; and, in the words of Sanford Pinsker, "We are awash in projects out to bolster one's sagging self-esteem or to provide spirituality on the cheap."

A therapeutic "gospel" makes God a genie whose power we can manipulate to obtain success, happiness and earthly benefits. Personal blessing becomes the focus of the message, not personal salvation. The Church seeks growth through being congenial and obliging, not by being consecrated and humble.

The result is that instead of sin, there are problems, hang-ups, needs, sometimes generic evils, or whatever is the latest therapeutic emphasis. The therapeutic plays to a psychologically seduced society. The concept of sin is lost on us. We now focus on getting rid of bad feelings, not sin. We want to feel good again instead of humbly repenting before God for sin committed against Him. In the process, God's character usually gets distorted to fit the therapeutic model; and the biblical focus on repentance is discarded or down-played. Of course such a no-sin, no-repentance "gospel" soon becomes a saltless gospel, without savor, and contributing enormously to the amorality of our public conscience.

Instead of the Good News, we preach nice news. The Good News—the Gospel—is good because there is bad news: we sin, and deserve and face judgment. But we have hope because God loves us and sent our Savior Jesus Christ, who died for our sins. We are to come to God in faith and repentance. Jesus didn't die to meet our needs, or solve hangups and problems. He died for our sins; He went to the root of our problems.

The nice news plays to the therapeutic. The therapeutic gospel is really a form of religious humanism—focusing on ourselves. Bob Sutton spoke of one form of religious humanism as, "charismatic humanism that center[s] on man and God's obligation to meet his needs." Sutton, a charismatic, also said, "The greatest danger to the church is not atheistic humanism, but religious humanism that is filled with religious activity but is void of content, sacrifice and power."[11]

We do have a lot of needy and hurting people, of course. And the church must minister and counsel with a loving attitude to help and uplift those people. Shepherds must nurture people, as our Lord would want. We are not calling for harshness. We are calling for balance.

If the therapeutic becomes our gospel, then we essentially consent to this generation being damned, the victim forever of our enormous and egregious heresy and allowing men and women to go to hell feeling good about themselves!

A FALSE MINISTRY PROCLAIMS BLESSING WITHOUT REPENTANCE

Ahab's 400 prophets said plenty about Ahab's success and blessing he would have in his battle at Ramoth-Gilead. But they said nothing about repentance. We should probably expect nothing else from sycophants. But true preachers will call for repentance.

Warren Weirsbe said that proclaiming "consolation without true repentance is only giving a false hope; it's saying 'Peace, peace' when there is no peace." Weirsbe said of the false prophets who attacked the true prophet Micah, "These men espoused a shallow theology that had no place for either sin or repentance. 'We are God's special people,' they argued, 'and He would never permit these judgments to happen in the land' . . . What these counterfeit religious leaders forgot was that God's covenants involve precepts as well as promises, obligations as well as blessings . . . These false prophets were deceiving and robbing the people by giving them false assurance that everything was well in the land."[12]

There is a spirit of triumphalism that can get into ministry, into churches, and into preachers that goes beyond the glorious triumphant hope the Word of God proclaims. Triumphalism is an emphasis on blessing: having it all, finding our greatest hour as a church or nation, and being successful, and prosperous. Repentance is omitted. Triumphalism can fill the rhetoric of politicians in their campaigns and speeches; but ministers of the Gospel must be very careful.

F.C. Cook said, "It is a criterion of false teaching that it lightens the yoke or burden or responsibility of God's law—what God requires—removes God's fear from the conscience, and leaves man to his own nature; man does what he wants. And with this, man is only to ready to be content."[13]

By omitting repentance, we create heresy. We must ask ourselves: *If repentance is never mentioned and warnings never given, is the true Gospel of Christ even being preached?* If it is not, then is it "another gospel,"[14] under the censure of the Scriptures? The Apostle Paul turned Asia upside down and conquered it for Christ said, "But we preach Christ crucified, to the Jews a stumbling block and to the Greeks foolishness,"[15] and, "For I determined not to know anything among you except Jesus Christ and Him crucified."[16]

A FALSE MINISTRY AVOIDS WARNING

Ahab's 400 prophets only had a sunny, positive message for the king. Micaiah told him the truth. He told Ahab he would be killed.

The most compassionate thing we will do is warn—roar—the same as we would do when we see someone in grave danger. It is a false love, a fraudulent compassion that does not warn of sin and judgment.

Twice Jeremiah lamented, "Prophets and priests alike, all practice deceit. They dress the wound of my people as though it were not serious. 'Peace, peace,' they say, when there is no peace."[17] And later he said, "Do not listen to what the prophets and the prophesying to you; they fill you with false hopes . . . . They keep saying to those who despise me, 'The Lord says: you will have peace.'"[18]

The promise of peace by those false prophets was a devastating lie, a whitewash of sin. God was very clear in telling of the dreadful days ahead for the nation: "See, the storm of the Lord will burst out in wrath, a whirlwind swirling down on the heads of the wicked. The anger of the Lord will not turn back until He fully accomplishes the purpose of His heart."[19]

The dominating treachery of a false ministry is that it lies by what it omits, by what it doesn't say. The false prophets in Jeremiah's day omitted what the people really needed to know—that they were going to face judgment. The false prophets didn't warn!

A false message leaves out how heinous sin is to God, how sin brings judgment, and the absolute necessity of repentance.

A false minister ignores knowing that his nation is under judgment. He gives no consideration to the nation's sin that will bring it down. By these he becomes a charlatan who preaches a charlatan message which treats cancer with Band-Aids. "They dress the wound of my people as though it were not serious."[20] We can be charlatans whether we are evangelical, charismatic or Pentecostal.

False prophets place their own wisdom above the wisdom of God. If the Lord says we are to warn, that should settle the matter. False ministries, however, will not warn, because the false prophets think they know what to say better than God—they are only concerned with pleasing the people, while God is only concerned with saving their souls.

Most grievously, the tragedy of all this for our times is that on the one side, we have our society with blood running up to its knees from the killing of its unborn children, a drug epidemic, pornography, homosexual perversion, child abuse, AIDS, and violence all tearing at the fabric of society. And on the other side, we have a multitude of Christian ministries that are congenially focused on preaching and teaching "peace, peace" themes, never warning our nation of the Church about the consequences of their sins, or confronting them with the reality of God's dealings, and of judgment.

Such ministries commit treasonable acts against the Gospel of Jesus Christ and are unfaithful to the call of God. And like the false prophets of the Scriptures, they will receive God's searing rebuke.

The question I must ask myself is, "Will I warn them?" Or have I tried to be . . . peaceful and not stir up the waters, not cause any trouble for them and myself? On my day of accounting before the One who loves me and gives himself for me, one of the questions He will ask me is, "Did you warn them?" And if I answer no, He will ask me, "Why did you not?"

IN A FALSE MINISTRY, MEN AND WOMEN DO NOT TURN FROM WICKEDNESS

Jesus said that false prophets will be recognized by their fruit.[21] One fruit of a false ministry is that people do not turn from their evil ways as they do in a true ministry. Of false prophets, Jeremiah said, "They strengthen the hands of evildoers, so that no one turns from his wickedness. . . .because from the prophets of Jerusalem ungodliness has spread throughout the land."[22] God's bottom-line evacuation for any of our ministries is, DO MEN AND WOMEN TURN FROM EVIL?

One of western society's dominant philosophies is pragmatism—what is practical, what works—especially in America, and many churches fall prey to this mind set. They suppose that if something produces what churches are supposed to produce today according to society's measure of success—a crowd, commitments, goals, excitement, money, growth—it's good, so let's have lots of it.

One consequence of such an attitude is that it may not be spiritual life that impels the church, but pragmatic, success-producing activities and programs. Today the pastor, evangelist, church leaders, or worker whom we might regard as successful might or might not be the most godly among us; but it is a strong possibility he or she could be the most success-producing. In fact, a minister who has once satisfied the basic spiritual requirements for ordination in his denomination can remain on that spiritual level for his entire ministry, and still be regarded as successful because he learns how to work pragmatically, learns how to produce success according to society's measurements. A *successful* ministry has become more important than a *faithful* ministry—and the two words are not necessarily synonymous.

So, for myself, I must allow the penetrating voice of God to ask the most important question about every aspect of my ministry: DO THE PEOPLE TO WHOM I MINISTER FORSAKE SIN? The issue is not, is there a large attendance, many adherents, and many decisions; but do people forsake sin? *Do they give it up; do thy they turn from their wicked ways and lead righteous lives?* A fruit of a false ministry allows men and women to remain comfortable in their sin, unrepentant and deceived about the consequences.

One fundamental aspect of the call to ministry that is both beautiful and terrifying is that God has called us because He intends to use us. This means it is our magnificent privilege to share the Word of the Lord. This demands seeking Him, waiting upon Him for direction,[23] and moving only in the direction He tells us to, speaking His Word. So as a minister, I must constantly ask myself, "Am I proclaiming every aspect of the Word of God, both that which is pleasant to our ears and flesh, and that which is unpleasant?"

A FALSE MINISTRY FACES JUDGEMENT

We have already heard Jesus say, "Watch out for false prophets. . . .I will tell them plainly, 'I never knew you. Away from me, you evildoers!'"[24] To His words, we must add the words from the Book of Revelation. "I warn everyone who hears the words of the prophecy of this book: If anyone adds anything to them, God will add to him the plagues described in this book. And if anyone takes words away from this book of prophecy, God will take away from him his share in the tree of life and in the holy city, which are described in this book."[25]

Why such harsh judgment and punishment? Because God's Word is crucial. If we get the message wrong, those who hear us get it wrong and perish. God says that if we "do not warn him [a wicked man] or speak out to dissuade him from his evil ways in order to save his life, that wicked man will die fro his sin, and I will hold you accountable for his blood."[26]

I might not be able to know where others stand or whether their ministries are true or false, but I can know where I stand. *I must know!* I do those am called to serve and me the greatest service when I am tougher on myself than on anyone else and when I allow God to search me while I lay on my face before Him.

Do I want God to call me faithful, or do I want man to call me successful? Do I want the approval of man or the approval of God? Do I have a heart that only wants His "well done" or man's "great job"? Do I do what a false prophet does: put my wisdom before God's, speak peace and fail to warn? Do I have Micaiah's attitude? Or Zedekiah's? THE BOTTOM LINE: DO I FEAR GOD, OR DO I FEAR MAN?

Truth invites examination and has no fear of it. Untruth hides and covers and rationalizes and points at others. So if any of us hides from our Lord's examination and dismisses His penetrating evaluation with a casual wave of the hand, that could be a sure sign of just which side our ministry is really on.

I can hide nothing from the Lord, so it is useless to try. He knows my motives and will weigh them in *His* scales, not in mine or on society's. Each of us, alone, must confront God's examination of the motives and integrity of our ministry. King David prayed, "I know, my God, that you test the heart and are pleased with integrity . . . ."[27] and "Create in me a clean heart, O God."[28]

I may tremble in anxiety and even fear, but I must be just as forthright as David about whether what I do for God is true or false and whether my ministerial heart is clean or marred with self-delusions and falsehoods.

O God, I want to be true and clean of heart before you!

All this is important because as our nation accelerates on its determined course in sin toward its impending judgment, we need that clear voice in the midst of all this that will roar the heart of God: "Come back to Me!" Such a voice cannot and must not be distracted by false emphasis, a sycophant spirit, fads, hype, celebrity and all that we have looked at here. If it is, that is an ultimate treachery.

It comes down to that question: Are our waving lanterns lit?

If it isn't lit, then we bear and deserve enormous censure.

In our degenerating, barbarian Sodom, may our lit lanterns wave with the pure light of the Word of God, anointed by the Holy Spirit. Let this happen in every church and parish; in every pulpit and ministry; in my heart and yours.

Now. Today.

Let that become a catalyst our Lord uses to send blessed biblical revival.

Let us join together in prayer: *Our gracious heavenly Father, our beloved America is deeply entrenched in its chosen lies, self-delusion and bold sinning. When we in Your Church treacherously do not proclaim Your Word as You desire, we hasten our nation's looming judgment. Forgive us for omitting anything from Your message, or for becoming enamored with some new truth or caught up in hype and the idolatry of celebrity. Forgive us for failing to warn and turn men and women from wickedness. We repent. Instead of deserved judgment, we appeal to Your mercy and ask for revival and spiritual awakening. May we in Your Church be instruments in Your hand for this. We ask in Christ's Name, Amen.*

CHAPTER 7 ENDNOTES

[1] II Timothy 4:2.

[2] Edward Morgan, *John Elias, Life and Letters*, (Banner of Truth, 1973), p.354.

[3] All references in this story come from I Kings 22 and II Chronicles 18.

[4] I Kings 22:23.

[5] Jeremiah 23:31-32.

[6] Jeremiah 23:16b.

[7] Jeremiah 23:26.

[8] Jeremiah 23:15.

[9] II Thessalonians 2:11.

[10] I Corinthians 2:1-5.

[11] Bob Sutton, *Humanism: Man as Master*, (unknown date).

[12] Warren Weirsbe, *Be Concerned, Selected Minor Prophets* (Colorado Springs: Victor Books, 1996), from pp 93, 94, 95.

[13] F.C. Cook, *The Biblical commentary, Vol 5 and 6, by F.C. Cook* (Baker Book House, 1981).

[14] II Corinthians 11:4.

[15] I Corinthians 1:23 (NKJV).

[16] I Corinthians 2:2 (NKJV).

[17] Jeremiah 6:13-14; 8:10-11.

[18] Jeremiah 23:16-17.

[19] Jeremiah 23:19-21b.

[20] Matthew 7:20.

[21] Jeremiah 8:11.

[22] Jeremiah 23:14-15b.

[23] Isaiah 40:31.

[24] Matthew 7:15, 23.

[25] Revelation 22:18-19.

[26] Ezekiel 3:18.

[27] Hebrews 12:10-11 (KJV).

[28] I Chronicles 29:17.

[29] Psalm 51:10.

PART THREE

A REVIVAL OF PERSPECTIVE AND PASSION

"Men of Issachar, who understood the times and knew what Israel should do."[1]

"Their judgment is based on this fact: The light from heaven came into the world, but they loved the darkness more than the light, for their actions were evil. They hate the light because the want to sin in the darkness. They stay away from the light for fear their sins will be exposed and they will be punished."[2]

"O God, you are my God, earnestly I see You; my soul thirsts for You, in a dry and weary land where there is no water."[3]

In Pat Frank's book, *Alas Babylon,* he imagines Florida under the pall of a fictional atomic attack. All electricity was cut off, gasoline supplies were exhausted, and life settled down to the basics. Cadillacs were traded for fat hens, and power boats for a shaker of salt. If and when a nuclear war strikes our world, the survivors will suddenly realize that most of the things we have been striving for and racking our brains to acquire are worse than useless. *If we could only discover this in time, perhaps the fate of Sodom and Gomorrah toward which we are moving could be averted."*[4]

—BILLY GRAHAM, COMMENTING ON
IDOLATRY IN AMERICA

America as a nation is ripe for judgment. The evangelical movement in this country is characterized by an arrogance that is almost beyond belief. The neglect of prayer, the involvement of Philistine methodology, the moral evils, and the doctrinal corruptions that characterize the movement are sufficient to cause Sodomites to wonder at God's justice in destroying their city while sparing the United States."[5]

—RICHARD OWEN ROBERTS,
LOOKING AT AMERICA AND THE CHURCH

A s I have looked back across the ruins and landmarks of antiquity, I have been stunned by the parallels between those societies and our own. For most of us the destruction of Carthage, the rise of the Greek city-state, and the Fall of Rome are mere ghosts of the past, history lessons long forgotten. And such things as the capture of Constantinople, the dissolution of the Holy Roman Empire, the collapse of the kingdoms of France and Spain, and the slow withering decline of the British Empire are much less clear and less memorable. Most of us do not remember much from our history lessons about the French Revolution. But this is the legitimate background of our culture. If we are to grasp the importance of our own place in history, it is vital that we reconsider the nature of life in those earlier times. For within those eras and movements are the seeds of the troubles we face today."[6]

—JIM NELSON BLACK, COMPARING
ANCIENT CULTURES TO TODAY

Part Three Endnotes

[1] I Chronicles 12:32.

[2] John 3:19-20 (NLT).

[3] Psalm 63:1.

[4] Billy Graham, *World Aflame*, (Westwood, NJ: Fleming Revell, 1965), p.39.

[5] Richard Owen Roberts, in his article on *"The Solemn Assembly."*

[6] Jim Nelson Black, *When Nations Die: Ten Warning Signs of a Culture in Crisis*, (Wheaton: Tyndale House, 1994) p.3.

8

OUR PRICELESS GIFT

"For You created my inmost being; you knit me together in my mother's womb. I praise You because I am fearfully and wonderfully made."

—THE PSALMIST[1]

And there these twain upon the skirts of time / Sat side by side, full summ'd in all their power / Dispensing harvest, sowing the to-be. / Self-reverent each, and reverencing each / Distinct in individualities / But like each other, ev'n as those who love.

—TENNYSON'S "PRINCESS." VII

IT IS TIME TO STOP, TAKE A LOOK AT SOMETHING VERY BEAUTIFUL, something that much of our culture is tossing aside, something that even the Church seems to be ignoring. But this something very beautiful needs to be re-understood, and re-taught to our children and grandchildren. It is the wonderful story of human life, our life: where it came from, and how special it is. We risk losing its uplifting story in a world that easily allows shedding the blood of its unborn children and rationalizes euthanizing elderly and terminally ill people.

Much of what we have said so far on these pages has focused on our terrible sins, our willfulness, our aggressive sinning. However, in a jewelry shop, many times a diamond is showcased against a black background; and the contrast highlights the diamonds luster and brilliance. Let that be the case now. Against the dark background of what we have already examined, let us place that diamond of eternal worth—the priceless gift of life.

Our human life started with a dream: God's dream. Its majestic story is found in the simple words of Scripture: "Then God said, 'Let us make man in our image, in our likeness, and let them rule over the fish of the sea and the birds of the air, over the livestock, over all the earth . . .' So God created man in His own image, in the image of God he created him; male and female he created them."[2]

Man's creation was a creation of ultimate excellence, as God took His own image and reproduced it in a very special creature that would be like Himself.

In the hand of God the very dust of the earth was transformed into a man as God "breathed into his nostrils the breath of life, and man became a living being."[3]

Each of us have a *God-given identity*—we are made in the image of God.

The God-implanted character would include a moral, intellectual, and spiritual likeness. Morally, man would have the power of choice, a free will. Intellectually, man would be able to learn, to grow mentally, explore, discover, and to invent. Spiritually, man would have capacity to know God, to fellowship with Him, and to live forever.

The relationship between God and man would be a relationship of love. Indelibly marked throughout the Scriptures are "For God so loved the world" and "God is love." The corresponding supreme command to man is "Love the Lord your God with all your soul and with all your strength."[4]

But we have received not only a God-given identity, but also a *God-given sexuality.* We are created in the image of God—male or female.

Man was very special, unique in that he was the only creature with ultimate destiny. He was made to rule, to have dominion, to be fruitful, and to be blessed by God. "God blessed them and said to them, "Be fruitful and increase in number; fill the earth and subdue it. Rule over the fish of the sea and the birds of the air and over every living creature moves on the ground . . . I give you every seed-bearing plant on the face of the whole earth every tree that has fruit with seed in it. They will be yours for food."[5] And it was so.

The mark of excellence upon man was affirmed by God after He had completed the entire creation, and just after He had made man. "God saw all that he had made, and it was very good."[6]

But in His creation of man, God had a very special gift, an extremely extraordinary gift, to bestow. The heavens He created would not possess it. Plant life would not. Insect life would not. Fish life would not. Animals of the land would not.

Only man!

This gift would so uniquely express God's essential character of life that man would be the only creature who would receive it, for man alone possessed God's moral, intellectual, and spiritual imprint.

The gift would be a love-gift because only man had the capacity to love. The gift would be a dream-gift because only man had the power to choose. The gift would be personal gift because only man had the potential for intimacy.

What was this special gift?

It was the *ability to procreate life by an act of will!*

The Creator would implant in man the ability to reproduce life, life that also would have the very image of God.

But it would be life conceived *by choice,* by an exercise of will, by an expression of volition, *by wanting to.*

Animals reproduce, yes; but they only do so by instinct. Their internal programming, put there by God, dictates when they mate, conceive and bear young.

But not man. His gift is unique: he chooses when to bring forth new life. God gave man the unique capacity to create life by an act of will. God created the first life; He formed the gene pool; He then gave man the ability to reproduce life in cooperation with Him—to procreate.

So we not only have a God-given identity and a God-given sexuality; but we have a *God-given fertility*—we have the capacity to create, or pro-create, human life by an act of will, by deciding too.

It is wonderful, all a part of the dream, all a part of our priceless gift!

To say that the significance of this is great is an immeasurable understatement. The implications are awesome. In the unfolding of history, man has populated the entire earth. On this planet, literally billions of persons have been brought to life. This multitude is not a collective, impersonal "mass of humanity," but a collection of unique individuals, each one so absolutely original that no two are the same." Each is a rarity. Each one a masterpiece.

Each one with his or her God-given identity, sexuality and fertility is an unrepeatable miracle! Wow!

You are an unrepeatable miracle. I am. Everyone is.

And not only is each person exclusively unique, but each one is especially valuable. This worth is expressed through such care by the heavenly Father that even minute details are recorded. The very hairs on the head of each person are counted, and the record kept up to date.[7]

Indeed, Jesus would put each person's eternal worth and uniqueness in perspective when He said, "What good will it be for a man if he gains the whole world, yet forfeits his soul? Or what would a man give in exchange for his soul?"[8]

The profoundness of each person's specialness is brought powerfully home when we grasp that every single human being, has been *given life by the choice of* two individual human beings, who in turn were given the same life by the choice of two other individuals human beings, and on, and on, and on, all in cooperation with God!

Mankind is the marvel of life, and God's gift to His special creations. You and me!

But when God gives this beautiful gift, He arranges to present it in an unparalleled plan. God takes all the essentials of man's nature He implanted—moral, intellectual, social, and spiritual—and combines these with the genders He forms: male and female.

The first results: Adam and then Eve, the first two of the race.

It was a joyous time when God fashioned Adam and placed him in Eden, the garden planted by God. Adam was given the oversight of the garden "to work it and take care of it"[9]

According to the story we know so well, as Adam went about the work that God had given him, God saw a need in Adam. God said, "It is not good for the man to be alone. I will make a helper suitable for him"[10] Adam was to receive a specially created gift—from God.

Combine all the excitement and happy emotions of every Christmas gift given; join it with the joyous feelings of every beautiful birthday gift ever bestowed; add the bright anticipation of every anniversary, graduation, every occasion whenever a loving gift has been given. All this does not approach the divine emotion when God made the woman. "So the Lord God caused the man to fall into a deep sleep; and while he was sleeping, he took one of the man's ribs, and closed up the place with flesh. Then the Lord God made woman from the rib . . . and he brought her to the man."[11]

Adam responded, "This is now bone of my bones and flesh of my flesh; she shall be called 'woman,' for she was taken out of man."

Of the creation of woman, the poet John Milton beautifully wrote in *Paradise Lost:*

> Under His forming hands a creature grew,
> Man like, but different sex; so lovely fair,
> That what seemed fair in all the world, seemed now
> Mean, or in her summed up, in her contained,
> And in her looks,
> Grace was in all her steps, heaven in her eye,
> In every gesture dignity and love.

There in the Garden of beautiful Eden, God performed the first marriage ever. Before Him stood the man He had given that first life in His own image, and the woman He had made in love to be the companion of the man. Together they would enter a sacred and joyous union so fully intimate that they became one flesh. "The man and his wife were both naked, and they felt no shame."[12]

Into that special union God placed His gift, the creation of life by an act of will—their God-given fertility.

The beautiful act to beget new life would be wrapped in the bounds of sacred matrimony. Into this relationship would come two separate wills, a male will and a female will. In their commitment to each other in marriage they would have one will. That joint decision would be the coming together to conceive new life in the intimacy of sexual union.

And so man and woman possessed the power to reproduce life—to procreate—by choice, a gift bestowed by God.

God designed marriage and made it sacred.

The plan of marriage was simple. "For this reason a man will leave his father and mother and be united to his wife, and they will become one flesh"[13]

This Scripture explains that every marriage has two essential parts. One is *a public commitment*, the other *a private consummation*. The public commitment is expressed by the scriptural statement, "A man will leave his father and mother and be united to his wife." Every time a man and a woman are married, they declare their vows openly before the community. The Christian wedding ceremony is a formalization of this principle.

The requirement for such a public commitment means there is no such thing as a secret marriage. Such is a contradiction.

The public commitment itself has two aspects: *a leaving* and by contrast *a cleaving*. First, there is the leaving of father and mother. The closest relationship apart from marriage is parent and child. But at marriage there is a commitment to an even closer relationship. So the public commitment says that the man and the woman hereby leave the priority of the relationship with parents to form a new primary relationship together. Of course, the leaving of mother and father does not mean a leaving in the sense of honor, but a leaving in the sense of priority. Children, the Scriptures affirms, are always to honor mother and father.

The second aspect of the public commitment is the aspect of "vow" or "cleaving," as the King James Version of the Bible so aptly expresses it. The cleaving is to each other. This is the public declaration of the vows.

The wedding ceremony reflects this. ". . . to have and to hold from this day forward; for better, for worse; for richer, for poorer; in sickness and in health; to love and to cherish; 'til death do us part, according to God's Holy ordinance; and thereto I pledge thee my troth."

Then, in addition to the public commitment, there is a *private consummation:* "And they will become one flesh."

Following the recitation of vows before the community, the man and woman alone complete the marriage with sexual union. After the open affirmation of their commitment to each other, the couple privately seal their wedlock in physical oneness.

This oneness is a relationship of their own creation. It combines the husband's maleness and every aspect of his emotional, spiritual, and social being with the wife's femaleness and every aspect of her being as they join in an act of married love.

And so a man and a woman are married. It was so with Adam and Eve. And into this divinely conceived plan of marriage, complete with all the public and private commitments shared by the two wills and complemented by a male and a female, God placed his unique gift: *the reproduction of life by the exercise of will.* We can join with our Lord when He "saw all that He made, *and it was very good."*

Some ask, "When does human life begin?"

Does it start at birth? Does it start at mid-gestation when the mother feels the first movements of the baby? Does it start at conception?

Of course, we understand what this question means and know how it is to be answered. But in a majestic and ultimate sense, life does not start at birth, at mid-gestation, or at conception. Life has only one beginning: when God created the first human life in His image. Into that initial gene pool He placed all the potential for all human life that was to follow.

He gave the procreative right, the right to continue to reproduce that life in cooperation with Him, to Man and Woman, who were committed for life to each other. Their beautiful, joyous, and loving union by choice would bring forth children, "a heritage from the Lord!"[14]

Life is sacred! It is to be celebrated!

Such a celebration was expressed by Jesus when He spoke of the reason for His coming to be our Savior: "I am come that they may have life, and have it to more abundantly."[15]

We have been given a tremendous gift.

It is part of God's dream. That's where human life started!

These are the central, primary *facts of life*. These are the first things our children need to know at the proper time in their development. Little children, when they begin to understand anything, can understand their own *God-given identity*, that they are made in the image of God. Later on children can understand their *God-given sexuality*, that they are made in the image of God, male or female. They can know that they are special little boys or special little girls. These first two facts can be re-enforced again and again at natural times by parents, grandparents and the Church.

Then, still later (perhaps several years later), at an appropriate, natural moment, children can easily understand their *God-given fertility*. Facts about it can be given as appropriate for their maturity. At the time when body changes begin to come and puberty starts, more facts can be given. As information about their God-given identity, sexuality and fertility is shared over time, the *sacredness of marriage* can be included. They can be told how God wonderfully placed male and female together in matrimony, and their physical union is to be celebrated within their marriage (perhaps sharing teaching from Genesis 2:24).

So let parents and grandparents—*especially grandparents*—and ministers and others teach these happy fundamental facts of life, instilling as appropriate at a very early age. At every point, let children sense the wonder of their God-given identity, their God-given sexuality, their God-given fertility, and the beauty of marriage. And let them know again and again that they are unrepeatable miracles for whom Christ died.

Let grandparents be deeply involved in this. I remember when I was about age 15. I was living with my grandmother and her father, my great-grandfather. My grandmother, who had been widowed at age 46, was taking care of her father in his final years. One day I happened to be sitting across the kitchen table from my grandmother; no one else was there. I do not know how, but something about marriage and sexual matters happened to come up. It was not a long conversation, but it was memorable; and it built a moral wall around me. I will never forget the one notable and beautiful moment in that brief discussion. My widowed grandmother looked across that table at me; her face was soft and reflective, with perhaps some moisture in her eyes. She had an unmistakable radiance, and coupled with what she then said, her radiance was what riveted me; there was a certain attractive purity in it. She looked at me and said with deep conviction, "Son, sexual intercourse is one of the most beautiful gifts God has given us in marriage." Did that hit me. Something just echoed in my own heart, "That's what I want in marriage. That's what I want with the woman I marry!"

So grandparents, get involved in transferring the joyous facts of life to your grandchildren.

Of course, one of the great questions of every civilization has been, "What will we do with this gift?"

And in the collapse of each society, one can always look back and ask, "What did they do with the Priceless Gift?"

What have we done with our gift of life, the sanctity of marriage, and the specialness of married intimacy between a husband and a wife? Sadly we only have to look at the millions of our unborn children we have destroyed and continue to destroy, the violence among us, the violence we use for entertainment, and the sexual licentiousness that we accept and even promote, from heterosexual fornicating and adultery to pornography to homosexual practice and same-sex marriage.

Giving impetus to all this is the same attitude Sodom had— "arrogance, gluttony, indifference to the poor and the needy," and the wanton practice of "detestable things" before God.[16]

Sodom "was done away with," was destroyed, by God in fiery judgment. Leonard Ravenhill said, "Remember, Sodom had no preachers. Sodom had no gospel broadcasters. America has over seven thousand . . . The lights are flashing in the world around us; our civilization is on the edge of disaster and only a heartbeat from judgment; *but who is warning us?"* [17]

Will we even consider the implications for ourselves?

Let us pray together: *Our gracious heavenly Father, thank You for Your priceless gift of life. We thank You for making us each unique and special, an unrepeatable miracle. May we freshly rejoice in this, and teach it to our children and grandchildren. Thank you for the beauty of marriage and intimacy. Forgive us as a nation for allowing fouled values come into our land so that we easily kill our precious unborn children and rationalize sexual licentiousness whether heterosexual or homosexual. May the revival You send also see a rebirth of celebration of the life You have given us. In the Name of Jesus our Savior and Lord. Amen.*

CHAPTER 8 ENDNOTES

[1] Psalm 139:13-14.
[2] Genesis 1:26-27.
[3] Genesis 2:7.
[4] Deuteronomy 6:5.
[5] Genesis 1:28-30.
[6] Genesis 1:31.
[7] Matthew 10:31.
[8] Matthew 16:26.
[9] Genesis 2:15.
[10] Genesis 2:18.
[11] Genesis 2:21-22.
[12] Genesis 2:25.
[13] Genesis 2:24.
[14] Psalm 127:3.
[15] John 10:10.
[16] See Ezekiel 16:49-50.
[17] Leonard Ravenhill, from *America Is Too Young To Die*.

9

GOD'S URGENT CALL

"Seek the Lord while He may be found; call on Him while He is near. Let the wicked man forsake his way and he evil man his thoughts."
—GOD, SPEAKING THROUGH ISAIAH[1]

"Since there was no repentance, or heeding to the national signs of disaster that were lovingly sent to those who had ignored the Word of God written and announced by His messengers, God would be obligated to send His wrath and judgment on that nation."
—WALTER KAISER[2]

GOD WONDROUSLY EXTENDS GRACE TO US SO WE CAN REPENT. And written large on such extensions is one word: "Urgent!" In other words, this is important, take heed, take action, repent now, and do not delay.

There is urgency to repent because there is the limit of time, the intrinsic boundary of both nations and individuals. We have short periods of existence on this earth. "What is your life?" James asks. "You are a mist that appears for a little while and then vanishes."[3]

"God can punish whole nations as easily as He can particular persons and for this purpose God has many national judgments which He can utilize," Reverend Thomas Foxcroft said in a sermon in 1724.[4] "If a people sin, they lay themselves open to such judgments." To emphasize the urgency of repentance, Foxcroft added, "If they are finally impenitent, divine justice calls aloud for their utter destruction. *When a people are obstinate and irreclaimable, after a long time of trial and much waiting upon them, God represents Himself as weary with repenting and obliged to proceed to their destruction.*"

Yet men and nations—even the Church—largely do not consider the seriousness of the shortness of life that we have, nor do they usually include the urgency of repentance in their reflections on what is important in the grace of God that is continually extended to us.

Nations are not immortal. They are neither indestructible nor deathless. History is littered with the corpses of every nation, every society, every culture that has risen before us—there are no exceptions. The Roman Empire is gone. The Greek Empire is gone. Babylon is gone. Nineveh is gone. The Aztecs are gone. The Israel of the Eighth Century B.C. is gone. Some whose names are still with us have declined—the British Empire, Spain, France, and on and on.

Yet during their years of glory and power each of these societies assumed an aura of immortality and invincibility. There was that self-deceptive view of themselves and the assumption that their cultures in all their grandeur and magnificence would last, well, forever. Many cultures in their early years of course, established some sort of law and framework of society that gave them a foundation to exist; however, like stubborn, reckless teenagers reveling in the strength of their youth and bent on living as they please without regard to consequences; so nations, at ease in their supposed indestructibility. They acted arrogantly and indifferently, allowed evil, decay and degeneracy ate at their souls.

Jim Nelson Black spoke of the Roman Empire: "This was only one manifestation of the Roman devaluating of human life. Eusebius, the Christian historian who wrote during the fourth century, says that on some days Emperor Diocletian ordered as many as a hundred men, women, and children slaughtered in the arena, and he adds, 'There was not one filthy, dissolute act of which he was innocent.'"

Black quotes Edith Hamilton, author of *The Roman Ways*, who described the terrors that drew the Roman crowds: "How savage the Roman nature was which the Roman law controlled is seen written large in Rome's favorite amusements, too familiar to need more than a cursory mention: wild beasts hunts—so called, the hunting place was the arena; naval battles for which the circus was flooded by means of hidden canals; and, most usual and best loved by the people, the gladiators, when the great amphitheater was packed close tier upon tier, all Rome there to see human beings by the tens and hundreds killing each other, to give the victor in a contest the signal for death and eagerly watch the upraised dagger plunge into the helpless body and the blood spurt forth."[5]

Our great scandal—make that our unconscionable scandal—is that we so easily sin against God's beautiful grace, ignoring and even scorning and disdaining it. We, as nation or individual have acted selfishly and foolishly and evilly in the very times when God is providing us with His wondrous grace. We have scorned God while He smiled on us.

As a nation we have been blessed by God from our Declaration of Independence to our Constitution, and from our very earliest settlers to those who pioneered the west, from the men at Valley Forge to every man or woman who has sacrificed or died in war for us, from the great natural resources in our land to the magnificence of our technology, from the struggle of our forefathers to the highest standard of living ever on the planet; all of it is because of the grace of God.

Life is a gift to us from God. Yet we heartlessly reach into 4,000 wombs a day and chop up the lives there in the name of freedom and choice.

The wonder of married sexual intimacy is a gift to us from God. Yet we perniciously flaunt more and more fornication, adultery, homosexual practice and pornography in our movies, music and televisions. Our forefathers have pledged us to "In God We Trust" and to be "under God," yet we excommunicate Him from our public squares.

Our children are our greatest heritage, yet we "cause them to sin" in a hundred ways, and have placed a millstone of judgment around our necks. To say we are unthankful wretches is understatement.

WE CONTINUE AS A NATION BECAUSE OF GOD'S MERCY

Considering the arrogance and self-absorption of our nation in its chosen sins, the marvel is that we even continue to exist as a nation. The reason we do continue to exist—and the only reason we do—is the mercy of God.

Notwithstanding, and sadly, there is no urgency to return to the Lord, to come to Him in humility and repentance. It is not in our nation. It is not in our churches.

We've adopted that terrible miscalculation that because God is gracious that He doesn't care if we sin, and that He is indifferent to our evil. We think that because judgment has not yet come down on us, that this means there is no judgment, and that we are not accountable for our iniquity, that God is neutral, like Judah's attitude: "The Lord will do nothing, either good or bad."[6]

After a litany of sins, God says in Psalm 50, "These things you have done and I kept silent; you thought I was altogether like you. But I will rebuke you and accuse you to your face. Consider this, you who forget God, or I will tear you to pieces, with none to rescue."[7] But any urgency which the reality of such judgment should provoke in us is brushed aside as we treat God's mercy with nonchalance.

It is amazing to see how we banish from our minds all thoughts of God, and neglect Him; but not only neglect God, but also hold Him in contempt, and a most awful mark of contempt at that, as when He graciously calls us, we turn our back on Him instead of turning to him our face, like the obdurate Pharaoh to Moses, "Who is the Lord, that I should obey Him . . . I do not know the Lord."[8]

However, God's grace is unfathomable, and in the face of our persistent obstinacy, He yet reaches to us in love, He still calls us back to Himself. It is evident that He is a God not rushing to judgment. or we would already be judged, it would be over for us; but He is a God of immeasurable forbearance. With what cold-heartedness have we received His compassion.

Incredibly our great God still speaks to us, wanting us to understand where we are, where we are headed, and our need to return to Him. However, Dr. Walter Kaiser's warns, "Is anybody listening? Is anybody at home?" as he recounted the numerous times God has spoken to America through "event after event." And Dr. Kaiser further warns, "If our nation, our generation will not rise to the call of God for repentance and revival, He's got to judge us! And He will! And we are crazy if we think it won't happen here. It is time for pastors to lead the way."[9]

Certainly God has been speaking to America. To put that in perspective, let us go to a fairly well known Scripture, II Chronicles 7:14, a text that has become almost a mantra among believers who desire the "healing of the land." "If My people, who are call by My name, will humble themselves and pray and seek My face and turn from their wicked ways, then will I hear from heaven and will forgive their sin and will heal their land."

The downside to much-used Scriptures such as II Chronicles 7:14 is that they tend to lose their contextual setting. (How many of us have really studied the verses which precede and follow the great John 3:16?) To fully grasp the full meaning, we must begin with II Chronicles 7:13. "When I shut up the heavens so that there is no rain, or command locusts to devour the land or send a plague among My people . . . "

Now when God stops sending rain or sends locusts or a plague to the nation, those are judgments. In Scripture, we usually identify two kinds of judgments: 1) Remedial and 2) Final. Take the second one first, final judgments. They are as their name indicates final—when the curtain falls on a culture and there is no tomorrow. Final judgments came to Israel, Judah, Nineveh, Babylon, etc. Final judgments are coming to this world and for every lost soul.

REMEDIAL OR CORRECTIVE JUDGMENTS

However, ahead of final judgments, there are remedial, or corrective or restorative judgments. There are five factors in these judgments: 1) they are rooted in God's mercy; 2) they are intended to arrest the attention of a distracted, wayward people, to shake them up so they will listen; 3) they are to get them to face themselves; 4) they portend final judgment; 5) they are meant to restore by stirring repentance and humility in sinning people.

"The Lord disciplines those He loves," Hebrews tells us. Quoting Proverbs 3:11-12: ". . . and He punishes everyone He accepts as a Son."[10] Philip Hughes spoke of the "merciful effect" of judgment, Augustine said that for God to allow crimes and vices to go on unpunished is a more terrible judgment than for Him to curb them by afflictions.[11] So when God wants to get a nation's attention, He might take strong actions that will jolt the nation. He might shake up the economy, which of course what happened when He stopped rain, or sent locusts which affected agriculture, the foundation of an agrarian economy. It is better for a nation to lose its money than to lose its soul.

In Amos 4:6-11, God tells of taking forceful measures again and again. He sent famine, drought, locusts, blight, mildew, plagues, the sword, and even overthrew some cities like Sodom and Gomorrah. Why did He take these "terrible" actions? *Because He loved His people enough to do them; because He wanted them to come back to Him.* Five times God punctuates what He did to Israel with the lament, "Yet you have not returned to Me!" Come back to Him, that's what God wanted the nation to do. But they did not—they would not; they remained rebellious! God was heartbroken.

Of course, sending famine, drought, plague and all are not the first ways that God speaks. He does that through His Word. God's prophets first voiced God's message to the people. Through Amos we hear God's passionate voice trying to awaken the willfully sinning nation to the urgency of their approaching judgment. "The Lord roars from Zion and thunders from Jerusalem; the pastures of the shepherds dry up, and the top of Mount Carmel withers."[12]

However, after God graciously had Amos (and Hosea) proclaim His word again and again and again to the prodigal nation, and following one strong yet merciful action after another, all from famine to sword imploring Israel to return to the Lord, the nation did not heed. It did not use that time of grace—that "window of mercy"—to attend to the urgency of repentance to save them from coming disaster.

So, with the nation stubbornly sinning, their time was up. No more grace. God would "no longer turn back [His] wrath."[13] Israel faced judgment. "Prepare to meet your God,"[14] the Lord sharply declares. This means *final* judgment. There could only be great grief for Israel at that moment of reckoning.

Why wouldn't they listen? What kind of national self-deception caused them to so cavalierly set aside all that God was saying and doing to get them to come back to Him? Why does it take coming to the moment of final judgment for a nation to have the first inkling that something is wrong. Israel is like the five foolish virgins before the shut door. Israel is like others who glibly thought they were

okay; who, when they hear the awful sentence of their final judgment were so surprised and devastated that they vented their
stunned anguish in weeping, wailing and gnashing of their teeth.
Israel is like Laodicea who swaggered they were rich and needed
nothing, only to be shocked as the Lord "spits them out of His
mouth."

Why doesn't our nation, led by its pastors and churches, use its
seasons of grace as they are intended—to focus on the urgent matter
of coming back to God? As Richard Owen Roberts says, our early
forefathers did this, "Early Americans, despite their faults, knew
that God hated sin and punished it in the unrepentant, including
unrepentant believers and churches. Because they feared God and
His ability to punish, they sought lead their people in quick and
thorough repentance.

"They were alert to signs of God's manifest displeasure among
them. Natural calamities, which some of us treat with a shrug of the
shoulder, were dutifully examined, prayed over and improved by
godly men of old. Even the unexpected death of a pastor, a youth, a
government official, a farmer or a housewife had the power to
provoke them to inquire if God had a grievance against His
people."[15]

As an example, on November 3, 1727, the day after a violent
earthquake shook Newton, Massachusetts, a special time for prayer
and reflection was set aside. Reverend John Cotton preached from
Psalm 119:120: "My flesh trembleth for fear of Thee; and I am afraid
of Thy judgments." Among Cotton's observations were, "I persuade
myself that this text has so often employed the thoughts of so many
of us since we felt the awful shaking and trembling of the earth
under us that we have been and are now ready to cry out 'My flesh
trembleth for fear of Thee; and I am afraid of Thy judgments.' It is a
day of no little distress, concern and fear; and it may well be so, for
what a holy and provoked God may be about ready to do with us,
He alone knows. One thing is certain, our transgressions have been
multiplied, and our iniquities testify against us.

Cotton also said, "In past years the Lord has been, in various awful ways, testifying to His anger and displeasure against us, and we may be wisely afraid He will do yet more awful and terrible things. I am convinced that this is the great fear of everyone that truly fears the great God today."[16]

The reason for such seriousness was that Christians at that time had a deep fear—a loving respect—of God. They believed His Word. It shaped the public conscience. This helps explain why George Mason said at the Constitutional Convention, "Every master of slaves is born a petty tyrant. They bring the judgment of heaven upon a country. As nations cannot be rewarded or punished in the next world, they must be in this. By an inevitable chain of causes and effects, Providence punishes national sins by national calamities." Or why Thomas Jefferson said, "I tremble for my country when I reflect that God is just; that His justice cannot sleep forever."

HOW GOD MIGHT HAVE BEEN SPEAKING TO US

How might God have spoken to us in America and the West to stir us to seek Him? Are there such events, as Walter Kaiser termed them? Here are several possibilities which most of us have lived through: THE STOCK MARKET CRASH IN OCTOBER, 1987; THE GULF WAR; AIDS; PRESIDENTIAL SCANDALS; THE 2000 ELECTION DEBACLE; AND 9/11. Are these remedial judgments? Let's review them.

The Stock Market Crash? I was on a ministry tour of Australia and New Zealand in October, 1987, when the America Stock Market crashed. Immediate panic hit the Western world. How did this happen? What must we do to fix it? I remember being interviewed by a major television station in Adelaide for their evening news, and was asked if I thought the crash was the judgment of God. I said I thought it was, and explained. Others agreed.

That crash did what a corrective judgment is to do; it shook us up by causing our markets to take a dive. It pointed to final judgment, the kind seen in the Book of Revelation when "economic Babylon" falls and the curtain falls. But it was a merciful judgment. We didn't completely collapse, although we certainly thought about it! It made us think, even fleetingly, of what we are trusting in, and how tenuous are those material things on which we place so much focus. I recall watching an American television special on the market crash which was rebroadcast in Australia. One economist likened an economy to knitting. He said that if you cut a thread at a critical place, you can unravel all of the knitting. So it is with an economy. And apparently something like this unraveling had happened. Consider our economy, this massive materialistic foundation that we so trust, *as secure as knitting!*

"Come back to Me!" our gracious God was saying. What should we have done? Scripture tells us what we are to do, which we will examine a little later. But briefly, what we should have done is fall on our faces and sought the Lord, repented of our materialism and for putting our confidence in anything so flimsy as money and the assets of this world.

God in His loving grace was confronting us with our materialistic sinning, calling us to Himself. Understanding this, we in the Church should have canceled our programs and agendas, and led our nation in repentance. But we didn't, and as soon as the market crash crisis was over, we joined the world again in their materialistic frolic. We sadly even had our own materialistic doctrinal fads focused on prosperity that mirrored the world's.

The Gulf War? And as it happened, once more I was in Australia and New Zealand for ministry. Again, the world was shaken. A headline in Australia blared: "Are we heading toward Armageddon?" The headline alluded to an atomic bomb type of Armageddon. We didn't know for sure whether Iraq had that bomb or not. "Armageddon" is the language of final judgment which loomed as for a moment we considered the implications of a nuclear war and the holocaust it would cause. But nothing like that happened; we only thought about it. God was gracious. He lovingly was trying to get our attention to realize how uncertain this world is. The only absolute certainty is the Lord Himself.

"Come back to Me!" our gracious God was saying. What should we have done? The same as mentioned before, we should have fallen on our faces and cried out to God in humble repentance. We in the Church should have led the way. But we didn't as we didn't seem to understand the moment. So as soon as the war was over we joined the world in life as before.

AIDS? This is an ongoing judgment on willful, sinful, sexual behavior—heterosexual and homosexual, and by sharing contaminated drug needles. It is a self-inflicted judgment. Stop the sinful, sexual behavior, and the disease is stopped. R.C. Sproul said, "The Bible makes it clear that God punishes sin. There can be no doubt that infectious diseases like syphilis, gonorrhea and AIDS are Divine punishments for fornication. It is amazing to observe news commentators and liberal Christian spokespeople who deny this."[17]

MESSAGES FROM THE AIDS TRAGEDY

There are a couple of messages that can be drawn from AIDS. One is that AIDS is like sin. Normally when you get it, it's fatal. However, there is a wonderful difference. With sin there is a remedy that has divinely been provided through the blood of Christ our Savior and God's love for the world—all of us. *There is forgiveness, deliverance, and healing in Jesus Christ for those with AIDS and for those in the homosexual lifestyle, if they will repent of their sins, confess them to Him, ask His forgiveness, and make Him Lord of their lives.*

The other message comes from the sanctity of marriage. By contrast AIDS highlights the blessing and protection of sexual faithfulness within marriage. An uninfected husband and wife who have only known each other intimately do not need fear getting AIDS. (They could get AIDS, of course, from contaminated blood in a transfusion, but that is not the issue.) A husband and wife's pure marriage bed is their protection by God's design. AIDS is a call back to chastity before marriage, and faithfulness within marriage.

Consider the implications of AIDS and all venereal diseases from the following verse: "Marriage should be honored by all, and the marriage bed kept pure, for God will judge the adulterer and all the sexually immoral."[18] In our world now so grievously infected with AIDS, the Church and the pulpit should lovingly and strongly affirm the themes of this verse that are both grand and sobering.

Presidential scandals? This is NOT a political statement in any way, but the two presidential terms of William Clinton revealed our dominant national character. It is as if God held a giant mirror up before us to let us see ourselves. We winked at lying (even in a court of law). We tolerated sexual impurity in the White House, behavior that would have gotten a military officer court-martialed, a school principal fired, or a corporation executive thrown out. We did not protest at unbiblical definitions of adultery when we know that ALL sexual contact by a married person outside of his or her marriage is adultery. We exposed the fouled side of our collective character. It is as if the Lord saw that we wanted lies, we wanted whoremongering, and lowered standards, so He let us have them. We elected ourselves twice. It was a time to show us to us—for after all the only way we can repent is to understand ourselves and the sin we are to repent of.

Yet it was a mercy. God was saying, "Come back to Me!" What should we have done? The same as said before, we should have repented in great sorrow and humility before our gracious God.

Some may object to the collective "we" being used here. This is certainly understood. First, the "we" is an editorial usage. Second it reflects what the majority did. Third, it denotes biblical identification such as Daniel and Nehemiah when they prayed, "We have sinned."[19]

The 2000 Election Debacle? For 36 days we were at a standstill, poised between two markedly different futures as we waited to see who our new president would be—Al Gore or George W. Bush. We were shaken as aspects of our Constitution were debated and as we argued in state, federal and Supreme courts.

The election revealed "the cultural and religious divide in our country," as one TV talking head observed. The split in our national character was bared by the stark contrast in voting between minorities and whites, rural and urban, men and women, married women and single women, pro-life and pro-death, Christians and secularists, pro-traditional values and pro-immoral values, impeachment-backers and impeachment-opponents, and so on. In addition, the voting left the Senate split and the House almost even with a six-vote margin for the Republicans. Those six seats were won by fewer than 5,000 total votes, one of the seats by around 100 votes. Once more it was a time to show us to us.

Most sobering was how we divided over public sins. Voting for Al Gore were those who believe that shedding the innocent blood of our unborn children should be permitted, and who have a very liberal, permissive attitude toward sexual licentiousness and such evils as same-sex marriages. Voting for George W. Bush were those who believe our unborn children should be protected and welcomed into life; sex is exclusively to be celebrated within marriage; and marriage is only between a man and a woman.

It is fair to say that if Al Gore, the candidate who favored shedding the innocent blood of the unborn children had prevailed, both he and the majority of those he appointed to his cabinet, administration, and especially the Supreme Court and the federal judiciary would have reflected his viewpoint. It is also fair to say that probably most of his appointees would have come from that side of the political spectrum which takes a permissive view toward sexual decadence. In addition, we know there are assertive movements in America, such as feminism and gay rights, who are thoroughly committed to agendas of unhindered abortion and sexual license. Plus they work particularly in school to have our children indoctrinated in their agendas. It is realistic to believe that if Gore had become president, they would have been very happy and likely freshly energized.

Here is the point: America is so entrenched in its chosen lies and is sinning so boldly that it is not stretching reason to say that putting yet another very pro-abortion administration along with refired, outspoken pro-abortion movements into our aggressively wicked country could have been the flashpoint for a sobering scenario, one where our nation virtually abandoned any remaining restraints toward killing our unborn children—and other national sins. Our pride could have become more unyielding, our indifference toward our sin more pronounced, our complacency in our materialism more deadening, and our hostility toward God more prominent—our sin, like Israel's, could have "broken all bounds" of restraint with "bloodshed following bloodshed," *and our cup of iniquity could have overflowed. Our judgment would have been hastened!*

However, we do not have that scenario, although it still looms. What we have now is a gracious "window of mercy" from our Lord. We deserved to be "given up" to speed toward our judgment, but our beautiful Lord has given us still another chance and more time to repent and humbly seek Him. We believe this came because of the earnest intercession of so many across the nation and world, so many who understood the moment.

"Come back to Me!" our Lord was and is saying, because we're still in this corrective judgment. We are in the "window of mercy." This moment of grace we dare not—*we dare not*—treat carelessly! What should we do? We should do what we haven't done before in such times of grace. We should give ourselves to the urgency of falling on our faces in humble repentance before our gracious, forbearing Lord, implore Him to forgive us for our terrible personal and national sins, to repent of our bloodshed, and ask Him for a deep, genuine revival in His Church and a spiritual awakening in our land.

9/11? We'll not go into detail as in the others. But simply say that what has been said about the others can apply now. And since we are living in the post-9/11 time, let us hear our Lord call, "Come back to Me!" We are in a window of mercy.

God help us as a Church if we dissipate this season. God help us if we abandon our nation at this time. God help us if we do not seize the moment. If we treat this time with nonchalance, then we may well miss the sweeping revival that could well be birthed and the harvest of souls it would produce.

We've long talked of revival. Now in this window of mercy, let's fervently present ourselves before our gracious, Sovereign Lord to seek Him for one.

WHAT ARE WE TO DO?

Well, what ARE we to do? The Scripture is much more specific than just the general exhortations that have come forth on these pages. We return to that grand Scripture, II Chronicles 7:14. We know that it flows right from verse 13 which describes remedial judgments God might send upon the nation. So the Lord is saying, when you see Me send remedial judgments that come from My concern and mercy and are intended to shake up people, get them to face themselves and turn back to Me in repentance . . . when you see Me send such corrective judgments, I want you, My people, to move into action—special action that can bring healing to their land.

"If My people, who are called by My name," the Lord says. There is a double reference here to the same group, "My people,"and those "called by My name." This is to give emphasis, with the second statement amplifying the first. It's like the emphasis you or I use when saying, "I, myself." But also, here the statement of emphasis— those "who are called by My name"—is intimate, flowing from tenderness and love. It is the voice of a caring father, because every father gives his name to his family. God is saying, when you see Me, send corrective judgments in love, then I want you, My people, My family, to do certain things. Those certain things are: *humble yourselves, pray, seek My face, and turn from your wicked ways.*

"Humble ourselves." This is the hardest because pride is such a fundamental, insidious sin. Pride made a devil out of an archangel. Pride lurks in preachers' hearts. Pride infects churches and parishes. Pride infects Christians. In fact, religious pride is the most insidious pride, and the one to which we are most blind. Have we seen churches split and divide? Somewhere there is pride. Have we seen preachers fall? Somewhere there is pride. Have we seen or, sadly, been a part of church power struggles or congregational politics? At the root is pride.

Apathy is a form of pride. Apathy is the ultimate expression of arrogance and self-delusion. It is essentially saying to God, "I don't need any more of You; I am satisfied like I am."

We are to humble ourselves. We are to become ruthless, brutal, and fierce against our pride, our arrogance, and our apathy. We're to do as Jesus did: "He humbled Himself."[20]

We live in a proud, arrogant culture. We are to humble ourselves if we want to see our land healed.

"Pray." Refers to intercession: praying for others, for family, for community, and for our nation. We'll look at this more extensively a bit later.

"Seek My face." In the metaphor of Scripture, to have God's face upon us is to have His smile, His approval, and His blessing. To have His face turned away is to have His disapproval and His displeasure. We are to implore that His face once again be turned to us.

In a sense the face of God could be contrasted with the hand of God which is a metaphor for things God might do for us, His blessings, and His benefits. There is everything right about receiving such from our Lord. He desires to bless.

Notwithstanding, we are to seek God's face. To seek His face *is to seek God for Himself without regard to benefit. Just to know Him is its own reward. Just to know Him is enough, whether He blesses me or not.*

The healing of the land and revival will come as we seek the face of God, to joyously aspire to simply know Him! Again, let's return to this later.

"Turn from their wicked ways." God's people, called by His name are to repent. The nation certainly must repent, but repentance in the nation starts with God's family. Judgment *begins* in the house of God. Is there pride in the nation? Is there pride in you or me? Where will God start? He will start with you and me. Is there worldliness, lust, covetousness, bitterness, pornography, immorality, filthy talking, and lying in the world around us? Are these sins among us? Where will God start? He will start with you and me. *God, the perfect Father, will not permit in His house what He will judge a world for!*

God uses the word "wicked." We are to turn from our WICKED *ways.* This is a stunning usage of "wicked," a description usually given to those outside God's family. Wicked means corrupt, evil, profane, reprobate, and debased. God calls His people to turn from *their* wickedness. It is in His people that God sees wickedness—debasement and corruption. It is among those called by His name that He views profaneness, worldliness, and compromise. How God's view differs with ours, blinded as we can be by self-justifying pride. We would not tend to use the word "wicked" in describing ourselves. We might say that we are mistaken or at fault or bad, or have erred. But "wicked"? Not likely. Humility will allow us to see ourselves the way God sees us.

We are to repent. "Therefore, let all the godly confess their rebellion to You while there is time, that they may not drown in the floodwaters of judgment."[21] The command for God's people to repent in II Chronicles 7:14 mirrors Jesus' call to repent He gave to the Seven Churches. Later we want to look at specific wickedness we in the Church and pulpit must repent of.

"Then will I hear from heaven." The promise is sure, the Lord will hear us. His ear is open to our humble, repentant prayer. Let the

assurance that He will hear us implant faith and stir us to confidently do what He sets before us to do.

"*And will forgive their sin.*" God's hearing brings God's answer. Our sin is forgiven. Nothing—nothing—equals the importance of sins forgiven. Having our sins forgiven is the doorway to all the rest of what our Lord has for us. For us as a nation, it opens that most glorious of blessings: the healing of our land.

"*And will heal their land.*" This is what our Lord desires to do here in America and each nation. Instead of judgment, healing. Instead of sin, righteousness. Instead of bondage, deliverance. Instead of brokenness, health. Instead of decay, revival. Instead of moral decline, spiritual awakening. Only the Lord knows the wonders such a healing would bring to our prodigal nation.

To reiterate yet again, right now we have another time of grace. Within it is urgency—the urgency to give priority to hear God saying again, as He has so many, many times, "Come back to Me!" And, responding to this call, set our urgent priority to do what God says His "people who are called by [His] name" are to do to come back to Him.

For perspective, several questions: No doubt, if there ever is another 9/11-type of tragedy among us, there will again be enormous trauma, perhaps much worse than before. Will it take that to shake us to urgency? What will the Church's message be? Will we finally and courageously speak from the heart of God, "Come back to Me"? And lead the way in repentance?

Reverend Andrew Elliot, preaching on a public fast in Boston on April 19, 1753, spoke of the effect of repentance. "If we are once, by the influence of the Spirit of grace, brought to a sincere and thorough repentance, God, even our own God, will delight to dwell among us and to bless us, and things go well with us." Elliot then quoted from Isaiah 32:15-17, "If 'the Spirit be poured upon us from on high, and the wilderness be a fruitful field, and the fruitful field be counted for a forest, then judgment shall dwell in the wilderness,

and righteousness remain in the fruitful field. And the work of righteousness shall be peace; and the effect of righteousness quietness
and assurance forever.'"22

Oh, for the pure refreshment of such a healing of our beloved land!

Let us pray together: *Gracious Lord, how wonderful are Your
ways; how glorious is Your Grace. And how often have You graciously
spoken to us through Your Word and through corrective judgments.
Forgive us for not listening, particularly for not even considering that the
things that You have brought about are in fact You calling us to come back
to You. Lord, burn into my heart, and all of our hearts, the urgency
contained in grace, that grace is not to be ignored and trampled on and
brushed aside, but used to come to You. At this moment You have given
our nation a window of mercy in which we are to humble ourselves, pray,
seek Your face, and turn from our wicked ways. Oh, Lord, do whatever
You need to do to see that we do this. In the name of Your blessed Son,
our Savior and Lord, Jesus Christ. Amen.*

CHAPTER 9 ENDNOTES

[1] Isaiah 55:6.

[2] Dr. Walter Kaiser, *Revive Us Again*, (Nashville, TN: Broadman and Holman Publishers, 1999), p.232.

[3] James 4:14.

[4] Reverend Thomas Foxcroft, in his sermon, *"God's Face Set Against An Incorrigible People,"* preached at a public lecture in Boston, July 30, 1724.

[5] Jim Nelson Black, *When Nations Die: Ten Warning Signs of a Culture in Crisis*, (Wheaton: Tyndale House, 1994), p.224.

[6] Zephaniah 1:12.

[7] Psalm 50:21-22.

[8] Exodus 5:2.

[9] Walter Kaiser, Jr., speaking at *The Power of Gospel Preaching* conference in Atlanta, GA, October, 2000.

[10] Hebrews 12:6.

[11] Philip Hughes, from a promotion for his book, *Christians in a Secular Society*, Baker.

[12] Amos 1:2.

[13] Amos 2:6.

[14] Amos 4:12.

[15] Richard Owen Roberts, in the introduction to his article on *"The Solemn Assembly."*

[16] Reverend John Cotton, from his sermon, *"A Holy Fear of God and His Judgments,"* preached in Newton, Massachusetts, Nov. 3, 1727, the day after a violent earthquake shook the town.

[17]. R.C. Sproul, *Tabletalk*, May, 1991, p. 18.

[18] Hebrews 13:4.

[19] See Daniel 9 and Nehemiah 1.

[20] Philippians 3:8.

[21] Psalm 32:6.

22 Reverend Andrew Elliot, from his sermon, *"An Evil and Adulterous Generation,"* preached in Boston April 19, 1753, during a public fast.

10

OUR GRAND AMBITION

"Oh God, You are my God, earnestly I seek You; my soul thirsts for You, my body longs for You, in a dry and weary land where there is no water. I have seen You in the sanctuary and beheld Your power and Your glory."
—DAVID, SHOWING HIS PASSION FOR GOD[1]

"The more Thy glories strike my eyes / The lower I shall lie / Thus while I fall my joys shall rise / Immeasurably high.
—D. Thomas[2]

YEARS AGO, A SECULAR SPEAKER ARRESTED OUR ATTENTION with his opening sentence, *"The reason some people do not have any ambition . . . is because they do not have any ambition."*

He paused briefly, then he repeated the statement, this time unraveling it for us: "The reason some people do not have any ambition–or get-up-and-go and drive, is because they do not have any ambition–or any goal in their life."

Instead of "goal," I prefer "aspiration," which means a great yearning for something larger than ourselves, a grand ambition, something we are passionately living for, and something worth devoting your heart and soul to.

The poorest person is the one who, while having plenty of money and materialistic resources to live on, has little or nothing to live for.

The richest person is the one who, perhaps not having much money and materialistic resources to live on, has something to live for—a grand ambition.

Years ago, I remember attending a youth rally. The speaker, a minister in his fifties who communicated tremendously with young people, said that if the Lord were to say to him that he could have any gift he wished, he would select the capacity "to create spiritual hunger." Spiritual hunger was his grand ambition. He explained that when we have spiritual hunger we automatically deal with things like worldliness, and we set our priorities and standards.

We can be honorably engaged in many professions: We can be mechanics or machinists, schoolteachers or surgeons, plumbers or preachers, medical doctors or missionaries, truck drivers or traffic policemen, librarians or lawyers, farmers or fishermen, secretaries or scientists, waitresses or welders. All are worthy endeavors.

However, none of these, or any others like them, is worth the total devotion of a human soul.

The Pharisees, whose great goal was keeping the law, had one of their group ask Jesus, "Which is the greatest commandment in the Law?"[3] This was the kind of question we might expect a Pharisee to ask.

When Jesus answered that question, He not only named the greatest commandment, He also identified *the only thing worth the total devotion of a human soul*. He said, "Love the Lord your God with all you heart and with all you soul and with all your mind." And He also identified the second greatest commandment. "Love your neighbor as yourself."

Loving God with all we are is the only aspiration that merits the entire and absolute worship and passion of any of us.

What was it that made Moses who he was? Or the Apostle Paul? Or Joseph, Daniel, John the Baptist, Abraham, King David, Isaiah, Jeremiah, and other great men of Scripture? What was it that made John Wesley who he was, or George Whitefield, or Jonathan Edwards, or David Brainerd, or the great missionaries, or the honored preachers? What made even someone from your family or mine a godly person, such as my great-grandfather, Friedrich (Fred) Hofer, who emigrated to America from Switzerland?

A close look will reveal they each had one central focus, one grand ambition, one ultimate passion: *to love God with all his heart, soul and mind.* This is what set them apart, and made them who they were.

Look at Moses' grand ambition: "When he had grown up, refused to be known as the son of Pharoah's daughter. He chose to be mistreated along with the people of God rather than to enjoy the pleasures of sin for a short time. He regarded disgrace for the sake of Christ as of greater value than the treasures of Egypt."[4]

The Apostle Paul's grand ambition: "Whatever was to my profit I now consider loss for the sake of Christ. What is more, I consider everything a loss compared to the surpassing greatness of knowing Christ Jesus my Lord . . . I want to know Christ . . ."[5]

King David's grand ambition: "As the deer pants for streams of water, so my soul pants for You, O God. My soul thirsts for God, for the living God. When can I go and meet with God?"[6]

Whether well known or obscure, or whether famous or someone only known to your family or mine, they are the men and women who had that passionate desire to love God with everything in their being whom we honor as beautiful examples of godliness.

And the powerful result is that whether it was Moses leading Israel and becoming the one God used to give the Law, or it is my relatively unknown great-grandfather who in his church and community was so respected as a man of God and who played such a strategic role in my coming to Christ, these individuals profoundly impacted others. And they did so in sinful times—proud, distracted, compromised, immoral, violent, idolatrous times. They stood strong and true and straight in times bent by evil. They stood with one grand passion: to love God.

God was able to use them so effectively because they loved Him!

Our times cry for such men and women!

THOSE WHO KNOW GOD ARE NEEDED TO LEAD US

One great urgency for this hour is for those whose lives are wholly focused on loving God and knowing Him deeply to lead us. They are the godly men and women with the bearing of humility, the beauty of holiness, and the becoming love for our Lord who are needed to call us back to God. Those with that large passion to please only God are the ones we need to roar His message in this judgment-bound hour. We need them to rise in our pulpits, expound Scripture, and re-train our public conscience.

By refreshing contrast their lives will expose the veneer of ego-driven ministry. Their immense focus on loving God will bare the superficiality of hype. Their unpretentious genuineness will uncover the charade of celebrity. Their integrity with the Word of God will reveal the treachery of false prophets.

They will be concerned with what God—the One they know—is concerned about. Their message will flow from the Word of God and the heart of God, not from the latest fad or method or psychobabble. Their caring hearts will only be satisfied with believers growing in God's image, not settling for the shallowness of self-image. They will show that success is knowing God, not in attaining prosperity here. They will equip the Church not only for life now, but for life in eternity in the Presence of God. Their first focus for believers will not be happiness, but the joy of holiness, and knowing that in God's order we are happy when we are holy. Their ambition will be beyond the idolatry of building a ministry or constructing another ministry building, to unreservedly loving God. They will be known as passionate for God, not pragmatic in the work of God.

They cannot be silent because as their lives speak, their voices roar!

This generation needs an army of Christians and preachers just like this, a generation of men and women who discern with a different ear and eye in the midst of the profusion of distractions and distortions, who show us the true, and who lead us away from the false. We need men and women who have gained their discernment because they know whom most do not and what most care little about—*they know God!*

Their example will be one of the most refreshing aspects of deep, biblical revival.

Our most pressing need today is for men and women who *know* God—not know *about* God, but *know* God in the true intimacy of Father and child. How pivotal are such Christians!

It was the lack of intimate knowledge of God which was one of the basic reasons why Israel sinned—they knew *that* God was, but they did not know *who* he was. God indicted sycophant priests and prophets for the iniquitous environment by saying, "My people are destroyed from lack of knowledge."[7]

The nation was listening to the wrong voices—those who did not know God but who acted as if they did, false messengers with their spurious but popular messages built around triumphalism, blessing and prosperity. These false messengers gained the ear of the culture around them, and were a prime reason the true messages of Jeremiah, Isaiah, Amos, Hosea—virtually every true prophet—were not heeded, a message doubtless stronger than what the nation wanted to hear. The message which would have saved the nation was effectively silenced by the more acclaimed incomplete message of the mistaken preachers. Many times true prophets were either ostracized, or martyred, as if to get rid of the messenger was to get rid of the message.

But we can be thankful for those prophets who were true and stood true, those who knew God and loved Him supremely, such as the eminent Isaiah.

It was "in the year that King Uzziah died" that God gave Isaiah, through an awesome vision, a life-changing encounter with Himself. It was that year of national transition when God raised up the voice of Isaiah to speak for Him, a genuine, faithful voice who would speak because he had seen, and heard, the most breathtaking and wondrous of heavenly revelations.

I have never had a vision like Isaiah's. However, the wonder of Scripture and the intent of God is that the Holy Spirit can and does take what Scripture says and burn it into our hearts. Isaiah's vision can become reality for us. Isaiah's grand encounter in Chapter 6 of his book gave him a deep insight into knowing God and loving Him supremely. That vision brought to pass a deep work in Isaiah—a work that would give conviction and courage to him.

Isaiah saw "the Lord seated on a throne, high and exalted, and the train of his robe filled the temple. Above him were seraphs, each with six wings: With two wings they covered their faces, with two they covered their feet, and with two they were flying."[8] The late Derek Prince once pointed out that the action that the seraphs took with their wings was highly significant and important to us. Out of their six wings, he said, the seraphs used four to worship God and two to serve Him. Their relationship of two-thirds of their being and effort given to worship, and one-third given to service, Prince said, is what the relationship our being and effort should be in our work for God.

What a moment it was for Isaiah! He heard the worship of heaven as the seraphs called to one another, "Holy, Holy, Holy is the Lord Almighty; the whole earth is full of his glory." The triune "Holy, Holy, Holy" that Isaiah heard exalts God far above all human thoughts and conceptions. In one other place, Revelation 4:8, the thrice-repeated "holy" is given as John sees a vision of God and heaven similar to Isaiah's.

WE NEED TO HEAR "HOLY, HOLY, HOLY"

In an unholy world, our ears need to hear again "Holy, Holy, Holy." We hear so much "unholy, unholy, unholy." Every Christian, every minister of the Gospel needs to be stirred by "Holy, Holy, Holy" again. True prophets have heard "Holy, Holy, Holy."

Isaiah witnessed the doorposts and the thresholds shaking with the Temple filled with smoke. Majestic! And terrifying. William Eisenhower said, "Unfortunately, many of us presume that the world is the ultimate threat and that God's function is to offset it. But the biblical position is that God is scarier than the world by far."9

The most terrifying part of the encounter was when Isaiah saw himself. He saw himself before the holy God, and was shaken by the stark, immeasurable contrast between his earthly unholiness and darkness and the wondrous purity of God's holiness and glory. Compared to the absolute cleanliness of heaven, this world would be more like a moral and spiritual sewer.

Isaiah was gripped by the overwhelming weight of his sin. Every iniquity, flaw, shortcoming, lust, false motive, wrong word, everything even remotely evil in Isaiah was exposed. Laid bare were all those things that stay easily hidden in the pale light of human life.

In the piercing awareness of his own evil and need, Isaiah agonizingly cried, "Woe to me! I am ruined!"

In such a moment there was no ego in Isaiah, only deep humility. No self-righteousness, only the painful awareness of unrighteousness. Self-righteousness might be compared to a man swimming in a sewer and he sees a ledge just above the waterline. He grips the ledge, and with great effort pull himself up onto it. Then, standing, he eyes those still swimming in the sewer. And, with the filth and effluvia still dripping, he points his finger and taunts, "Aren't *you* dirty!" That's self-righteousness, something God likens to filthy rags.

Humility, that golden point of Christian graces, was deep in Isaiah. It is one of the marks of a true prophet. It marked John the Baptist who denied he was the Messiah, "One more powerful than I will come, the thongs of whose sandals I am not worthy to untie."[10] The man or woman God uses to speak effectively for Him will be known as humble, for God is not building a ministry in His spokespeople. He is putting Himself in them, so there will be no room for ego-driven labor.

Humility is an earmark of a true prophet.

"For I am a man of unclean lips," Isaiah said. It is as if the very sewer of this world oozed from his mouth. He might have been experiencing what Jesus spoke of when He said, "What goes into a man's mouth does not make him 'unclean,' but what comes out of his mouth."[11] Isaiah was devastated.

Isaiah's woe on himself was like David's anguish: "My bones have no soundness because of my sin. My guilt has overwhelmed me like a burden too heavy to bear. My wounds fester and are loathsome because of my sinful folly. . . I confess my iniquity; I am troubled by my sin."[12]

Isaiah felt the weight of sin and his guilt before God. The word "guilt" isn't popular. In fact, it's almost a cardinal sin for ministers to put people on a *guilt-trip*. Psychology has seduced us. "Guilt," however, is the proper word because we are indeed guilty, very guilty, of sinning before the holy God; and we must repent or be judged and punished. Certainly there is a false guilt that can afflict tender hearts, and we must avoid that. However, we in this nonchalant generation—individuals and nation—do not give much thought to our real and incriminating guilt. We are under judgment by the holy God. Our peril is real. And we need to face our guilt and repent in order to see forgiveness.

Isaiah pronounced woe on himself after having pronounced woe on others. In Chapter 5 he condemned evil practices from land-grabbing to drunkenness to denial of justice to the innocents. However, such pronouncements in a basic sense only reflected common decency, not necessarily spiritual eyesight. After all, women from the garden society might speak "woe" against pornography or prostitution, or men from the service club pronounce "woe" on stealing or drugs. But they would speak from customary virtue.

However, Isaiah now spoke woe because he had a vision of the awesome, holy God. It was a transforming moment. True prophets—and shepherds—do not speak against evil merely motivated by the best interests of mankind. They speak from the urgency of having seen God . . . and themselves.

An earmark of a true prophet is his abiding understanding of his own sinful poverty apart from God.

Then Isaiah looked around and saw everyone else, including you and me, in the same loathsome condition and continued, "And I live among a people of unclean lips." Isaiah saw only one condition in those around him—corruption. He didn't see the varieties of evil-doers—adulterers, fornicators, liars, murderers, abortionists, homosexuals, pornographers, the covetous, or the greedy. He saw everyone with a defiled mouth, just as he saw himself.

ISAIAH IDENTIFIED WITH WORLD'S SINFUL CONDITION

Isaiah identified with the condition of his world. He was a foul-mouthed man in a world of foul-mouthed people. He understood, and he could love and care.

True prophets don't stand aloof on some lofty, isolated pinnacle and shout pronouncements at the bad people below. No, they come down to walk among them, and identify with them. There is a "we-ness" in their attitude, like, "We have sinned. I have, you have. We must cry out to the Lord!" The godly Daniel understood this when he prayed, "We have sinned and done wrong. We have been wicked and have rebelled."[13] And Nehemiah understood. He said, "We have acted very wickedly toward you."[14]

Moses had the same spirit. When the Lord said He would destroy Israel for its sin, Moses cried, "But now, please forgive their sin—but if not then blot me out of the book you have written."[15] Centuries later the Apostle Paul said, "For I could wish that I myself were cursed and cut off from Christ for the sake of my brothers, those of my own race, the people of Israel . . . My heart's desire and prayer to God for the Israelites is that they may be saved."[16] The greatest example of identifying with the need of the world is our Lord Jesus Himself. Jesus had no sin, but "God made Him who had no sin to be sin for us, so that in Him we might become the righteousness of God."

True prophets speak with a deep conviction born of the awareness of their own sins. They speak with passion and compassion because they identify with the need around them. From that position, their words have great convicting power.

Then the vision shifted back to heaven—and a sequence unfolded that pictures the Gospel of Redemption. From the human standpoint there is no way Isaiah could escape his unholy condition. One of the seraphs took tongs and picked a live coal from the heavenly altar and flew to Isaiah. He touched his mouth with it, "See, this has touched your lips; your guilt is taken away and your sin atoned for." Isaiah was cleansed.

That live coal illustrated the cleansing of the blood Christ shed on the Cross. Because God loved the world, He sent His "Holy, Holy, Holy" Son into our world. Jesus Christ is the only One to come into this world holy, and leave as holy as He came. While He was here He died for our sins and arose from the dead. Then He ascended back to heaven, to the right hand of the Father.

Now through repentance of sin and faith in Him, we can be cleansed through His blood and declared righteous and holy!

Have you been cleansed? Do you remember when you came to Christ? I recall doing so when I was about 12 years old. God used the combined influence of my great-grandfather, Friedrich Hofer, the small church we attended, and my mother. My mother, who had drifted away from the Lord as a young women, had come to Christ a couple of years before in the first year of a very traumatic second marriage. The first marriage in which three sons were born, my two younger brothers and me, had ended in immense heartache when I was about six years old. For decades I never knew what happened to my biological father, a skilled and successful architect. Eventually I learned the sad story of his alcohol abuse which destroyed his successful architectural career, his consequent life as a hobo, and his death on Chicago's Skid Row.

I came to the Lord at home, late one night in my top bunk bed. My then 85-year-old great-grandfather was staying with us, and was sleeping across the bedroom. His ongoing joyous Christian testimony and open anticipation of going to heaven "to be with Jesus" had profound effects on me. I knew I wasn't going to heaven.

My mother sensed I had not been sleeping well (which I had not), and late one night stood by my bed and asked if anything was wrong. I said I didn't know if I was a Christian. She told me what we had both heard at the church, a smaller fundamental congregation, something to the effect that I needed to repent of my sins and ask Christ to be my Savior and Lord.

When she left I thought of my sins and tried to recall each one and repent of it, but the list seemed never-ending. I felt like the worst sinner on the planet, like my sins were a heavy weight piled to the sky. I started to weep quietly, gripped with a sense of desperation. Then with anguish I asked the Lord to please forgive me and be my Savior and Lord.

I will never forget that as I prayed, something came over me. It swept from my head down through my body. I do not know whether it was a powerful peace or a peaceful power, but it engulfed me. I was flooded with joy and love and a sense of cleanliness. No one had to tell me. I knew, I knew, I knew, I knew that something extraordinary had happened. I had experienced what folks at the church called "being born again." *I remember being cleansed.*

As memorable as that moment was, at various times since, I say with deep reproach, I settled down into the routine and ritual and rules of religious life. I forgot I had been cleansed.

I became a professional Christian.

And worse, since being in ministry, at times *I became a professional preacher.*

PROFESSIONAL CHRISTIANS HAVE LOST THE TENDER HEART

A professional Christian—or preacher—has lost that tender heart before God, gotten away from the deep awareness of the beauty of God's grace in his or her life, forgotten he or she was once utterly lost and a foul-mouthed man or woman; and are comfortable and at ease in the trappings of pious activity. It's abhorrent. It's deadly. It's abominable. But most of *all, a professional Christian has lost that grand yearning to "love God with all their heart and soul and mind."* They are not enthralled anymore with that large passion to know God. Because they're not captured by a lofty spiritual ambition, they lack energy and spiritual ambition. Aspiration has been replaced by apathy. Spiritual hunger has been displaced by worldly accommodation. *The only thing worth the total devotion of their soul* has been crowded out by a multitude of things that clutter their soul.

Professional Christians and preachers are the enemies of revival. They care little for the Lord. And they care little for their nation. By offering apathy they offer nothing to lift their nation, and this aids in its destruction; this furthers its demise.

How many of us are professional Christians? Or professional preachers?

If we are, our answer is repentance.

Here is where revival can begin—in you and me; in you and me desperately *humbling ourselves* and *seeking the face of our Lord in repentance.*

Well, when Isaiah's mouth was cleansed, his ears opened and he heard the Lord say, "Whom shall I send? And who will go for us?" The Lord was looking for someone to speak, to go to the world for Him. This is where the heart of God is . . . if we will let our ears hear it.

Isaiah's heart seemed to leap in response; and, with a cleansed mouth that he had confessed as filthy a few moments before, Isaiah declared, "Here am I. Send me!" Isaiah was ready. He wanted to go.

God said to Isaiah, "Go." And he did. For decades Isaiah went to his nation with the message of the Lord. He stood strong and spoke clearly, candidly, and courageously in times when the nation drifted spiritually, idolatry crowded in, empty worship became prevalent, and even when foreign armies invaded.

Isaiah had seen God. He had heard the holy worship of heaven. He had been personally overwhelmed by his own unholiness. He had been powerfully cleansed by fire from heaven. And he had fervently committed himself to going wherever God wanted Him to go.

Isaiah's grand ambition was to know God, "O Lord, You are my God; I will exalt You and praise Your name, for in perfect faithfulness You have done marvelous things."[17]

God commanded Isaiah to proclaim His message, "Raise a banner on a bare hilltop, shout to them. . ."[18] "Shout it aloud, do not hold back. Raise your voice like a trumpet."[19]

Isaiah raised that trumpet, "For Zion's sake I will not keep silent . . . 'til her righteousness shines out like the dawn, her salvation like a blazing torch."[20]

Oh may it be that those who know God and love Him supremely, who have walked the path of Isaiah, and whose wisdom is rooted in God's Word and God's heart; may it be them—and only them—who lead us!

Let us pray together: *Oh our great and mighty Lord, give our nation Isaiahs—men and women who know You and will speak Your Word into our heart and conscience. Give us men and women who have that large aspiration to love You with all of their being, and are motivated by Your heart. Forgive us in Your Church for those times too often when we have become professional Christians or professional preachers. Forgive our apathy which offers nothing to stop the decay of our world. How we sin against Your love when we are this way. Oh Lord, give us revival, biblical revival centered around loving You with all our heart and soul and mind. In Jesus name, Your Son and our Savior and Lord, Amen.*

Chapter 10 Endnotes

1 Psalm 63:1-2.

2 D. Thomas, *The Revelation of St. John the Divine*, (Pulpit Commentary, Eerdmans, 1950), p. 466.

3 This encounter comes from Matthew 22:34-40.

4 From Hebrews 11:24-26.

5 From Philippians 3:7-10.

6 Psalm 42:1-2.

7 Hosea 4:6.

8 This entire account comes from Isaiah 6:1-9.

9 William D. Eisenhower, *"Fearing God,"* (Christianity Today, Feb. 7, 1986), p.34.

10 Luke 3:16.

11 Matthew 15:11.

12 Psalm 38:3b-5, 18.

13 Daniel 9:5.

14 Nehemiah 1:7.

15 Exodus 32:32.

16 Romans 9:3-4, 10:1.

17 Isaiah 25:1.

18 Isaiah 13:2.

19 Isaiah 58:1.

20 Isaiah 62:1.

PART FOUR

A REVIVAL OF PRAYER AND THE MESSAGE!

"Say to them, 'This is what the Sovereign Lord says.' And whether they listen or fail to listen—for they are a rebellious house—they will know that a prophet has been among them . . . You must speak My words to them."[1]

"I am compelled to preach. Woe to me if I do not preach the Gospel."[2]

"Now prophecy all these words against them and say to them: 'The Lord will roar from on high; He will lift His voice from His holy dwelling and roar mightily against His land. . . He will bring judgment on all mankind and put the wicked to the sword,' declares the Lord . . . Look! Disaster is spreading from nation to nation."[3]

And we as Christians today, what are we saying? We are saying that we want reformation and we want revival, but still we are not preaching down into this generation, stating the negative things that are necessary. If there is to be a constructive revolution in the orthodox, evangelical church, then like Jeremiah we must speak of the judgment of individual men great and small, of the church, the state, and the culture, for they have known the truth of God and have turned away from Him and His propositional revelation. God exists, He is holy, and we must know that there will be a judgment. And like Jeremiah we must keep on so speaking regardless of the cost to ourselves."[4]

—FRANCIS SCHAEFFER, ON WHAT
IS NEEDED IN OUR MESSAGE TODAY

I yearn to hear a voice that declares God's judgment on the godlessness he sees around him. Where is the denominational leader who has the Gospel boiling in his veins as Jeremiah did in Chapter 20? Many of our preachers seem incapable of being volcanic. Many sermons have become religious entertainment and move no one to tears of repentance.

"The true prophet of God is not concerned first of all about the nation or even about the Church. He is concerned that God is insulted openly."[5]

—LEONARD RAVENHILL,
ON GREAT PASSION NEEDED
IN PREACHERS TODAY

Gentlemen, there is one matter to settle before I take this position. Do you want my head of my feet? You can have one or the other, not both. I can run around doing this and that and drinking tea, if you wish me to; but don't expect me to bring you something that will shake this city."6

—ALEXANDER MACLAREN,
TO A CHURCH'S DEACONS
BEFORE HE BECAME PASTOR

Repent is the prophetic word . . . God's just and righteous character is the keynote to which society must be tuned, and principles of justice in His kingdom are the notes on the score which society must play . . . Measuring human sin and social injustice against the character of God and the principles of His kingdom, a prophet is compelled to tell the truth and cry, 'Repent'. . . The sad truth is that Christian are not prone to call themselves to repentance . . . Old Testament prophets invariably called the people of Israel to repent of their sins before they could claim the promise of God to change the pagan world. The truth still stands."7

—DAVID MCKENNA,
ON THE PROPHETIC MESSAGE TODAY

PART FOUR ENDNOTES

[1] From Ezekiel 2:4-7.

[2] I Corinthians 9:16.

[3] From Jeremiah 25:30-32.

[4] Francis Schaeffer, *Death in the City*, (Downers Grove, IL: InterVarsity Press, 1969), p.76.

[5] Leonard Ravenhill, in *America Is Too Young To Die*.

[6] Alexander Maclaren, quoted by Leonard Ravenhill in *America Is Too Young To Die*.

[7] David McKenna, *A Pure Note Above the Noise*, in United Evangelical Action, Winter, 1982.

11

"OH"

"Oh Lord, hear me as I pray; pay attention to my groaning. Listen to my cry for help, my King and my God . . . Oh God, You take no pleasure in wickedness; You cannot tolerate the slightest sin."[1]

—DAVID, PRAYING PASSIONATELY

"Oh that Thou wouldst the heavens rend / In majesty come down / Stretch out Thine arm omnipotent / And seize us for Thine own."

—CHARLES WESLEY

WHEN WE LOOK OUT AT OUR SOCIETY'S BOLD SINNING coupled with its indifference and even hostility towards God's gracious calls to return to Him, what should be our response? Retreat? Fear? Panic? Nonchalance? Resignation?

No! Never! When the great prophet Isaiah looked out at his world, a world not unlike ours, he urgently cried to God, "OH." *"Oh, that You would rend the heavens and come down, that the mountains would tremble before You"* (64:1). Martyn Lloyd-Jones said of Isaiah's "Oh," "I would remind you again that true praying is always characterized by the use of that word, 'Oh.' 'Oh that thou wouldest rend the heavens.' There is no word that is more expressive of longing than that word. It expresses the thirst of deep desire, it is the cry of a man at the end of his resources and waiting and looking for, and longing for, God."[2]

Isaiah's "Oh" is a groan of grief over a nation's sins and its rebellion against God. His "Oh" epitomizes his whole anguished intercessory prayer found from 63:7 through to the end of chapter 64, a prayer that is fervid and agonizing. It moves from pleading to confessing and back to pleading and again to confessing, all streaming from the depths of Isaiah's soul because he is so stirred by how acutely his nation needs God.

In the face of America's sin, may Isaiah's intense "Oh" pour from our hearts today on behalf of our beloved nation, our communities, and our churches. May "Oh" saturate our prayers, prayers in the pulpit, prayers in prayer meetings, prayers in home meetings, prayers for one another, prayers of spiritual warfare, even prayers of grace before we eat. *Let "Oh" be the roar of intercessory prayer!* Let it birth revival.

In 63:15, Isaiah fervently beseeched God to "look down from heaven." He wants God to "see from [His] lofty throne, holy and glorious." *Isaiah wanted the face of God.* No doubt Isaiah knew Deuteronomy 31:16-18 where God says what will happen should Israel "prostitute" herself to "foreign gods." "I will hide my face from them and they will be destroyed. Many disasters and difficulties will come upon them . . . I will certainly hide my face on that day because of their wickedness in turning to other gods."

The nation vainly imagined it could get along without God, but Isaiah knew that not having the gracious face of God—His smile, His approval—was the worst of tragedies for any nation, or any individual. It is the maximum catastrophe, the utmost calamity. So Isaiah urgently implored the Lord to turn His face back toward them, to "look down."

Then in 64:1, Isaiah cries "Oh" to the Lord to split the skies and *"come down." Oh, how he wanted the presence of God!* He knew there was nothing—*nothing*—as magnificent and powerful—and needed—as the holy presence of the Lord. When God is present "mountains tremble"—immovable obstacles are no match for Him. When God "comes down" it is like "fire [setting] twigs ablaze" which "causes water to boil"; and God's Name is made known to His enemies and the nations quake before Him.

Isaiah could not live without the presence of God. God is not expendable! And Isaiah knew the nation could not survive without God's presence.

So Isaiah's fervent "Oh" came from his consuming understanding that revival *is* the presence of God with His people! It is in the Lord's glorious presence where the beauty of His holiness, the radiance of His love, and the wonder of His grace and mercy are displayed in their splendor. It is in the Lord's righteous presence where every hindrance is leveled, every hostile enemy is defeated, every chosen lie is exposed, every boldly sinning rebel is revealed, where the weight and foulness of sin is discerned, and the terror of judgment is comprehended.

So, it is no wonder Isaiah cried "Oh" for the Lord to "come down." Such passionate prayer is missing from professional Christians, professional preachers, and certainly false prophets. But is essential in true spiritual warfare.

May our churches and we in ministry cry for the awesome awareness of God's presence and glory in our meetings. May we yearn for it, obtain it, maintain it, and absolutely depend upon it. It makes little sense for us to rail at the world about their sins unless the presence of God is in our midst. In His presence is the power of conviction, and therein lies the only hope for change. In His presence is revival—His presence *is* revival!

"Oh" is at the center of that grand text on prayer from James, "The effectual, fervent prayer of a righteous man availeth much."[3] It is the fervency of "Oh" in a righteous man's or woman's prayer which makes it so effective and "avail much." Just as He does with preaching, God, who could work without us, has wonderfully designed to work through us.

FERVENCY FIRST A CONVICTION

Right here is where many of us get intimidated about praying. We presume we are not fervent. We equate fervency with praying a long time with emotional vigor. But *fervency and urgency are primarily a matter of conviction*. a conviction that God is our only hope, and He answers our prayers. "This is the assurance we have in approaching God," John affirms, "that if we ask anything according to His will, He hears us. And if we know that He hear us—whatever we ask—we know that we have what we asked of Him."[4] And Jesus said, "My Father will give you whatever you ask in My name. Until now you have not asked for anything in My name. Ask and you will receive, and your joy will be complete.."[5]

Fervency reflects an assurance, a certainty of the truth of these promises. Although fervency, quite expectably, might at times result in extended and intense prayer or even travail, these do not define it. Jesus travailed in the Garden of Gethsemane for us; we so rejoice that He did. But His other prayers, such as those for the sick and demon-possessed, were prayed differently. In all there was fervency.

But still many struggle over the length of their praying and its intensity, feeling they do not measure up in prayer with some of the men and women in the Bible or some "super-prayers" today. So they get down on themselves, feeling themselves to be so ordinary in prayer, and even sub-standard, that well, they just aren't effective, and tend not to pray.

PRAYER TIME OR PRAYER LIFE

Perhaps they confuse a prayer time with a prayer life. It is to a *prayer life* that God is calling us. A prayer time may be a part of a prayer life, but a prayer time is not necessarily a prayer life. This is what I had to learn. When I was 15 years old, having been a Christian for three years, I began trying to pray. I was at a point where I was concerned about the up and down, roller coaster, way my spiritual life was going. I wanted it to be more steady, and more consistent. I remembered what ministers said about our need as Christians to pray. So, although I had no instruction about what I should do, just an inner conviction, I thought I would spend five minutes a day in prayer. So I knelt at my bed, eyed the big hand on my wind-up clock on the bed stand to calculate five minutes, and started to pray. For about 30 seconds I roamed in prayer for the missionaries, for the pastor, and for immediate family members. Then my thoughts went to school activities, to sports, whatever. Some minutes later my mind suddenly jolted, "Oh, no! I am supposed to be praying." So I took 30 seconds off my five minutes and started again, doing virtually the same as I had just done: praying randomly about this or that, allowing my mind to wander, suddenly "waking up," reproaching myself, taking some time off the five minutes, and starting again. I continued this herky-jerky "praying" so that my five minutes took me about an hour.

Each day it was the same. I tried to pray five minutes, but would end up taking twelve times that long. A couple weeks later I even increased my basic time to ten minutes, and that would take an hour and a half or more.

As this continued, I came to hate praying. I detested it, to put it mildly. But I was afraid to quit because I had said I would pray, and the thought of quitting brought overwhelming condemnation and a sense of devastating failure to my soul. So I plodded on. I was like a man with an excruciating headache who knows he needs his head; but it hurts unbearably to keep it.

Finally, in a moment of great despair, I cried out with an anguished "Oh." "Lord, if I am going to pray, *help me to want to!*" I am still stunned and awed by the Lord's gracious answer to that prayer. Within a short time, just a few days if memory is right, I was wanting to pray. And in just a short time, my basic time was up to an hour a day (and by then included reading the Word). And *the hour took an hour.* It was divided into three 20-minute segments: before school, during lunch hour (I lived only a block from my high school), and before going to bed.

I do not pray that way now. Now prayer has evolved. But I learned that the Lord is calling us to a prayer *life*, not just a prayer time. What if a husband and wife's relationship was only "married time," when each day for 30 minutes they met at the kitchen table to talk? And then what if they said goodbye and parted, not seeing each other or communicating until "married time" the next day? Absurd. Husbands and wives are to be in a married *life* 24 hours a day. The same for prayer. It's a life, a life growing and knowing the Lord—His Word and His heart.

PRAYER IS A NAME FOR KNOWING THE LORD

Prayer is a name we give for knowing the Lord! It is a relationship, around-the-clock communion with our beautiful Lord, living before Him continually, or as some used to say, "Coram Deo" (before the face of God). Prayer flows naturally from that grand ambition of "loving God with all our heart, soul and mind."[6] As we have seen, King David exclaimed, "My soul thirsts for God, for the living God. When can I go and meet with God?"[7] And Paul cried, "I want to know Christ."[8] A prayer life issues from such desire.

In a prayer life we can be at our employment and do our work excellently with focused attention; and all the while, carry the heart of prayer. Or we can be at home, driving the car, in the mall, visiting friends, on vacation, on a walk, fishing, or in bed—wherever life takes us (we can even be in church), and we can be before the Lord in the spirit of prayer. We will have a "time" of prayer or devotions, but that will be only a segment in the *life* of prayer lived continuously with the Lord.

As we live in a prayer life, some of our greatest intercession may be five to ten seconds at a time. It need not be out loud if, for example, it is when we are at work or in a supermarket. But coming from the heart, such intercession will not lack fervency, intensity, or travail. It will not lack "Oh." *And God will answer!*

As we live a prayer life, we'll find ourselves gripped by special prayer needs for our family, our church or parish, our pastors and others in congregational leadership, our community, and our nation. We'll carry such concerns—an inner travail—perhaps for days, weeks, months, or even years, interceding for them again and again and again wherever we are. We'll fast. And there may be extended, intensive times of intercession. It's part of a prayer *life! And God will answer!*

A prayer life is for "ordinary" believers. Our Lord wants us, regular members of His family, to understand the blessedness, beauty, and power of knowing Him in a life of prayer. Prayer is not to be made mysterious. It is not to overwhelm us. It is not something that only spiritual superstars do. No, prayer is a name for knowing the Lord. We say with Elijah, "As the Lord, the God of Israel, lives, *before Whom I stand,*"[9] meaning the God before whom I live, the One I worship and serve. And speaking of Elijah, the Apostle James uses that notable prophet as an example of an ordinary person praying. He describes Elijah as "a man just like us."[10] He describes his fervent prayer as availing much.[11] Elijah prayed it would not rain in Israel and it didn't for 3 1/2 years; then he prayed it would rain, and it did.[12]

We should remember that just a short while before he prayed for rain, Elijah prayed for fire to fall on a sacrifice, a prayer that takes about twenty seconds, and the fire fell. That occurred during that momentous confrontation with the prophets of Baal on Mount Carmel.

BELIEVERS' POWERFUL POSITION IN PRAYER

The powerful position of ordinary believers in prayer is driven home in Ezekiel 22. This chapter summarizes the flagrant sins of Jerusalem to demonstrate why the city faced judgment. One kind of sin is mentioned seven times in just the first 13 verses. Here are excerpts from those verses—*which sin is mentioned the seven times?* "Son of man, will you judge her? Will you judge this city of bloodshed? Then confront her with her detestable practices . . . O city that brings on herself doom by shedding blood in her midst and defiles herself by making idols, you have become guilty because of the blood you have shed and have become defiled by the idols you have made. You have brought your days to a close, and the end of your years has come . . . . See how each of the princes of Israel who are in you uses his power to shed blood . . . . In you are slanderous men bent men bent on shedding blood . . . . In you men accept bribes to shed blood . . . . I will surely strike my hands together at the unjust gain you have made and at the blood you have shed in your midst."

What was the sin repeated seven times?

Shedding blood. Bloodshed. The nation had become violent. The repetition of the sin being practiced in multiple ways is to demonstrate how rampant bloodshed had become and how it was "breaking all bounds with bloodshed following bloodshed," to again use Hosea's language.[13]

Judgment loomed because the city was indifferent to such violence. There was no shame, no outrage, and certainly no repentance.

Two chapters later God says, "Woe to the city of bloodshed;" "For the blood she shed is in her midst;" "Woe to the city of bloodshed!"[14] And earlier, in Chapter 16, verse 21, "You slaughtered my children and sacrificed them to the idols." "Because you gave them your children's blood . . .I will sentence you to the punishment of women who commit adultery and who shed blood. I will bring upon you the blood vengeance of my wrath and jealous anger" (verses 36 and 38). And in Chapter 20, "When you offer your gifts—the sacrifice of your sons in the fire—you continue to defile yourselves with all your idols to this day"(verse 31).

The city was awash in blood, brutality, barbarity.

And was unrepentant.

But there was another rampant evil: immorality. Immorality, like bloodshed, had reached a defining level, revealing how seared Jerusalem's conscience had become and how full her cup of iniquity was. God laid open a particularly abhorrent form of immorality which men in Jerusalem were nonchalantly practicing. It is found in the discreet language of the first phrase of verse 10: *"In you are those who dishonor their fathers' bed."* Or "In you men sleep with their fathers' wives" (NLT). Men were having sex with wives of their fathers.

Now a father might have more than one wife, so the reference does not necessarily mean that sons were committing immorality with their own mothers, an unspeakably revolting indecency. *However, a son having sex with a wife of his father carried the same level of appalling, sickening repugnance as if he had done so with his mother!* Or at least it should have carried the same repugnance. But not in Jerusalem. Apparently immorality had become so debauched and so casual that men easily debased themselves with wives of their fathers. The indifferent, untroubled indulgence of men in such unmentionable depravity reveals how corrupted Jerusalem's standards had become.

Other odious licentiousness furthers the case: "In you one man commits a detestable offense with his neighbor's wife, another shamelessly defiles his daughter-in-law, and another violates his sister, his own father's daughter." (verse 11)

Jerusalem's violence and gross lewdness revealed how comprehensively sin had lost its gravity and judgment its terror. Their cup of iniquity was full as the Lord cried "Oh." "Oh city that brings doom on herself . . ." (verse 3) "You have brought your days to a close" (verse 4)

But it gets worse! Both the political and the spiritual leadership of the city were abetters of the sins. God said that Jerusalem's princes were "like roaring lions . . . they devour[ed] people . . . and [made] many widows within her." (verse 25) Her officials were "like wolves . . . they shed blood and kill[ed] people to make unjust gain." (verse 27)

He said that the priests did violence to God's law and were indifferent about holiness and the standards between the clean and the unclean. (verse 26)

God said the prophets whitewashed the city's outrageous sins, likening their misleading message to "repair[ing] cracked walls with whitewash." What these prophets did was use their prophetic ministry, no doubt a self-anointed prophetic ministry, to announce so-called words from the Lord to the people. "'This is what the Sovereign Lord says,' when the Lord has not spoken." (verse 27).

Now these prophets might have been quite sincere in saying the Lord was speaking, but sincerity doesn't insulate us from error. Indeed we can be quite sincere and still "see false visions." Sincere or not, a false message is still "untempered mortar" or whitewash!

What God was saying was that if they were true prophets—if indeed He was speaking through them—then they would have named Jerusalem's sins and warned the city of judgment just as the true prophet Ezekiel did throughout Chapter 22 and elsewhere. Naming sin and warning of judgment are not the only ingredients in Ezekiel's message, as any study of his book will show, but they were an essential part of it. The same is true for other genuine prophets such as Isaiah, Jeremiah, Amos, Hosea, etc.

By omitting sin and judgment while the proud city was deeply into bloodshed and immorality, the unfaithful prophets, sincere or not, whitewashed those evils. Inexcusable!

GOD'S JUDGMENT ON FALSE PREACHERS

Ezekiel 13 is God's judgment on false preachers. It is withering. He calls them "jackals among ruins" (verse 4) God was against (verse 8) these prophets of whitewash who misled the people with pretensions to prophecy—sunny messages filled with promises of prosperity but with no mention of sin and certain judgment. God declared, "They lead my people astray, saying 'Peace,' when there is no peace," (verse 10). John Wesley said the message of false preachers "suggests to sinners that which tends to lessen their dread of sin, or their fear of God." Wesley called them "the most dangerous seducers."[15]

What had happened in Jerusalem was that they had reached a point of ultimate peril. They were flagrantly, yet complacently, sinning. Their civil authorities also were doing so. Their cup of iniquity was ready to overflow. Their judgment was looming. And all the while, their priests and prophets were giving a sugarcoated message.

What about America? Are there parallels?

Bloodshed? Certainly we are awash in violence, epitomized by killing our unborn children.

And like Jerusalem, our collective conscience is seared. Killing our unborn children, our own flesh and blood, and the most defenseless members of our society has been reduced to an issue, a political football, a choice where the politically correct position is neutrality—sitting on the fence. To us as a nation, bloodshed is not horrendous, not sickening, and does not grieve us. There is no shock. We are not appalled. We are not scandalized. And we could not imagine repenting for it. Plus we get combative when told that our officially sanctioned bloodshed is a society-ending sin, a watershed iniquity that is writing "terminal" over us.

Many of our secular leaders are advocates for the "right" to kill our unborn children. While thankful for spiritual leaders who do speak up about this national sin, many in our pulpits will not say anything. Sadly, when it comes to national or community sin, they remain mute prophets.

Immorality? Is there any kind of degeneracy in America which carries the repugnance of a man having sex with the wife of his father? Or at least should? *What about teaching our children to sin?* By any account, that would more than match it. Brainwashing our children in the ways of evil is epidemic. Child pornography and child molestation are generally condemned, although we are hearing debates rationalizing sex between adults and children. But whether approved or not, these remain a national cancer. What about exposing our children to fornication, adultery and violence in movies, TV, music, sex education, and the Internet? Or the de facto pornography we show them in music videos? Or instructing them to use condoms? Or helping them have abortions without their parents' knowledge (a major sin for us)? Or dressing grade school girls in skimpy outfits, adorning them with make-up and adult hairdos, and having them dance provocatively to rock music as part of the entertainment for parents' night or for a beauty contest?

What about the huge abomination we are committing when we indoctrinate our children in school or elsewhere that homosexual practice is right and normal? Certainly we are seeing our brazenness to dump our children into Sodom's sewer by such things as visits by homosexuals and lesbians to classrooms to provide "diversity education," and by our widespread vilification of the Boy Scouts for not allowing homosexual Scout leaders. Plus at least one school board in a well known city has voted unanimously to hire a full-time advocate for homosexual and lesbian students in their school system.

Added to all this is how more and more our children are understanding how utilitarian has been our decisions to allow them to be born. We've taught them about abortion, it being their right and all. But now it is sinking in that they have "older" brothers or sisters who were pulled apart in the womb. And the only reason they're here is that they came along at a convenient time.

Many of their homes are broken. Their fathers are not around. Many of them are poor. And although some do live in nice places, Mom and Dad are not around a whole lot. A lot of them came of age when President Clinton then taught them that oral sex is not sex, so they and those younger are making that form of indecency their immorality of choice.

Too many of them have a lot of rage and are taking guns to school and shooting their classmates. Or shooting themselves. (Suicide now ranks as the second leading cause of death among teenagers—just behind car accidents.) Their rage is part of the rising rage around them; as Dorothy Anne Seese said, "School rage, along with road rage, soccer-mom rage, bar room rage, and sporting events rage is evidence that America has lost a lot of self-control. We have 'self' in everything else, but we lack self-control."[16]

Coupled with our indoctrination of our children into depravity, we have subverted their moral education. We've pulled down the Ten Commandments, taken prayer out of their schools, and generally sterilized their public environment of anything that is not secular. We're not teaching them the values embedded in the Declaration of Independence, the Pledge of Allegiance, the Constitution, our national motto "In God We Trust," or a host of other concepts fundamental to our nation.

We don't need to go on, although each of us might add to the list of how extensively we are teaching our children to sin. However, as we have seen, teaching our children to sin might not be so loathsome to us, but it is very abhorrent and repugnant to our Lord, who said, "Whoever causes one of these little ones who believe in Me to sin, it would be better for him if a millstone were hung around his neck, and he were drowned in the depths of the sea."[17]

We've got the millstone is around our necks. And the sea below.

However, the alarming part is, we're yawning, including many of us in the church and pulpit.

WHAT ARE WE TO DO?

So, what are we to do? So far in Ezekiel 22, our discussion has been pretty grim and dark. Can there be any good news? One response could be what we shared in the Prologue: We could look at our obviously sinning country and exclaim, "Judge it, Lord; bring down your fist on us; we deserve it." And we do deserve it. We might look over our shoulder toward our Lord, expecting to see His fist raised, poised to slam down on us. But what we might be surprised to see is, instead of His fist, see His open hand and arm outstretched. And then, looking beyond His open hand, see His face; and instead of the harsh lines of fierceness, we see tears, tears of compassion, tears of grief, tears that just might have an "Oh,"—"Oh, come back to Me!"

It is this attitude of compassion we find in Ezekiel 22. Did Jerusalem deserve judgment? Was God just in judging the city when He finally did? Of course. Do we deserve judgment? Will God be just in judging us? Without question.

But in Ezekiel 22, do we find God rushing to judgment, fist raised, looking for ways to bring down the city's sins on its head? Not at all. What we find is God looking for something else. We find Him looking for someone—anyone—to do something very important. "So I sought for a man among them who would make a wall, and stand in the gap before Me on behalf of the land, that I should not destroy it; but I found none."[18]

The Lord was looking for an intercessor.

The gap in the wall is drawn from the imagery of a city wall broken through by an invading army, where immediately troops go to defend. The Lord is looking for someone to go to the gap in intercession on behalf of the land. There, they stand before the Lord and His judgment. They stand there in prayer—prayer that avails much.

Abraham was such an intercessor who pleaded with God to spare wicked Sodom. He asked the Lord if He would spare the city for 50 righteous, then 45, then 40, all the way down to 10. Each time the Lord answered He would.

Moses was such an intercessor, "Therefore He [God] said that He would destroy them, had not Moses His chosen one stood before Him in the breach, to turn away His wrath, lest He destroy them."[19]

Amos, who heard God's roar, was such an intercessor. He saw two visions of coming judgment: one of locusts and the other of fire. Both would devastate the land. But Amos stood before the Lord and intensely cried, "Oh." "Oh Lord God forgive, I pray! Oh, that Jacob may stand, for he is so small." The judgments were stopped. "So the Lord relented concerning this. 'It shall not be,' said the Lord."[20]

Daniel was such an intercessor who "set [his] face toward the Lord God to make request by prayer and supplication, with fasting, sackcloth and ashes." Again and again Daniel repented for Israel, "Oh Lord our God. . .we have sinned." And he passionately cried, "Oh Lord, hear! Oh Lord, forgive! Oh Lord, listen and act! Do no delay for Your own sake, my God, for Your city and Your people are called by Your name."[21]

Jesus our Lord was the great intercessor, whose agonizing in Gethsemane caused Him to sweat blood. He cried "Oh"—"Oh My Father, if it is possible, let this cup pass from Me; nevertheless, not as I will, but as You will."[22] Jesus is still making intercession for us (see Hebrews 7:25, 9:24 and I John 2:1-2).

Such intercessors are who our Lord is looking for in America— and in every nation of the West! Intercessors who take that pivotal position in the gap. Intercessors who who know the privilege and the power of a prayer life. Intercessors who understand they can lift their fervent petitions at all times, and do, because they know that God hears their prayers. Intercessors like Moses and Amos who know that the broken wall, the gap, means that judgment is certain unless someone stands in that gap before the Lord. Intercessors who are grieved over their society's sins, and who, like Daniel, repent for their nation and name its sins in contrition. Intercessors who, as John Wesley said, "Interpose between a sinful people, and their offended God, and entreat for mercy." Intercessors who, in the place of God's judgment, cry to the gracious Lord, like Isaiah, for His presence, "Oh, that You would rend the heavens! That You would come down!"

May the roar of "Oh" in intercessory prayer be heard across our nation, from my house to your house to the White House. Let it rise in the Congress and in every congregation. Let it be humble and repentant and passionate.

We face certain judgment. We are under judgment. We need a national prayer meeting. We need a national sacred assembly like Abraham Lincoln called. We need solemn assemblies in cities, towns and villages. We need the Church to lead the way.

John Knox, the Scottish reformer prayed, *"Oh God, give me Scotland or I die!"*

From our pulpits to our public squares, may God give America and the West a host of men and women with the heart of John Knox. May his passion burn in our prayers.

With our judgment on the horizon, we must not—we dare not—misuse this "window of mercy" God has given us!

With the urgency of "Oh," may we seek Him.

Let us pray together: Oh Lord, when we look at the egregious sin of our nation, we weep. You have abundantly blessed us, yet we are pushing You aside while we push on into our evils. We deserve judgment. We are under judgment. The only reason we remain a nation is because of Your mercy. We see Your gracious hand outstretched toward us, and hear You calling us to return to You. Oh Lord we do return. We are grieved for our enormous sins. Forgive us. And Oh Lord, come down among us. We so want you in our midst because Your gracious presence brings life—revival! In the blessed Name of Your Son, and our Savior and Lord, Amen.

CHAPTER 11 ENDNOTES

[1] Psalm 5:1, 2, 4.

[2] D. Martyn Lloyd-Jones, *Revival, Can We Make It Happen?* (Great Britain: Marshall Pickering, 1986), pp 304-305.

[3] From James 5:16 (KJV).

[4] I John 5:14-15.

[5] John 16:23-24.

[6] Matthew 22:37.

[7] Psalm 42:2.

[8] Philippians 3:10.

[9] I Kings 17:1.

[10] James 5:17.

[11]12. James 5:16c.

[12] James 5:17-18.

[13] Hosea 4:2.

[14] Ezekiel 24:6,7,9.

[15] John Wesley's *Notes on the Bible, Ezekiel 13:10.*

[16] Dorothy Anne Seese, in her column March 6, 2001, after a school shooting in Santee, CA, the day before which left two dead and 13 wounded.

[17] Matthew 18:6.

[18] Ezekiel 22:30.

[19] Psalm 106:23

[20] Amos 7:1-6.

[21] See Daniel 9:3-19.

[22] Matthew 26:39.

12

GRAVITY AND TERROR

*"The outcry against Sodom and Gomorrah is great, and
. . . their sin is very grave."*[1]

—GOD, SPEAKING TO ABRAHAM

*"You who now hear of hell and the wrath of the great God,
and sit hear easy and quiet, and go away so careless; by
and by will shake and tremble, and cry out, and gnash
your teeth, and will be thoroughly convinced of the vast
weight and importance of these things which you now
despise."*[2]

—JONATHAN EDWARDS,
SPEAKING ON EZEKIEL 22:14

IT WAS A MOMENT OF SOBERING DRAMA—AND A MOMENT OF
truth.

Comfortably camped east of the Jordan River in an area with a
lot of acacia trees, the men of Israel were enticed by the women of

Moab to come to the sacrifices to their Midianite gods, sacrifices that included the grossest of obscenities.[3] Soon the Israeli men were engaged in open revelry, an orgy of whoring, riotous feasting and worship all in honor of the god Baal-Peor. They were "joined to" this god, which made Israel guilty of both physical and spiritual whoredom.

Israel's blasphemous debauchery brought God's judgment, and a plague began. People began dying. God ordered that the ringleaders of the revelry at the idols of Baal-Peor be executed.

The withering judgment so jolted the people that they gathered at the entrance of the Tabernacle where they began to weep "over the divine judgment and the punishment,"[4] prompting Matthew Henry to say "they were sanctifying a fast in a solemn assembly, weeping between the porch and the altar, to turn away the wrath of God"[5] from them.

The gravity of sin and the terror of judgment gripped them.

And then it happened. While the awful plague was going on and the people wept, a man and his lover of the moment strode brashly into the camp. They were Zimri, son of a leader in the tribe of Simeon, and Cozbi, daughter of a leader in Midian. The two paraded boldly right in front Moses and the weeping people, right past the Tabernacle, the house of God, and on into a tent for another tryst.

It could not have been more shocking. One who saw it was Phinehas, son of Eleazar the High Priest, and grandson of Aaron. Phinehas jumped up and went and found a spear. Then he rushed to the tent, burst in, and, catching the adulterers in the act, with a mighty thrust drove "the spear through the man's body and into the stomach of the woman." As the Knox Translation puts it, "And [Phinehas] followed this Israelite into the place of shame; man and woman both he pierced through, groin to groin." The plague stopped, although 24,000 had died.

"Because he was zealous for his God," God commended Phinehas. "He was as zealous as I am for My honor." God said that Phinehas' spontaneous action had "made atonement for the children of Israel."

To gain perspective on Phinehas' commendation, imagine the response of a father who comes home and finds a large man in the act of raping his ten-year-old daughter. In his shock and in desperation to save his daughter from the brutal assault, the father grabs a knife and stabs the man to death. Wouldn't the father's strong action be expected? Even necessary?

Most people would probably commend the father. Well, consider that thousands in Israel were dying in a plague while others were being executed in judgment for their appalling, brazen depravity. People were gathered, sobbing in anguish over their sin and the punishment. Then amidst this, a man and woman in full view of all, swagger to a tent to indulge in more indecency.

It seems that at that instant Phinehas saw arrogant, presumptuous sin as God saw it and hated it as God hated it; and he acted in holy indignation. For us, Phinehas example is not to plunge spears into wicked people, but to desire to see as God sees and be impelled to humbly but firmly stand and take action, even alone, against whatever is compromised, worldly, and vile.

The enemy of such zeal is tolerance—tolerance of sin. To be tolerant of immense and shameless sin shows a heart far from right towards God. May the holy zeal of Phinehas rise again in the Body of Christ!

WHY ZIMRI AND COZBI'S SIN WAS SEEN AS REVOLTING

Zimri and Cozbi's open lewdness was revolting not just because it was worse than numberless other such acts that had taken place (and probably were still taking place) in that wicked time; *it was revolting because it occurred at a moment when its shamelessness, naked vileness, and bold insolence could be clearly seen. Their sin was intensified by its stark contrast with the penitential sorrow and plague all around them.*

It was this glaring contrast which made the gravity of their sin plain to see!

Ananias and Sapphira had the same presumptuousness.[6] And their "lying to the Holy Ghost" amidst the powerful revival that began on the Day of Pentecost set their sin in contrast with the holy atmosphere that permeated the Church. The sword of God fell on them.

Sadly, surrounded as we are by so much sin, we get acclimated and indifferent to it, even comfortable with it. We get to the point where we do not look at sin—your sin or my sin—as heinous, detestable or filthy. Undeniably most of us do not view pride as depravity or vileness. And certainly most of us, including those of us in the Church, do not view the massive killing of our own flesh and blood in the womb as a ghastly, homicidal atrocity. It just doesn't register that when we take unborn human life whose only impediment is that he or she is still in the womb, and dice it up, suction it into a bag and throw it away like so much toilet tissue, that this is a judgment-bringing crime of bloodshed.

Dr. Carl F.H. Henry believes our sin is bringing near our judgment. He writes, "I think we are now living in the very decade when God may thunder his awesome *paradidomai* (I abandon you or I give them up—Romans 1:24ff) over America's professed greatness. Our massacre of a million [unborn] a year; our deliberate flight from the monogamous family; our normalizing of fornication and of homosexuality and other sexual perversions; our programming of self-indulgence above social and familial concerns—all represent a quantum leap in moral deterioration . . . *Our nation has all but tripped the worst ratings on God's Richter scale of fully-deserved moral judgment.*"[7] (Italics added)

If "our nation has all but tripped the worst ratings on God's Richter scale of fully-deserved moral judgment," what will it take for us to be stirred by this grim fact? Will it take a "Zimri and Cozbi" event for us to be sobered for our sin and shaken by the certain horror of our looming judgment? Will it take, as we asked earlier, another 9/11, some other national tragedy, economic disintegration, war, terrorism, natural disasters, some unknown epidemic or scourge, massive electric power outages, or something unforeseen? Would these even stir us? Or, are we so determined to go our own way, so self-deluded with our chosen lies, so indifferent and complacent about judgment, and so hardened in our national sin that we simply will refuse to change and repent?

Are we are in a post-repentance time when we could repent, but we will not repent?

Certainly it is imperative that we in the Church and the pulpit speak—roar—of these issues. However, what if during that idolatrous time of revelry when Israel was licentiously frolicking at the idol of Baal-Peor and God's judgment was falling and people were dying with others being executed, instead of Moses and the people gathering at the entrance of the Tabernacle to weep in repentance over what was happening. Moses had called for a conference on success. What if he had been concerned with how to have your needs met or prosperity, or self-esteem, or some trendy prophetic fad then making the rounds? What if Moses had arranged for some big meeting "to get all the religious groups together"? Moses had a good record on seeing miracles happen: a Red Sea had opened, ten enormous plagues had decimated Egypt; water had come from rocks; his staff had turned to a snake and back to a staff. What if he had succumbed to the celebrity which such miracles could have commanded, and permitted hype about himself to capture the moment. What if he had allowed Joshua and other minions to use his celebrity to call people together to hear this "great man of God, Moses." What if the hype surrounding Moses had suggested to people that when they came, more miracles could well happen?

Ludicrous. Of course. It is unthinkable, even traitorous that anyone could or would have thought of engaging in such fanciful activity in Israel during those serious, dangerous days when they so grievously sinned at the idols of Baal-Peor. Any individual or group who would have been so superficial during that somber time would have had to be ranked with Zimri and Cozbi in indifference and perfidiousness.

Moses and the people did what they should have done, what the times demanded. They are an example to all of us. They gathered to weep and repent. They had a solemn assembly.

Assuredly today we in America and the Church are in a time not unlike Israel at Baal-Peor. We may not be seeing the plague Israel saw—yet. But we've seen other, perhaps lesser, remedial judgments, and we are clear that the fundamental reason we remain as a nation is only His mercy.

However, like Israel and a host of other nations, the anger of the Lord is roused against us. The weight of our sin is immense, and the fearfulness of our coming judgment is real. Is it not traitorous for us during such a time for us to be caught up in fads, hype, celebrity and psychobabble?

Martin Luther said, "If we profess with the loudest voice . . . every portion of the truth of God except precisely that little point which the world and the devil are at that moment attacking, I am not confessing Christ, however boldly I may be confessing Christ. Where the battle rages, there the loyalty of the soldier is proved, and [it] is mere flight and disgrace if he flinches at that point."

BIBLICAL PREACHING ALSO PAVES THE WAY FOR REVIVAL

As we saw in the previous chapter, intercessory prayer and the cry "Oh" for the Lord to come down among us paves the way for revival. When God wants to send revival, He will set us to praying.

But there is something else: biblical preaching—biblical preaching that become compassionate roar. *Such preaching could well become what God uses to pave the way—the catalyst—for the revival so many desire.*

But it is biblical preaching that includes the gravity of sin and the terror of judgment. These essential tenets are mostly lost in the Church and pulpit today. It is a catastrophic, ruinous loss which is reflected in our easy distraction with worldliness and materialism as well as with fads, hype and celebrity; and the loss of the respectful fear of God in both the culture and the Church.

Historically, when there has been anointed, forceful, biblical proclamation of sin, judgment and God's character (perhaps beginning with God's character), the effect has been believers sobered and grieved anew over their compromised, worldly lives. This is accompanied by humble, earnest repentance that wonderfully births fresh passion to know God and serve Him with love and joy. *Revival.*

In such an atmosphere, sinners are convicted by the enormity of their iniquity and the lostness of their souls. They come to Christ in repentance and faith for salvation. *Harvest!*

And, hopefully, the larger community and nation is jolted to remorse over the lies it has chosen to believe, its self-righteousness, arrogance, bold sinning, and judgment. Hopefully, they, too, repent and humbly return to God. *Spiritual awakening.*

So it can be said that *revival in the Church comes down to: 1) the fervent cry of its praying, 2) the biblical integrity of its preaching, and, 3) the godly character of its people.* To give principle substance to these three, understanding the tenets of three other things—sin, judgment and the character of God is vital.

This means that if we are serious about our commitment to the Word of God, and we truthfully want the anointing of the Holy Spirit, then we should not hesitate to use the language the Holy Spirit put in Scripture about sin, judgment, or the character of God.

The Holy Spirit anoints *His* Word! Can we say we are anointed by the Holy Spirit if we avoid speaking of sin and judgment, the grievous realities that sent Christ to Cross? *We do not understand grace and mercy and the depths of God's love until we understand these.*

Jesus said that when the Holy Spirit "has come, He will convict the world of sin, and of righteousness, and of judgment—of sin, because they do not believe in Me; of righteousness, because I go to My Father and you see Me no more; of judgment because the ruler of this world is judged." One thing the Lord is saying to His Church and His preachers is, *Clean up your message!*

The Holy Spirit uses forcible language in Scripture to impress us with the gravity of sin and the terror of judgment. Romans 3:13-18, using excerpts from the Old Testament, describes sin: *"Their talk is foul, like the stench from an open grave. Their speech is filled with lies. The poison of a deadly snake drips from their lips. Their mouths are full of cursing and bitterness. They are quick to commit murder [or 'to shed blood' as another translation says]. Wherever they go, destruction and misery follow them. They do not know what true peace is. They have no fear of God to restrain them."* (NLT) Can we picture an open grave, with its rotting body and its stench? Or snake poison dripping, oozing, from someone's lips?

About sexual immorality, the Holy Spirit says in Romans 1:24, "They did vile and degrading things with each other's bodies." (NLT) Eugene Peterson's *The Message* translates this verse, "It wasn't long before they were living in a pigpen, smeared with filth, filthy inside and out." An analogy for fornication, adultery and homosexual practice could be two people rolling around in a barn-yard smearing each other with the droppings.

II Peter 2:22, quoting Proverbs 26:11, describes going back into sin as, "A dog return[ing] to his own vomit." About bloodshed, it "pollutes the land." (Numbers 35:33)

Concerning judgment, the Holy Spirit uses graphic words and phrases like "fire," "wrath," "anger," "cast out," "darkness," "weeping and gnashing of teeth," to describe its terror. And He shows us wrenching scenes of terror-filled people, as in Revelation 6:15-17: "Then the kings of the earth, the rulers [including presidents, governors, senators, congressmen, etc], the generals, the wealthy people, the people with great power, and every slave and every free person—all hid themselves in the caves and among the rocks of the mountains. And they cried to the mountains and the rocks, 'Fall on us and hide us from the faces of the One who sits on the throne and from the wrath of the Lamb. For the great day of their wrath has come, and who will be able to survive?'" And in Luke 16:19-31, the rich man in hell is in "torment" and "agony" in the "flame."

Let's remember that any human metaphor, no matter how shocking or graphic, still does not illustrate adequately what it is describing. Thus, *stench, poison, defilement, vomit* to describe sin; or *fire, wrath, cast out, darkness, bringing about weeping and gnashing of teeth* to speak of judgment, while gripping metaphors, do not completely depict them. The stark, absolute realities of sin and judgment are worse yet . . . infinitely worse.

Much of our church talk includes "love." But love, God's love certainly—the love of Romans 5:8 or John 3:16, cannot be understood unless we understand the gravity of our sin and the complete terror our judgment for sin will be. The same must be said about mercy which cannot be comprehended, and certainly not appreciated, unless justice is also grasped. Or grace, which cannot be understood until we also know the law.

Right here the objection will rise: "But we don't need 'fire and brimstone preaching' on sin and judgment. That was for another time. All it did was breed legalism and bondage. This is now. People have different expectations and they won't come for that kind of preaching."

Well, shame on us if our message is dictated by the "expectations" of the crowd. That's preaching to tickle ears and a selling out of the integrity of ministry. However, it is precisely "fire and brimstone preaching" that we do need. We do not need to be afraid of it.

But it must be *"fire and brimstone preaching"* *with tears, with grief, with* *compassion, with "Oh" saturating it.* That's the kind that will stab into the heart of our hearers.

That's the kind that will roar in our barbarian Sodom—and birth *revival!*

Granted there may have been some "fire and brimstone preaching" in the past which came out of harsh hearts and severe attitudes and did produce legalism and bondage. That was wrong, absolutely so. However, we must not throw out the proverbial baby with the bath water. For if their notably harsh preaching produced legalism and bondage; our notably un-harsh preaching is producing lukewarmness and worldliness. And ours is equally wrong, and absolutely so.

The tenets of sin and judgment must be clearly and definitively proclaimed with brokenness, tears, and deep love for those to whom we are speaking to, accompanied by the command of God to repent. This means we must know the character of God.

JUDGMENT BEGINS IN THE HOUSE OF GOD

Most of us probably realize that God's judgments begin with His people, "For the time has come for judgment to begin at the house of God."[8] Such judgment, or chastening, or discipline, is to produce character—"the peaceable fruit of righteousness."[9] The producing of character will always be a fruit of genuine revival. In fact, real revival will have aspects of judgment or discipline to bring believers to humble repentance of sin. It will not move from having a purifying effect on character. Any alleged revival which does not have this character-building aspect is, at best, suspect.

In Ezekiel 8 to 11, God gave Ezekiel a sobering vision of judgment in the house of God. It was a vision in which God revealed the hidden idolatry being practiced by the seventy elders, and by women and men. The consequence was a dreadful judgment in which compromised people were ordered killed and the glory of God departed.

God first showed Ezekiel the shocking, secret "wicked and detestable things" the seventy elders were doing "in the darkness, each at the shrine of his own idol."—*in the house of the Lord.* Self-deception marks them, "The Lord does not see us; the Lord has forsaken the land."[10] The audacity, arrogance and disrespect for God shown by these elders, who were supposed to be the spiritual leaders of the nation, ranked with that of Zimri and Cozbi and the men of Israel at the idols of Baal-Peor.

Likewise, the brazen idolatry of women scorned God, "mourning for Tammuz" *in the house of the Lord;* and the idolatry of about 25 men who were worshiping the sun *in the house of the Lord.*[11]

Before God allowed the judgment to proceed, He had one group protected from the slaughter, "*those who grieve and lament over all the detestable things that are done.*"[12] These were those who prayed with that anguished "Oh" over the sin in their nation. "Slaughter old men, young men and maidens, women and children," God ordered, "*but do not touch anyone who has the mark.*"[13]

God commanded the fierce judgment to begin at His sanctuary, "So they began with the elders who were in front of the temple." As the massacre unfolded in his vision, a deep "Oh" poured out of Ezekiel as he fell "face down, crying out, "Ah, Sovereign Lord! Are You going to destroy the entire remnant of Israel in this outpouring of Your wrath on Jerusalem?"[14]

God answered, "The sin of the house of Israel and Judah is exceedingly great; the land is full of bloodshed and the city is full of injustice"—*suggesting a cause-effect relationship between the secret idolatry in the house of God and the massive bloodshed out in the nation!*

How might such a cause-effect connection be made? We are "the salt of the earth," Jesus said, indicating the preserving, beneficial effect of true believers on their larger culture. Their "salty" presence restrains evil. However, idolatrous leaders or laymen in the house of God are salt that has lost its savor, worthless in inhibiting evil. By not restraining evil, they, in effect, advance and encourage it. There's no zeal of Phinehas. So, because of "saltless," idolatrous leaders and people in the Temple, out in Jerusalem there was unrestrained bloodshed—bloodshed that has "broken all bounds."[15]

The execution of the "saltless" hypocrites in the house of God was an equity, a justice. Bloodshed fell on the aiders of bloodshed!

What if today the Lord exposed the hidden idolatry in His Church starting with the "elders," us in ministry and those on church boards or in eldership? What if He laid bare how ego-driven we are; how other goals such as growing a church have replaced that grand ambition to love the Lord, how success in ministry supercedes growing in Him, how we have pragmatically learned to use methods to bring in more people, but we're really backslidden in heart; how we overlook and excuse sin in ourselves and the congregation; and how we try to hide it by being captivated by the latest doctrinal fad? What kind of a sword might the Lord send on us?

It is estimated that one out of five of those in ministry are into pornography, particularly Internet pornography. What if that idol were uncovered by God for all to see?

What if the Lord exposed the women in the house of God who are idolaters? Variously their "Tammuz" could be materialistic success, fashion, position in the church and other superficial things. Idolatrous women have no passion after God, they find it easy to gossip; and, while they wouldn't think of looking at the pornography men look at, they can get quite caught up in afternoon soaps and salacious TV. One pastor's wife spoke admiringly of a highly rated one-hour TV sitcom she said she liked to watch: "It does have some bad words in it and sometimes there is immorality, but the story lines are wonderful."

And then what if the Lord revealed the men in His house who are idolaters, who get caught up in everything from work to sports and from pornography to church politics?

Whatever our idolatry, it is "detestable" to God, and audacious. In Ezekiel's vision, the judgment started "in the sanctuary"—and in the sanctuary, it began with the elders. God will *not permit in His Church what He will judge a world for!*

In repentance for our idolatry, may a humble "Oh" pour from our hearts—"Oh Lord, forgive us!"

THE CROSS: WHERE SIN'S GRAVITY AND JUDGMENT'S TERROR ARE SEEN

If we are hesitant to speak of sin and judgment in our message, then perhaps we should stop and take a long look again at a place where these issues are vividly and intensely displayed, a place that is integral to our Redemption. We should look at the Cross, the Cross of our Lord Jesus. And when we look at that Cross, and the difficult, eternal issues that were resolved there for us, we may find ourselves, in thanksgiving, impelled, like the Apostle Paul, to "resolve to know nothing. . .except Jesus Christ and Him crucified."[16]

It is at the Cross where we see the graphic revelation of the gravity of sin and the terror of judgment. These were the reason for the Son of God to go to that Cross and die there for us—our Salvation, our Atonement, our Propitiation for sin and judgment was wrapped up in what our Savior did.

Because the Cross of Christ is so absolutely central to our Redemption, and the issues settled there so critical to the integrity of our message, let us pause and re-visit what happened there: Let us follow Jesus in those hours along His trail of blood: It winds through three special places—Gethsemane, Gabbatha, and Golgotha. As we walk with Him, may we be sobered again—or for the first time—by the realization that what He did was only because our sin was so grave and judgment for it so eternally final. On that trail of blood, Christ bore our sin and judgment.

We start with our Lord in Gethsemane. Although He is with His disciples, He is really alone. In keen awareness of the awesomeness of humanity's burden upon Him, Jesus agonizes in prayer, His "soul overwhelmed with sorrow to the point of death."[17] He cries, "My Father, if it be possible, may this cup be taken from me."[18] This happened three times. His anguish built, His body strained beyond measure, so great that the capillaries burst in His sweat glands and blood oozed from His pores.

We can only surmise, but perhaps in His mind's eye there flashed before Jesus the faces of untold billions of souls, of you and me, and everyone throughout all time who would be redeemed through what He did. And all would perish forever if He didn't take the cup. The decision was made—not that Jesus hadn't known it before—and He said to the Father, "Yet not as I will, but as You will." Jesus took the cup, knowing full well the terrible road ahead. Never has a person been so alone, left with such responsibility.

He was arrested, and first taken before the high priest. Then the Sanhedrin. Then, to Pontius Pilate, to King Herod, and back to Pilate. Here was the second trail Marker — Gabbatha, the judgment hall of Pilate.

Unable to get Jesus released, Pilate relented to the riotous crowd and allowed Jesus to be crucified. But first he had Jesus scourged—a Roman scourging lived up to its nickname—"halfway death."

Jesus was stripped, His back exposed, and securely tied. Then a soldier took a flagellum, a short wooden handle with several long leather strips attached and in the end of each was fastened a piece of sharp iron, rock, or bone.

Jim Bishop, in his classic work 'The Day Christ Died,' paints a vivid picture of the event: "The soldier moved to a position about sex feet behind Jesus, spread his legs. The flagellum was brought all the way back and shifted forward and made a dull drum sound as the strips of leather smashed against the back of the rib cage. The bits of bone and chain curled against the right side of the body and raised small subcantaneous hemorrhage on the chest. A moan escaped the lips of Jesus and He almost collapsed. The knees bent, then, by effort, straightened.

"The soldiers murmured approval because they had seen others who passed into unconsciousness before the punishment was fairly underway. The flagellum came back again, aimed slightly lower, and it crashed against the skin and flesh. The lips of Jesus seemed to be moving in prayer. The flagellum now moved in slow heavy rhythm." (Harper Brothers, New York, 1957, P.291).

Thirty-nine times the scourge hit his bleeding, mutilated back. For most victims, the punishment would have stopped there. But Jesus was subjected to even more humiliation and torture as a crown of razor sharp thorns was pushed down upon His head. Then, He began the last segment of His journey—to Golgotha.

UNSEEN ENEMIES ARRAYED ON GOLGOTHA

Popular depictions of Golgotha have shown us the spectacle of crying and mocking people with Jesus surrounded by soldiers and priests. Yet beyond what could be seen visibly, there were others there on that hill, a most awesome array of enemies.

Sin was there. Not just sinful men, but sin itself. All the world's sin, my sin, your sin; ugly, filthy and vile beyond imagination.

Judgment was there. It was there in the terror of that final day when men would be called to account for their deeds and would receive their just retribution.

The Law was there. The Law which cannot save, but only condemn and expose all men's sins.

We can be sure that the enemy of God, and our enemy, Satan, and all His wicked horde, was there. Ready to rejoice at Jesus' death.

Death was there. Silent, lurking, certain of utter victory—who could escape Death?

And the fires of Hell were there. Invisibly burning, ready to claim another soul.

Jesus arrived at Golgoltha, though weakened physically, His eyes revealed an inner resolve and strength. Amazingly, they bespoke love. And within that love, an absence of fear.

Jesus was hung on a cross with spikes driven through His wrists and ankles, and the cross raised. With strength ebbing from His body, His hair matted with blood that ran into His eyes and blurred His vision, and struggling for breath, He compassionately prayed for His accusers—"Father, forgive them, they don't understand what they're doing."

But it was to unseen enemies that were at issue. Sin was the burden on His battered back; sin was what nailed Him to that cross. Judgment, in all its fearfulness, was poured out on Jesus' broken body and He took our guilty verdict. The law pressed forward, demanding fulfillment, ever-insistent upon the shedding of blood. The fires of Hell surged at the foot of the cross. And Death, silently awaited the final blow.

With the cry, "It is finished!" Jesus expired. Then, it was over. Sin was dealt with, Judgment resolved, the Law satisfied, the chains of Hell broken, and Satan defeated—the bruised heel of Jesus crushing Satan's head.[19] Plus, three days later, Death was conquered, as Jesus, in His resurrection, became the final victor!

We should add another reality that Jesus faced on that cross: the wrath of God. Jesus bore the eternal wrath that should have come down on your and me that was to be meted out for all eternity in hell. The wrath of God was vented upon Jesus so that we could escape eternal damnation. It was released upon the Savior so that God could be both just in His judgment, and also the justifier of those who believe.[20] It was loosed upon the Innocent Lamb of God, so that God's holy righteousness could be perfectly satisfied and yet demonstrate mercy toward us.

W.E. Vine, in his *Expository Dictionary of Old and New Testament Words*, more formally describes propitiation as follows: "Man has forfeited his life on account of sin and God has provided the one and only way whereby eternal life could be bestowed, namely, by the voluntary laying down of His life by His Son, under divine retribution. . . Through the propiatory sacrifice of Christ, he who believes upon Him is by God's own act delivered from justly deserved wrath, and comes under a covenant of grace" (pp. 223-24)

On the Cross, Jesus became the perfect sacrifice for atonement, His blood permanently covering our sins. The Cross transformed God's judgment to mercy for those who believe, bringing cleansing and redemption.

We should remember that there are only two places for our sins to be: either on us, or on Jesus; there's no other place. If they're still on us, then Jesus hasn't become God's propitiation for us and eternal damnation yet remains. If they're on Jesus, God's judgment is already passed, the trial is over, and our records are clean, hidden beneath the precious atoning blood of Jesus. Which one will it be?

So, may we focus again on the Cross. There the watershed issues of sin and judgment were faced by our Lord, and our Redemption was provided.

But our society and sinners must know they have sinned and will be judged. They will not know if we who are mandated by our Savior and Lord to preach the Gospel do not declare these essentials.

In Revelation 21:8, the Word that we are to preach describes those who go to damnation as, "cowardly, unbelieving, vile, murderers, sexually immoral, sorcerers [those who practice magic arts], idolaters, and liars"—*they are identified by categories of sins*. Their fate: the Lake of Fire, the Second Death. The next chapter, in 22:15, the same Word identifies the lost in much the same way, but adds the depiction of them as "dogs." Jolting terminology, but lost sinners as "dogs" only emphasizes the gravity of their evil. And they are said to be "outside" the eternal "Holy City" where the redeemed are forever in the presence of God.

Knowing the sad, gripping doom of the unregenerate, how can we not speak of sin and judgment now. To not speak of these is like whispering in a burning house. It is the opposite of the zeal of Phinehas. It is showing indifference to the indecency of Zimri and Cozbi. It is turning a blind eye to the idolatry of the seventy elders. It is giving Ananias and Sapphira a pass. In another sense, it is like opening the Holy City to the "dogs."

The Apostle Paul stood before the Roman governor, Felix, and reasoned with him "about righteousness, self-control, and *the judgment to come*."[21] Felix was terrified, and told Paul to leave. The Holy Spirit, through Paul, commanded us to "Preach the Word"—the whole body of Scripture, nothing excluded; and from all of Scripture to "correct, rebuke and encourage." And to do so "with great patience and careful instruction"[22]—which means being motivated by love.

There is a deepening sense among many people that something is terribly amiss in our country. Let America and the West be confronted with their sin and the certainty of their judgment. Soon. Now. It must come from those who understand the biblical issues involved.

Ezekiel understood those issues. And he was commanded by God to "confront [Jerusalem] will all her detestable practices."[23] True compassion for our nation and for its soul, and for the souls of men and women, will compel us to so confront. So from Honolulu to Houston, from Portland, Maine, to Portland, Oregon, from Syracuse to Sacramento, from Wichita to Washington, D.C., and from

Anchorage to Albuquerque to Atlanta, *may America be confronted with its sin and its judgment.* Let it be with the pure zeal of Phinehas. Let it be motivated by the caring heart of our great and holy God. *Let it be a roar!*

It will be one of the most loving things we will ever do for our nation!

And it could well be part of the birth of revival and spiritual awakening!

Let us pray together: *Our gracious Father in heaven, too many of us are leaving out essential parts of Your Word, the sobering truths of sin and judgment. And we are doing this to our shame, in the face of enormous and imperious sin going on around us, and our judgment looming. More and more people recognize there is something deeply wrong in our nation, morally wrong, spiritually wrong. Forgive us in the Church, and those of us in the pulpit, for being silent at a time like now. May we raise our voice and expound clearly Your Word on sin and judgment, remembering that these terrible issues were at the center of why Your Son went to the Cross. In Your Son's Name, Jesus Christ, our Savior and Lord, Amen."*

Chapter 12 Endnotes

[1] Genesis 18:20.

[2] Jonathan Edwards, in his sermon on Ezekiel 22:14. From *The Works of Jonathan Edwards* (Banner of Truth, 1974), vol. 2, pp.81-83.

[3] This entire story is found in Numbers 25:1-15.

[4] Numbers 25:4 (Amplified).

[5] Matthew Henry in his commentary on Numbers 25.

[6] See Acts 5:1-11.

[7] Carl F.H. Henry, *"Reflections—Classic and Contemporary Excerpts,"* The Christian Century (November 5, 1980), p.32.

[8] I Peter 4:17.

[9] Hebrews 12:11.

[10] See Ezekiel 8:6-13.

[11] See Ezekiel 8:14-16.

[12] Ezekiel 9:4.

[13] Ezekiel 9:6.

[14] Ezekiel 9:8.

[15] Hosea 4:2.

[16] I Corinthians 2:2.

[17] Matthew 26:38.

[18] Matthew 26:39.

[19] Genesis 3:15.

[20] Romans 3:26.

[21] Acts 24:25.

[22] II Timothy 4:2.

[23] Ezekiel 22:2.

13

THE PROPHETIC ROAR

"Warn everyone to tremble! The judgment day of the Lord is coming soon. It will be dark and gloomy . . . The day of His judgment day is so terrible that no one can stand it."[1]
—THE PROPHETIC JOEL

"We have awful reason to fear that God has been provoked by our former want of sincerity at Solemn Assemblies. Let this day call our sins to remembrance and the sins of this people. Let us think of the guilt we have contracted . . . It is only by repentance that we can avert the judgments which are brooding over us."[2]
—ANDREW ELLIOT, PREACHING DURING A PUBLIC FAST IN 1753 IN BOSTON

IT WAS MEANT AS HUMOR, BUT GEORGE S. KAUFMAN'S 1925 ONE-act play, *The Still Alarm*, could be a parable depicting today. It centers around two businessmen, Bob and Ed, who are told by the bellboy that the hotel they are in is on fire. However, they are informed in the manner of English drawing-room comedy with everyone acting calmly and politely as though it were an invitation to a cup of tea.

At one point Bob looks out the window and discovers the fire has reached the floor right below. The bellboy says courteously, "Yes, sir. The lower part of the hotel is about gone, sir." Bob, with his head still out of the window and wanting to be optimistic, looks up, "Still all right above, though."

The courtly manner continues when firemen arrive. They show little interest in fighting the fire or saving people, but are glad to make small talk and practice the violin. It concludes with one of the firemen entertaining the group with a violin solo done in the manner of a concert violinist while everyone wipes their brows from the heat, and Ed enjoys a cigar lit from the fire outside. The fireman plays, *"Keep the Home Fires Burning."*

The whole play screams for someone to run in and shout, "Get out of here!" This, of course, doesn't happen because the play is a parody. However, after smiling at the humor, we might cry, "Hey, this is us!"

Several year ago I met former members of a notorious motorcycle gang who had recently become Christians. They exuded the joy of their new life in our Lord and had a great concern for men still in the lifestyle they left. They were bold in their testimony which was evident in the message emblazoned on the back of their black T-shirts, *"Turn or Burn,"* intended to "tell it like it is" to those men.

Whatever we may think of the in-your-face toughness of "Turn or Burn," it is at least unambiguous, which is rather refreshing. It's the unfuzzy sort of message true prophets gave when the nation's destiny was in the balance because judgment loomed due to the nation's bold sinning. One question must be asked: *Are America and the West headed toward judgment?* The short answer is yes! Then a second question: *What should America and the West do?* The answer: Return to the Lord in humble repentance. And a third question:

What should the church do? The answer: Speak strongly on the first two questions—raise a compassionate roar!

Again, America and the West will not go on ad infinitum as it is going. We face the consequences of our evil choices. We're slaughtering our unborn children, and their blood pollutes our land as their collective cry beseeches God for justice. We're brazen in our licentiousness with heterosexual sin rampant. We're going beyond Sodom's sin by wanting same-sex marriage pushed into both public policy and holy matrimony. We're already seeing apostate churches and ministers approving and performing such marriages. On top of all this, *we're egregiously teaching our children to sin. No, we're educating our children to go to hell!*

It is this evil, teaching our children to sin, that particularly marks us just now. It is almost unbelievable how aggressive we have become in doing this to our children. We seem to be throwing down all restraint. For instance, look at the momentum that seems to be building insidiously for homosexual-praising curricula and policies in public schools. It is like an enormous tyranny over parents' objections. And look at the denigration the Boy Scouts are receiving for not permitting homosexual scout leaders.

Added to our bloodshed, licentiousness, and perversion, teaching our children to sin is damning us. Our cup of iniquity is spilling over. It is time we understood Matthew 18:6 where our Savior, in unambiguous language, condemned teaching our children to sin. The millstone is around our necks, and we're teetering.

Into all this must be a voice expounding the clear Word of the Lord. Let that prophetic roar come from the Church and its pulpits. Our society needs to be confronted with our "detestable practices," faced straight on about them, warned of our certain judgment for them, and commanded to repent. When it happens it could well be the catalyst our gracious Lord uses to send sweeping revival to the Church and spiritual awakening to the nation.

America and the West don't right now need another year of the church calendar, another doctrinal fad, another round of hype, another teaching on prosperity, another night of church entertainment, or another article or book on psychobabble, self-help or self-image. These will only treacherously continue to distract us from examining how deeply we have sinned against God, keep us from repenting, and divert us from the fierceness of our looming national judgment. In addition they will hold back that blessed revival so many are wanting to see.

What we need is the Church proclaiming God's Word with urgency, the kind of urgency of the man who warned a bridge was out. I was on a speaking itinerary in Australia several years ago when my schedule took me to Hobart, Tasmania. I was being driven by a friend to my next engagement, and as we approached the long, high-arching harbor bridge, my friend recalled the night years before when a large ship accidently rammed and knocked out one of the bridge's huge center pillars, bringing down a whole section. Speeding automobiles, he said, began plunging into the abyss. However, one driver, a friend of his, somehow saw the danger and stopped his car just at the edge. His friend carefully got out and ran back down the bridge urgently waving his arms and yelling to warn others. To his horror drivers ignored him and sped on to disaster. But he didn't quit warning, and eventually traffic was stopped.

WHAT WILL IT TAKE TO AWAKEN US?

As asked before, what will it take to awaken America and the West? *What will it take to awaken the Church?* Our retribution is fast approaching, and we weep to consider that it will in fact take judgment itself for the truth of our self-deception and the finality of our punishment to hit us.

We must consider that God's judgment might now be in abandoning us as He did Israel. Are we being "given up," in the words of Paul in Romans 1? Our forefathers in the faith certainly weighed this. Reverend Joseph Rowlandson in 1678, preaching on a special day of fasting and humiliation, a Solemn Assembly, said, "God's forsaking the people He has been near to is a thing of such weight and solemnity and has such bitter effects that it is a very difficult subject, especially in a dark and mourning day, for ministers to speak of and for people to listen to. But servants of God must warn of the danger and the people of God must act so as to avoid such a judgment. *As God presence is the greatest good His people can experience on this side of heaven, so His absence is the greatest misery they can know this side of hell.*"

And Rowlandson added, "God's forsaking a people is a sore judgment in that it exposes them to all the other judgments."

Just a few years ago, John MacArthur commented on Romans 1, "[Paul's] words . . . are strikingly applicable to the predicament of contemporary society . . . He reveals that those who ignore or suppress their conscience risk a dreadful judgment: God ultimately abandons such people to the devastating effects of their own sin. That is exactly what we see happening in our nation. It is also the record of human history—nation after nation being abandoned by God after they first abandoned Him and became hopelessly enthralled with their own sin."[3]

And Maurice Roberts said in 1993, "The wheel of history has come full-circle. We are, as a civilization, rotating back to the state of affairs depicted by the apostle Paul in the first chapter of the Epistle to the Romans . . . Society is repeating the very vices which always provoke God to give the world over to its own sensuality and self-destruction."[4]

But it doesn't have to be judgment itself that finally awakens. We could be awakened by the penetrating Word of the Lord clearly proclaimed from the Church and pulpit if we will but do it. Good places in Scripture to begin might be the messages and stories of the prophetic giants, men God used to define the moment at pivotal, watershed times, men who raised a compassionate roar! Here are several.

JONAH. As we know, Jonah did not want to preach in Nineveh, so he took a ship to get as far away as possible. (*See Book of Jonah.*) It took a fierce storm, being thrown overboard, swallowed by a large fish where he spent three days for Jonah to get things sorted out with God. After the fish vomited him out, Jonah heard the Lord again tell him to preach in Nineveh. This time he went. And he delivered the message God had for that pagan capital city of the Assyrian Empire. It was direct, it had a "Turn and Burn" tone: "Forty more days and Nineveh will be overturned."[5]

What an impact Jonah's message had! The city repented. From the king to the peasant, they repented in sackcloth and cried to God for mercy. And God "had compassion on them and did not bring upon them the destruction He had threatened."[6]

Jonah's message was the catalyst for one of the greatest spiritual awakenings in history.

People ask, *"Have we in America and the West gone too far?"* Well, Nineveh had gone pretty far. They had only forty days left. Yet they humbly and wholeheartedly repented and sought the Lord. And look at what happened. If there ever was a "deathbed" spiritual awakening, Nineveh had it.

Right now our nation needs to hear a Jonah-type message: "America your judgment is near!" "Forty days" could be four days, forty weeks, forty months, or whatever is in God's design.

Nineveh repented. Will we? The Church should model repentance and lead the nation to the same place. It brings tears of joy to contemplate a Nineveh-level awakening in our beloved America. May it happen. It happened in Nineveh. It can again.

PETER. (*See Acts 2:1-41*) "Save yourselves from this corrupt generation," the Apostle Peter called to the crowd in Jerusalem on the Day of Pentecost, sounding that urgent prophetic roar which God's genuine spokesmen have all had. Peter called his generation corrupt. He put the same face on the world that God does.

"Corrupt," meaning depraved, debauched, and completely sinful; with morals, religious activity, entertainment, music, sports, business, and politics. Whatever sinful man had touched was affected by sin.

Earlier during his message—expounding from Scripture that Jesus was Messiah, Savior and Risen Lord, Peter boldly named the sin of the crowd there before him: *bloodshed.* He charged them with the death of Christ: "You, with the help of wicked men, put Him to death . . . this Jesus, whom you crucified."[7] Seven weeks before, they had crucified—murdered—the Son of God, the most innocent blood ever shed, and Peter faced them with that. He used the word "you." *You did it!*

The impact was profound. "When the people heard this, they were cut to the heart"—stabbed in their consciences and convicted of their sin. The Holy Spirit, who had just come to the Church, took the Word of God Peter preached and penetrated the very souls, spirits, joints, and marrow of Peter's hearers. (See Hebrews 4:12.) They were jolted awake them to their lost condition, something that the predominantly religious crowd, who had no sense of the gravity of their sin, needed.

Let America's sins be named: *bloodshed, licentiousness, perversion, teaching its children to sin, and pride.* And America told there are consequences. Let's not shade and shape our message to avoid hard truth. Hard truth is still truth.

May we pray that America and the West will be cut to the heart. This is more urgent than creating a new social program, balancing the budget, upgrading education, cutting taxes, or saving Social Security. Our only "social security" is in returning to the Lord in humble repentance; and if we do not do that, Social Security will not be worth having.

At the end of Peter's message, about 3,000 responded and were baptized. *A revival was birthed by which we are still affected today!*

John Wesley saw this kind of response. Wesley believed in "speaking of death and judgment, heaven and hell," as George Catlin said of him, "to arouse men to consciousness of their actual, present, damnation-deserving sin." He wrote about what happened when he preached at a factory: "A large number . . . were employed. The whole conversation of these was profane and loose to the last degree. But some of them stumbling in at the prayer meeting were suddenly cut to the heart. These never rested until they had gained their companions. The whole scene changed . . . . No more lewdness or profaneness were found; for God had put a new song in their mouth, and blasphemies were turned to praise."[8]

SAMUEL CONFRONTS KING SAUL

SAMUEL. King Saul was supposed to destroy the Amalekites "and totally destroy everything that belongs to them." But Saul did not. (*See I Samuel 15.*) When confronted by the prophet Samuel because he had not done what God told him to do, Saul at first protested that he had done what God wanted; but when forced to admit he had not, twice tried to excuse himself by saying that the best of the sheep and cattle had been saved to offer as a sacrifices to God. Here is Samuel's memorable answer, a message that needs to be implanted in the heart of the Church and nation: *"Does the Lord delight in burnt offerings and sacrifices as much as in obeying the voice of the Lord? To obey is better than sacrifice, and to heed is better than the fat of rams."*[9]

Saul finally confessed that he had sinned; in fact he did that twice, but each time there was a contingency in his "repentance." It was false repentance, the "I have sinned, *but*" kind, filled with face-saving self-interest. After his first admission he'd sinned, Saul added, "I was afraid of the people, so I gave into them." The second time, to look good, he implored Samuel, "I have sinned. But please honor me before the elders of my people and before Israel." Because of Saul's dishonesty he lost his kingdom, and perhaps his soul.

In our time of self-delusion, chosen lies, and easy grace spawning easier forgiveness, the message of Samuel and the tragedy of King Saul carry powerful lessons for us.

ELIJAH. (*See I Kings 18.*) Picture Elijah today thundering into our society where only the names of the idolatries are different, but the double-mindedness and decadence are the same. Picture him standing before morally ambivalent preachers and political leaders, and giving that signature declaration: "How long will you waver between two opinions? If the LORD is God, follow Him; but if Baal is God, follow him!" What might happen today?

There are two pivotal reasons why the Church and America needs to be confronted with Elijah's challenge. One, *America is wavering between its Christian heritage and secularism.* We're seeing enormous pressure being exerted from secularists to remove our nation from "under God." The effect has left Americans ambivalent—wavering between God and Baal. We're cutting off our roots.

Peter Marshall, Sr.'s powerful message on this text in 1944 still states the issue excellently: "Today we are living in a time when enough individuals choosing to go to hell will pull the nation down to hell with them. The choices you make in moral and religious questions determine the way America will go."

Let the Church speak as Mr. Marshall who also said, "We must decide and decide quickly who is chief, whom we will serve. Millions of people in America live in a moral fog. The issues are not clear for them. They cannot face the light that makes them black or white. They want grays and neutral tints. They move in sort of a spiritual twilight. Modified morality on the basis of cleverness guides millions of people. Modified dishonesty within the letter of the law is the practice of millions more. Surely the hour is late when we must decide, and the choice before us is plain. Jehovah or Baal. Christ or chaos. Conviction or compromise. Discipline or disintegration."

The other reason America needs to be confronted with Elijah's challenge is *we have made a moral virtue of sitting on the fence!* From killing in the womb to fornication to homosexual perversion, we're commending neutrality. Today our preferred morality is amorality, no-opinion morality, cop-out morality. "Some of my friends are for this, some of them are against. I'm with my friends." The code words are "pro-choice," "tolerance," "non-judgmental."

How can America now have the blood of some 40 million of its unborn children on its conscience? How can America be so enmeshed in teaching its children to sin? How can America and the liberal Church be so casual about going beyond the sin of Sodom as we move toward including same-sex marriage in holy matrimony? How can America have so little sense of the gravity of its sin? How can America be so at ease in its hastening judgment?

Fence-sitting.

But fence-sitting won't absolve us of accountability. To think so is to live in a fool's paradise. Pilate made a virtue out of moral neutrality when he had Jesus on trial before him. He tried to absolve himself of responsibility for Jesus' death by ceremonially washing his hands in a basin of water and intoning, "I am innocent of this man's blood."[10]

MORAL NEUTRALITY WON'T ERASE ACCOUNTABILITY

Claiming moral neutrality didn't work for Pilate, and it won't work for us. We have blood on our hands because of the holocaust against our unborn children, and we're training our children to go to hell. We can wash our hands all we want over a basin of self-professed pro-choice neutrality, but it won't spare us from judgment. Can we imagine God awaiting feminists to present their pro-choice arguments at the bar of heaven before He rules on whether or not shedding innocent blood is sin? No, we stand answerable to God, and now our guilt is piling up like water rising behind a dam, ready to br released in our coming hour of judgment.

Our nation and every nation in the West could be headed to our own "Judas-moment." Judas betrayed Jesus for a bit of silver. Then when he saw Christ condemned to death he was smitten in conscience and rushed to the priests and threw down his blood-money crying, "I have sinned, for I have betrayed innocent blood"[11]

For a bit of silver—material benefit—we've betrayed our unborn children and had them killed. Could the day be arriving when, like Judas, we're shaken to see that we have indeed betrayed innocent blood, and the weight of that pierces our indifferent conscience? Will we cry in remorse, "We have sinned, for we have betrayed innocent blood of our children?" May that day not be too late like it was for Judas!

As mentioned in the Prologue, Peter Marshall, Sr. concluded his sermon on Elijah's penetrating call this way: "We need a prophet who will have the ear of America and say to her now; '*How Long Halt Ye Between Two Opinions, If the Lord be God follow Him, but if Baal be God follow him—and GO TO HELL!*'"

NATHAN. King David had committed adultery with Bathsheba and then covered it by having her husband Uriah killed in battle. Nathan courageously went to David, and, wisely told the king a story about a rich man who took his poor neighbor's one sheep to feed his guests. (*See II Samuel 11 and 12.*) David angrily denounced the rich man.

Nathan's unforgettable answer, " You are the man," pierced David's heart. And David repented deeply and openly. He didn't blame Nathan or anyone for exposing his sin. No excuses. That's true repentance. David had a personal revival.

Nathan's prophetic heritage is not only David's repentance, but also Psalm 51, which David penned in his shame. That psalm is an eloquent expression of David's humble remorse, a moving soliloquy in which David tenderly shows us the traits of which true repentance consists: deep humility, admitting truthfully that we have sinned, confessing that our sin is first against God, and having a desire to be cleansed, passion to have a pure heart and wanting to be restored to fellowship with God. Let Psalm 51 be studied deeply by every congregation!

We should remember that even after he repented so deeply, David still paid a fearful price under God's judgment for his adultery with Bathsheba and the murder of Uriah her husband. After his year-long cover-up of these sins, David was sternly rebuked by the prophet Nathan. The baby he fathered in his adultery died. He was overthrown from his throne for a while by his son Absalom. His concubines were publicly humiliated by Absalom. There were rape and murder in his family. And there was national disgrace.

At a time when our nation does not admit its sin, and we in the Church avoid speaking of it, let it hear Nathan's story told again so it pierces our calloused hearts, and when we react, let us be told, "You are the man!" Let our congregations and America come to grips with how honestly and thoroughly David repented, the judgments he suffered, and Psalm 51.

The welcome effect God could be that David's personal revival becomes our national revival!

JOHN THE BAPTIST. (*See Matthew 3:1-12; Luke 3:1-19.*) Scripture says that John the Baptist preached the Gospel—the "good news." "With many other words John exhorted the people and preached the *good news* to them."[13] And if crowds mean success in preaching, then John the Baptist had great success because he had crowds. But he treated those crowds differently than we might. He spoke strongly to them, "John said to the crowds coming out to be baptized by him, 'You brood of vipers! Who warned you to flee from the coming wrath?'" John, like other genuine spokesmen of God, knew that fallen men and women can be artful liars, and artful liars can be artful repenters, so he confronted "easy" repentance. He knew that true repentance is verifiable. "Produce fruit in keeping with repentance," he challenged the crowds. "Every tree that does not produce good fruit will be cut down and thrown into the fire!"[14] John spelled out for them what such repentance will look like.[15] To say the least, confronting crowds like John did is different from the way many today think preaching the Gospel ought to be done!

Of course, John was a humble man. This was enormously essential for such direct preaching. When asked if he were the Messiah, John answered, "One more powerful than I will come, the thongs of whose sandals I am not worthy to untie."[16]

Can ministry include rebuking a national leader? For John it did (and of course for Nathan, Samuel and Elijah and others). John rebuked Herod for his relationship with Herodias, the wife of Herod's brother "and all the other evil things [Herod] had done."[17] This part of John's ministry resulted in his beheading.

What might have happened say in 1993 if a modern John the Baptist had confronted Bill Clinton about his immoralities? And what if the president had repented deeply? We probably would have been spared years of scandal. What a blessing that courageous John the Baptist would have been. But we didn't have one.

On the other hand, what if a modern John the Baptist had confronted the president in 1993 and throughout his presidency about his immoralities "and all the other evil things he had done," and the president, like Herod, had not repented? Many preachers may well have condemned that modern John for being "unloving," "unforgiving," "harsh," "not using wisdom," etc., and effectively destroyed his ministry. The equivalent to beheading him. Who can forget the standing ovation several thousand clergy gave Mr. Clinton at a ministers' conference in 2000. This was a president who vetoed a ban on partial-birth abortion twice—something which alone should have brought him a John the Baptist type of rebuke. And he received cheering applause from ministers! Can we imagine John the Baptist, or Samuel, or Elijah, or the Apostle Paul or the other faithful preachers applauding?

John received no condemnation from Jesus, only the strongest commendation: "Among those born of women there has not risen anyone greater than John the Baptist."[18]

There are other prophetic voices we could examine such as the Apostle John. "Light has come into the world, but men loved darkness instead of light because their deeds were evil";[19] or Amos—"Prepare to meet your God"[20]; or Habakkuk, who proclaimed, "Woe to him who builds a city with bloodshed;[21] or Zephaniah, who declared, "The great day of the Lord is near and coming quickly";[22] or Nahum, who warned, "The Lord is slow to anger and great in power; He will not leave the guilty unpunished."[23] In the next chapter, the Epilogue, we will examine two more: Joel and Hosea.

Since "all Scripture is God-breathed and is useful for teaching, rebuking, correcting and training in righteousness,"[24] let the prophetic roar from Scripture be heard. Let it pierce the consciences of the Church and our nation. Without question this could be the most timely, patriotic, and fruitful thing we could do.

If it needs to be said, this is not a call to harshness and finger-pointing. It is a call to true compassion, to a true prophetic voice. Our national house in on fire, our society's bridge is out, we're playing on the street of destruction, we're teetering on the cliff (to recall some of the metaphors we've used in these pages to describe our peril). True love will confront, warn, and show the way back to our gracious God, and will do so fervently and urgently.

False compassion will not speak; it will not confront. But true compassion will impel us to. *"Preach the Word! [Being] ready in season or out of season [to] convince, rebuke, exhort, with all long-suffering and teaching."*[25] And as God's righteous dealings with us unfold, we will need those who know God and His Word to define the moment and show us what to do.

If it is true that when God begins to judge a nation the first thing He does is give His people cowardly preachers, then the timorous, accommodating attitude we are seeing in many churches and pulpits might now be a graphic signpost of our nation's looming judgment.

But let us speak. Let us not betray our calling. Gripped by the Word of God and the motivated by heart of God, right now, during this window of mercy, while our barbarian Sodom is frolicking at ease on its way to hell, let us raise the prophetic roar. The "hotel" below us is on fire.

Could we see another awakening as Nineveh had, national repentance as David did, or an outpouring of the Spirit as Jerusalem saw? We believe we could. May our gracious Lord grant it!

Let us join in prayer: *Our great and Sovereign Lord, Your Word records what You have spoken through men at crucial and wicked times, giving the exact answer to the situation. We need to hear that Word. Oh Lord, may the famine of such a Word be over. May we in Your Church and we who stand in the pulpits raise a heartfelt, clear prophetic roar that will cut to the heart of our nation and bring it to repentance, and back to You. May we in the Church lead the way in this. And gracious Lord, may You be pleased to pour out Your Spirit, and may our beloved land have a sweeping awakening. In the Name of Jesus, Your Son, and our Savior and Lord, Amen.*

CHAPTER 13 ENDNOTES

[1] Joel 2:1, 2 & 11 (Contemporary English Translation).

[2] Reverend Andrew Elliot, in his sermon, *An Evil and Adulterous Generation*, given April 19, 1753, in Boston during a public fast.

[3] John MacArthur, from his book, *The Vanishing Conscience*, pp 58-59.

[4] Maurice Roberts, "God Gave Them Up," The Banner of Truth, October 1993, pp 3-4.

[5] Jonah 3:4.

[6] Jonah 3:10.

[7] Acts 2:23 and 36.

[8] George Catlin, *The Anglo-Saxon Tradition*, (London: Broadway House, 1939), p.191.

[9] I Samuel 15:22.

[10] Matthew 27:24.

[11] Matthew 27:4.

[12] I Kings 18:39.

[13] Luke 3:18.

[14] Luke 3:7-9.

[15] Luke 3:10-14.

[16] Luke 3:16.

[17] Luke 3:19 and Matthew 14:4.

[18] Matthew 11:12.

[19] John 3:19.

[20] Amos 4:12 (starting with verse 6).

[21] Habakkuk 2:12 (and the section from 2:6-19).

[22] Zephaniah 1:14 (and on through 2:3).

[23] Nahum 1: 3 (and on through verse 10).

[24] II Timothy 3:16.

[25] II Timothy 4:2.

Epilogue

Lord, Send Revival

"I will give you abundant water to quench your thirst and to moisten your parched fields. And I will pour out My Spirit and My blessings on your children. They will thrive like watered grass, like willows on a riverbank."
—GOD, SPEAKING THROUGH ISAIAH[1]

"The propriety of setting apart days for national humiliation is questioned by none except those who despise all religion, or those whose extravagant principles of liberty lead them to set at nought all human authorities . . . We have reason to be thankful that this nation is now called in the most solemn manner to humble itself before God."
—CHARLES SIMEON IN 1820

As said in the Preface, it is encouraging today to see a rising cry for deep, biblical revival coming from many who are dissatisfied with both the barrenness of their own spiritual lives and the superficiality of the message from parts of the

Church, and who see the need for the Church's clear, prophetic voice at this pivotal time. They passionately desire "fresh rain from heaven"—an outpouring of the Holy Spirit and revival. They are convinced that this is today's most urgent need.

Some years ago, I watched a TV documentary on the dust bowl of the 1930s, when drought devastated farms on the American prairie. The documentary had a short segment of film on one ravaged farm. It was black-and-white, grainy, and a bit jerky. As the camera panned slowly from left to right, you saw the arid fields and dust high up around the fence posts.

Then as the side of a ramshackle house came into view, something wonderful happened. It began to rain hard. The camera stopped and reversed direction a bit to show a family coming out of the front of the house: a father, mother, perhaps three young children, all poorly dressed. You did not see their faces, just their sides and backs, but by their body language you saw they were very happy. They just stood there in the pouring rain and looked toward the sky, allowing the rain to wash over their faces and drench their clothes.

Like the family in the documentary, many today are praying for the end of a drought, the spiritual drought in many local churches and parishes. They want to see a sweeping "outpouring from heaven."

One powerful promise for such an outpouring is Acts 2:17-21 where the Apostle Peter, preaching to that large crowd on the Day of Pentecost, quoted from Joel 2:28-30 to explain the phenomenon of the coming of the Holy Spirit which had just happened. Peter's quote actually contains two promises. It opens with, "In the last days, God says, 'I will pour out My Spirit on all people;'" and closes with, "And everyone who calls on the Name of the Lord will be saved." This last phrase is essentially the focus of Peter's message which follows.

While we modern Christians tend to focus chiefly on Peter's quote from Joel found in Acts 2, that crowd of "God-fearing Jews from every nation under heaven"[2] would have known the larger story. They would have known that Joel prophesied during a time when Israel had sinned and was under God's remedial judgment. They suffered from a plague of locusts and a drought which devastated the country, particularly its crops, and crippled the economy. One effect was that the basic elements used in worship—corn, wine, and oil—were destroyed,[3] resulting in empty worship. And the people were depressed. "The joy of the people [was] withered away."[4]

It was into this devastated, depressed situation that God, as He had done with prophets before and after, sent the prophet Joel. He sent him to give His Word for the difficult time the nation was in.

As he prophesied, Joel declared those things God wanted the nation to do to reverse the tragedy going on in the land and bring healing. He proclaimed hope by extolling God as "gracious and compassionate, slow to anger and abounding in love."[5]

GOD'S IMPASSIONED CALL

God wanted Israel to return to Him; and the devastation of the locusts and the drought were to stir them to do so. God gave an impassioned call, "Even now, return to Me with all your heart, with fasting and weeping and mourning. Rend your heart and not your garments."

"*Even now*" had in view the Day of the Lord—judgment. It was at hand. And it was dreadful. In such a fearful day, who would be able to stand? No one.

However, although the hour was late and things looked grim, *even now* the Lord called, "Return to Me. " Repent. Come back. In other words, even at that late, urgent time, there was hope if they would repent.

They were to come to the Lord **wholehearted**, *"with all your heart."* This meant true repentance, total commitment, no divided loyalties. They were to come *"with fasting and weeping and mourning,"* evidence of humility and genuine contrition, revealing a supreme passion to get back to God.

They were to return to the Lord **brokenhearted.** *"Rend your heart and not your garments."* Rending, or ripping, your clothing was a traditional way to show remorse. But such an action could easily become just a superficial ritual masking an unrepentant heart. No, the nation had sinned. It faced judgment. And only repentance from a heart torn by grief over their sin would save them. So God called them to be done with mere outward shows of repentance.

The reason they could return to the Lord is because the Lord is **tenderhearted**. He is a God of love Who "relents from sending calamity." So judgment could be stayed. "Who knows but that He may turn and have pity and leave behind a blessing—grain offerings and drink offerings for the Lord your God." Hope was proclaimed, rooted in God's compassionate character.

However even further, the repentance being called for was not only to be personal, it was to be corporate. Corporate sin was to be repented of corporately, together. So they were to come together in a **sacred or solemn assembly,** announced by blowing the trumpet.

Attendance at the solemn assembly was to be the priority for everyone. From elders to nursing babies, from the oldest to the youngest, all were to attend. Even a bride and groom were to leave their honeymoon and come. Nothing—*nothing*—was to take precedence over that solemn assembly.

By why such urgency? Because nothing less than the nation's existence was in the balance. And repentance needed to be thorough.

Of course a nation's future is its youth. Richard Owen Roberts has said, "If the youth of a nation are to live out their lives in a land of freedom and opportunity, they will do so because their parents had grace sufficient to humble themselves, pray, repent of their sins, and seek God's face in Solemn Assemblies."[6]

The nation's spiritual leaders were to lead in the repentance. "The priests who minister before the Lord [are to] weep between the temple porch and the altar," crying to God "Spare Your people, O Lord."[7]

And God promised to heal the land. (*See Joel 2:18 to 3:21.*) God would restore what the locusts had eaten, and the land would have abundant showers in the autumn and spring bringing "grain, new wine and oil, enough to satisfy [them] fully;" and their "threshing floors will be filled with grain [and] the vats will overflow with new wine and oil." The nation would know that God alone is God, they would rejoice, never again to be shamed.

Then came that tremendous promise of the outpouring of the Spirit, a promise happily still in effect today.

JOEL'S DAY AND OURS

We should note the sequence of events in Joel. First the people were called to earnestly and humbly return to the Lord in a Solemn Assembly. Then God graciously promised both to heal their land and pour out His Spirit.

Our nation mirrors the nation of Israel at the time when Joel spoke. As they did, we are sinning, apathetic, and facing judgment. We have the same need: a defining, prophetic voice to come among us and show where we are and what we are to do. We need to listen for its unmistakable earmarks: its clear and forthright message anchored in Scripture, and its tone flowing from the heart of God, humble and caring. Such a voice will call us "even now" to return to the Lord.

When we do, we will be candidly honest about our "wicked ways," and brutal with our pride, self-absorption, bloodshed in the womb, licentiousness, homosexual perversion, *and teaching our children to sin. We will admit that the millstone is around our neck.*

Speaking of teaching our children to sin and as an expression of our repentance, **let every biblically founded church make ministry to children one of their highest priorities. Let us evangelize and disciple the children of our nation!** This could be pivotal to the very future of our nation.

Usually we in the church focus on youth ministry, ministry to teens. This, of course, should continue. However, today the reality is that at earlier and earlier ages, many of our children are exposed to and saturated in sin. By adolescence, they are fairly hardened. The effect is that youth ministry is becoming effectively "salvage-ministry." So we need to push back our evangelistic focus to those younger whose hearts still are tender.

As we have seen, our children's saturation in sin comes from different directions. We have stripped moral education from them. Fathers are absent. They are being bombarded with filth and corrupted values from TV, movies, and music. In public school they are exposed to graphic sex education and "diversity" training where even homosexual practice is approved; they are growing up in a "third-sex" world. And on and on.

In spite of this, however, may we in the church and pulpit give our children the Gospel and disciple them. May we evangelize their homes.

And let's expand our thinking about revival. Certainly our Lord's heart is toward children, the "little ones." In any revival He might make children one of His primary focuses. His promise to pour out His Spirit included "sons and daughters." Without question, revival among our children would singularly benefit our future as nothing else.

Ministry to our children could be the most compassionate roar we'll give in our barbarian Sodom.

TIME FOR CORPORATE REPENTANCE

It's time again for corporate repentance. We say *again* because corporate repentance is part of our American heritage; it's been done many times. Many of our forefathers—both religious and governmental—believed national repentance was the means to avert national judgment, so they called for solemn assemblies at pivotal points.

There is the example again of Abraham Lincoln called for days of **National Humiliation, Fasting and Prayer** several times during the Civil War. Lincoln said of his day, "We have forgotten God." He asserted that the Civil War "may be but a punishment inflicted upon us for our presumptuous sins, to the needful end of our national reformation as a whole people." (What kind of punishment might Lincoln say would be just killing our unborn children?)

Even further, many of our forefathers believed that in all times of national need, seeking God was vital. For instance, on June 1, 1774, the Virginia House of Burgesses called for a day of fasting and prayer as an expression of solidarity with the people of Boston who were under siege by the enemy. On March 16, 1776, the Continental Congress recognized that the "Liberties of America are imminently endangered" and the country needed "to acknowledge the overruling Providence of God." They called for a day of humiliation, fasting and prayer.'" On June 28, 1787, during the debate of the Constitutional Convention, Benjamin Franklin, convinced of God's intimate involvement in human affairs, implored the Congress to seek the assistance of Heaven in all its dealings.

With all that is going on in our nation and world since September 11, 2001, urged by Scripture and instructed by the example of our forefathers, let us hold Solemn Assemblies today. Let established entities such as churches and governments call for them.

Let churches and parishes lead the way in urging them. Let them be held in every state and by the national government.

So, with the special challenges we now face, may the President of the United States and leaders of the Senate and Congress, make calling Solemn Assemblies a national priority.

May Prime Ministers and national leaders in other nations make calling them a priority.

May local ministers, mayors, governors and others make such a call a priority.

May pastors and ministers in local communities make such a call a priority.

Let them be held from the White House to every state house, to my house and your house.

There is urgency. For our national sins we will receive one of two things: judgment or mercy. If we continue to spurn God's mercy, we leave ourselves only one option: judgment.

Yet our holy and compassionate God desires mercy on us instead of judgment. He calls to us through Scripture, "Return to Me." He may use remedial judgments to stir us to do so.

Let our personal and national response "even now" be humble repentance. The well known II Chronicles 7:14 is our guide, "*If My people, who are called by My name, will humble themselves and pray and seek My face and turn from their wicked ways, then I will hear from heaven and will forgive their sin and will heal their land.*"

AS WE CONCLUDE OUR JOURNEY

As we conclude this journey, my mind goes back to that train ride referred to in Chapter 1, when my own heart was initially gripped by the issues and questions raised and discussed in this book. I go back to the time when God used the sin of killing our unborn children to open the larger issue of our nation's sins, our need of repentance, and the certainty of judgment if we remain unrepentant.

My mind also goes back to that pivotal Sunday morning service spoken of in Chapter 2, when a panorama of our nation's sins seemed to unfold as I spoke, and our Lord's heart seemed to be calling, "I love you. Come back." I remember that before and after that Sunday, I grappled with the need and the place of the voice of the Church in our world, and with the questions of true and false ministry (issues discussed in Chapters 2 and 7).

I must admit that I have wrestled with the gravity and the implications of our national sins, sins we've rationalized because of our pride and delusions we've purposed to believe, and sins epitomized by such evils as killing in the womb and teaching our children to sin. I've also been gripped by the prospect of our judgment. Assuredly judgment is a terror that no nation—or individual—ever wants.

Especially I have been awed again by God's grace. I have been freshly struck with the wonder of God's mercy. Our Lord is indeed a God of forbearance. We have sinned. Our sins are capital offenses. We deserve judgment. Yet here we are. There is an America. God's grace is truly amazing! Humbly, let us thank Him. And happily recommit ourselves to Him as a nation "under God."

Before a final word, let me briefly mention something which profoundly motivated what has been written here. It happened in August, 1990. Iraq had just invaded Kuwait and there was much discussion of war. Of course in just a few months, in January, 1991, we did go to war.

Details would take too long, but let me say that the Lord used that unsettling time leading up to the first Gulf War to place deeply in my heart and the heart of my wife Esther an insight as to how He wanted His Church to proclaim His Word in times like those. He wanted His Church to raise its voice, motivated by love, and urgently call the nation to return to Him, and to lead the nation in repentance. As the Church did so, the Lord would powerfully anoint. (You might want to read again II Chronicles 7:13 and 14, noting how verse 14 flows directly from 13.) However, time after time the Church has missed or ignored such times (such as those mentioned in Chapter 9).

As Esther and I prayed then, we made a commitment to our Lord that to the best of our abilities, we would try to do and speak as our Lord desired. This book is one small way we have tried to keep that commitment.

Once again, we will face our nation's sins. It is not whether or not we will face them, just how and when. We will face them either in repentance now, while there is God's mercy (as Nineveh did, and was saved) or we will face them in judgment later, when there is not God's mercy (as Sodom did, and was destroyed).

Since September 11, 2001, with the threat of terrorism and the war in Iraq, our world has changed. We all know it. And we know that the days ahead may see more change. More difficulty.

The times call for us to say with Hosea, "*It is time to seek the Lord.*" Hosea spoke to judgment-bound Israel, "Sow for yourselves righteousness, reap the fruit of unfailing love, and break up your unplowed ground; *for it is time to seek the Lord*, until He comes and showers righteousness on you."[8]

The nation had, Hosea said, "planted wickedness [and] reaped evil."[9] It was time to sow righteousness and reap the blessings of God's love. Hosea called on the people to break up their unplowed or fallow hearts, to break up their insensitive, callous hearts, and their indifference to the gravity of the nation's sin and the terror of its coming judgment. The hardened soil of their hearts needed to be plowed so there was new humility, a fresh sensitivity to God's Word, a restored tenderness to God's heart, and a renewed grand passion to know Him.

Only a plowed heart will discern God's heart for this post-9/11 moment. Only a plowed heart will receive the rain from heaven.

We are to seek the Lord *until He comes and showers righteousness upon us!* We look forward to the day when God's rain falls. We want to stand there, looking up, and getting drenched. And then we want to watch the crops grow.

Can there be revival?

Yes.

But it's late.

Let the Church from pew to pulpit raise a compassionate roar!

May that Spirit-anointed roar penetrate the heart and conscience of our world.

And may our gracious Lord use such a roar to send revival to local churches and parishes . . . to yours!

And from such revival, may we see spiritual awakening birthed across the nation from the White House to my house to your house!

I must confess that tears well up just now at the awesome prospect of what God might do as we raise a compassionate roar; at what He will do in an outpouring of His Spirit in a revival and spiritual awakening which He wants to send (and will send!) to every believer, every minister, and every church.

Oh Lord, may it happen!

May we pray a final prayer together: *Our wonderful heavenly Father, as we conclude these pages. We want to thank You for who You are: holy, loving, just, gracious, all-knowing, and all-powerful, to name just a few of Your awesome attributes. We rejoice that You are always with us. And no matter how evil the world is, You have given us every resource to stand. Now we ask that we in Your Church and Your pulpits will understand our moment, this window of mercy, that it is time to seek You and we will do so. And in our Sodom we will roar Your timely Word, and lead our nation to You. According to the promises of Your Word, may You be pleased to pour out Your Spirit. May Your rain of righteousness fall. Oh Lord, come down! Oh Lord, we cry for this. Our hearts weep for it to happen. And may our beloved land, a land You have given us, have a mighty awakening. Bless the one who is now reading this. And may he or she be a strategic instrument in Your gracious hand in these pivotal times. In the Name of Jesus, Your Son, and our Savior and Lord. Amen.*

EPILOGUE ENDNOTES

1 Isaiah 44:3-4 (NLT).

2 Acts 2:5.

3 Joel 1:13.

4 Joel 1:12.

5 Joel 2:13.

6 Richard Owen Roberts, in the introduction to his article on *"The Solemn Assembly."*

7 Joel 2:17.

8 Hosea 10:12.

9 Hosea 10:13.